Marcus Linear is a freelance writer concerned with
environmental problems and the ecological impact of
development, particularly in the poorer tropical countries.
A former planner, architect and cattle farmer, he has spent
much of his life in various parts of Black Africa and the
Middle East. He now lives in Europe, and has published
books in Germany and The Netherlands.

GW00758659

Marcus Linear

Zapping the Third World

The Disaster of Development Aid

Pluto  Press

London and Sydney

First published in 1985 by Pluto Press Limited,
The Works, 105a Torriano Avenue, London NW5 2RX
and Pluto Press Australia Limited, PO Box 199, Leichhardt,
New South Wales 2040, Australia

7 6 5 4 3 2 1

89 88 87 86 85

Set by *Sunrise Setting*, Torquay, Devon
Printed in Great Britain by Guernsey Press Co. Ltd,
Guernsey, C.I.

British Library Cataloguing in Publication Data available

ISBN 0 7453 0013 8

Contents

Abbreviations

EDF	Euro-Development Fund
FAO	Food and Agriculture Organization
FFHC	Freedom from Hunger Campaign
ICP	Industry Co-operative Programme
IFAD	International Fund for Agricultural Development
IIED	International Institute of Environment Development
ILO	International Labour Organization
IMF	International Monetary Fund
IUCN	International Union for the Conservation of Nature and Natural Resources
LDCs	Least Developed Countries
ODA	Overseas Development Aid
OECD	Organization for Economic Co-operation and Development
NASA	National Space Administration
TCP	Technical Co-operation Programme (of the FAO)
UNCTAD	United Nations Commission for Trade, Aid and Development
UNDP	United Nations Development Programme
UNEP	United Nations Environment Programme
UNESCO	United Nations Educational, Scientific and Cultural Organizations
UNICEF	United Nations Children's Emergency Fund
UNO	United Nations Organization
WFC	World Food Council
WFP	World Food Programme
WHO	World Health Organization
WWF	World Wildlife Fund

Introduction

Wealth and poverty are part of the same thing in the end. Both are relative positions along the length of a piece of string. We measure relative wealth and poverty against a sliding scale, a continuum which shows our distribution of or access to the products and facilities provided by our various societies for our survival and well-being. Upon this scale we set an arbitrary point, below which we feel that the individual's survival chances are not equitably ensured by society, and which we call the 'poverty line'.

Far from being a fixed position or value, this point along the line is almost infinitely variable, firstly in terms of the multiplicity of forms adopted by human society (and the consequent expectations of its members), each of which sets its own minimum standard, but also in terms of time, in as much as few if any societies today remain in a static state, and our perception of poverty within a given society increases with the general advance of material wealth. Even the remotest surviving 'subsistence economies' – the tundra-dwelling Eskimos, or the Kalahari Bushmen – are affected, and changed for better or worse, by the pervasion of technologies deployed by the more dominant, outreaching societies. The evolution of our technological societies over time, accompanied by the shifting standards of expectations and the rise or fall of the poverty line, are inevitably carried over in an involuntary 'transfer of technology' to all human communities, wherever and however they may choose or chance to live.

But the problem of the wealth/poverty continuum is rather more complex than this linear definition would seem to imply, for the continuum is limited by the nature of things at one end only. There is no absolute wealth, while absolute poverty means in practical terms a survival failure: death. Any degree of minimal survival above that extreme, from the most abject bare maintenance of life up to that offered at the 'poverty line' which societies set at what they perceive to be the tolerable minimum survival level, represents a value above absolute zero.

At the other end of the scale, however, wealth – and the power to create it – is limited only by the bounds of human ingenuity. There are no limits to growth, no insuperable natural constraints on human use of our habitat on the earth and beyond it, which we could not overcome should we wish to do so.

Apart from the odd brief respite of 'Golden Ages' in which virtue prevails, the history of this use has been the sorry record of men competing, by aggression and trade, to acquire control of a greater share of the earth's wealth and means of production. (One might fairly reformulate von Clausewitz's dictum to read, 'War is merely a continuation of trade by other means').

Success in this acquisitive struggle led to accumulation of wealth – and its concomitant, power – in the hands of a dominant minority; the majority, the masses, were automatically impoverished. The discrepancy became (and of course still is) part of a self-generating, or self-propelling, system. Accumulation of wealth increases power, which in turn means increased power of acquisition. This accelerates the drain of wealth from the powerless, the primary producers, who are thus forced ceaselessly to increase their production of wealth, by transmuting the earth's raw resources while enjoying an ever-diminishing share of its fruits. Poverty is created by the accumulation of wealth.

The formation of competing nation-states, ruled by stratified autocratic power structures, did nothing to disturb the established disparity between rulers and the ruled. Indeed they stemmed ultimately from the disparity and their main purpose was to maintain and enhance it. The objective of the rich and powerful has always been, must always be, the subjugation of the ruled, in order to reinforce their own position and to reduce any threat of insurrection. But as George Orwell pointed out, the 'proles' – the lower 85 per cent of the population – have never in reality presented a threat of revolt. 'The masses never revolt of their own accord, and they never revolt merely because they are oppressed. Indeed, as long as they are not permitted to have standards of comparison, they never even become aware that they are oppressed.'

The recent formation of the 'super powers', inheritors of the neoclassic empires of the nineteenth and early twentieth centuries, merely solidified and intensified the process. Moreover, their formation has practically eliminated the age-old phenomenon of 'territorial' wars between rival nation-states – with the exception of such minor aberrations as Mrs Thatcher's reconquest of the Falkland Islands (a nineteenth-century imperial hangover which brought about the collision of nineteenth-century minds, and found its catharsis in a nineteenth-century display of gunboat diplomacy and a little vicarious bloodletting), or the even older conflict between Iraq and Iran, whose lunatic leaders fan the fury of ancient hatreds in a conflict carefully inspired and fuelled by insidious outside interests. For the rest, the recurring outbreaks of armed conflict in various marginal areas of the world are entirely relics of colonial iniquity, or the result of external manipulation in furtherance of super-power neocolonial interests. Such atavisms aside, however, the territorial imperative has lost its driving force in modern human society. Today's technology has created a fundamental disruption of our dependency, for breeding and survival, on the possession of territory. The farther human societies progress away from their roots in nature, and the more obscure the relation between human communities and their existential base in the environment's natural resources becomes, so much greater become both the dangers of artificial manipulation of our lives for ends over which we have no control, and on the other side of the balance, the benefits of emancipation from the constraints and physical limitations which unsophisticated nature inevitably imposes.

To the perplexed and despairing today, it may seem that Armageddon rules the world – the ultimate perversion of human ingenuity locked into creation of destructive technologies has appeared. Yet the ultimate disaster can never occur. Though our masters be necrophilous paranoics to a man or woman, sharing ambitions of grandeur and delusions of persecution to shame the devil, the human race will survive.

Some defeated intellectuals currently believe that 'the system' is running out of control, and is now beyond the influence of the powerless masses. They are, however, unrepresentative in their discouragement, and ill-fitted to point out ways to future survival – about which, indeed, most of them are suicidally sceptical. Moreover, modern means of transport and communications have not only opened up new ways for our rulers to defend and exploit their privilege, as is sometimes claimed by such sceptics. Much more importantly, they have awakened consciousness of the need for international solidarity, providing at the same time practical media for the expression and achievement of this ideal. That these media are still underemployed is largely a result of their first having been developed at the behest of the established power systems, in whose control they mainly lie. Fortunately, the latter are powerless to prevent infiltration and vulgarization for these new pathways, or have no more than superficial control over their use to disseminate good will among the people they newly unite.

Faced with the constant imperative of the self-chosen few to accumulate wealth and concentrate power in their own hands, the mass of people throughout history, in all cultures and of all religious persuasions, has invariably shared and upheld an ideal of solidarity, of compassion for the less-well-endowed, and a compulsive tradition of equity in the enjoyment of whatever survival resources are left to them. Charity is not an invention of the rich, out of the generosity of their acquisitive, self-seeking hearts. It is a product of the survival urge of the poor, springing perhaps from an instinctive perception of the need to assure survival of the human race – or at least their own communal part of it. The rich, invariably, are concerned only with their own survival and that of their immediate kin – the survival of their kind may, indirectly, help to assure their own. For the rest, the devil take the hindmost.

Even world wars and their aftermath – in our day truly global, in contrast to the limited range of ancient 'world' conquerors like Alexander and the Caesars – have brought different peoples into intimate contact. After these conflagrations, particularly, the desire for renewal and for the panacea of peace and universal prosperity has incited world-wide efforts to level inequalities, counter injustices and remedy the pestilences and deprivations suffered by less fortunate lands.

Behind a smokescreen of this genuine good will, the acquisitiveness of the West produced its finest flowering with the invention of what has become the development aid industry, with such creations as the financial, trade and technical arms of the United Nations Organization (UNO) 'family' of agencies, the World Bank and its affiliates, and, in the background but very much at the helm for all that, the International Monetary Fund (IMF).

After the 1914–18 War, the short-lived League of Nations was born out of such compassionate sentiments. As, after the Second World War, was that present-day monument of our rulers' disunity, the United Nations Organization. Both of these ventures, conceived and launched by a coalition of national governments and elder statesmen as hopeful first steps towards an eventual world government, caught the popular will and mood of their time. The first, the League of Nations, now defunct except for a staff of functionaries still administering the self-perpetuating pension fund, effectively died with the rapid rise of fascist military might during the Spanish Civil War, and with Mussolini's Italy assaulting Abyssinia, until then the only African kingdom uncolonized since Pharaonic times.

The UNO, on the other hand, is still a minor force in the world – although far from that which its founders predicted. Its practical influence derives less from its principal role as 'talking shop' for international diplomacy and posturing, than from the panoply of specialized agencies it has spawned, reaching into almost every sphere of human activity. These agencies, even more than their parent body, benefit from relics of public good will and desire to help the less fortunate. But such relics are fast crumbling away as public awareness grows, bringing disenchantment with the manipulations and power plays practised by the paymasters of these bodies (and by the several caucuses of interests grouped within them), the self-serving nature of member governments' interest, and the growing gulf which has opened between their ostensible aims and the real impact of their 'aid' on the ground. We will examine the effects of certain activities of these agencies in some depth in the following chapters.

A second, more candidly interested exploitation of this praise-worthy public sentiment is embodied in what is known as 'bi-lateral aid'. With a handful of notable exceptions, this comprises government-to-government agreement for one to loan funds to the other, on condition that the borrower spends the money on products or services of the 'donor' country. In practice, such loan arrangements serve the lending country as export subsidies at taxpayers' expense, or to promote disposal of its otherwise unsaleable surplus production or manufacturing capacity.

The third arm of the aid industry – and by far the most powerful, in that aid is essentially a matter of money – is the World Bank and its affiliates, in alliance with the IMF. These, sitting on top of a hierarchy as structured as any of the old imperial systems on which the aid industry is modelled, control the purse strings of development of the poorer countries. All specialized agencies depend on World Bank funding for most of their major projects. As a condition for granting loans, the Bank imposes financial stringency upon borrowing governments – and also demands control of national economies and financial policies – which results inevitably in increased poverty for the mass of their populations.

We will also examine further the relationship of the World Bank and the IMF to the UNO system. Here, suffice it to say that for the poorest, whose survival is threatened, money is not the problem. This is why Robert McNamara was mistaken when, as president of the World Bank, he spoke so unctuously of the plight of those in the 'Third World' living in absolute poverty, and the need for his bank to do more for them. The people he had in mind, for instance, included my friends in the slums of Lagos in Nigeria. His error is perhaps best illustrated by a little personal history.

I was once given the task of acting as tour guide for a group of seven West German experts – economists, sociologists, development engineers and planners – who were to study the problems of 'Third World' slumdwellers for UNO's International Labour Organization (ILO). (I was given some such title as 'orientation consultant', and paid a fee for my services as astronomical as those of my 'real expert' colleagues, although the exercise was essentially one of upmarket tourism, the modern technological equivalent of 'slumming'.)

German development consultants work under the considerable handicap, as they see it, of having no recent colonies, at least none with coloured populations outside Europe, in which to gain field expertise without a language barrier, an advantage which other countries' ex-colonies offer. They claim, with a certain truth, that British (and consequently, also US), French, Belgian, Dutch and even Italian specialists can more easily acquire field experience in their countries' former colonies, nearly all of which have retained some degree of 'special relationship' with their former imperial masters, cemented by official use of the latters' languages and administrative systems. Thus it comes about that they are, to a greater extent than any of their international competitors, largely desk-bound consultants, exercizing an expertise which is predominantly theoretical, unsullied by the realities to be found on the ground.

My group's visit to Lagos was their first to a tropical country. My own functions were several: firstly, to guide them through the oblique paths of one of the most corrupt post-colonial administrations ever bequeathed to its former subject people by the departing imperial power; secondly, to smooth the team's introduction to their local 'counterpart' colleagues on the project; and thirdly, to calm their near-paralyzing fears of being robbed by every mendicant who approached them, short-changed or over-charged by every taxidriver they employed, or infected with some dreadful disease by every insect which bit them. Little could be done, however, to alleviate the cultural shock from which they all suffered, from first day to last of a six-week visit.

Early on in our slum tourism, one women expressed unconsciously the basis of prejudice and false expectations in which much of this cultural shock was rooted, when she indicated the local inhabitants around us and asked: 'But how can they be so happy?' And in fact, looking at the laughing brown babies rolling in the dust, or older children happily playing rowdy games alongside, and sometimes even in, the foetid effluent of open sewer and storm-drain trenches, which are often their only play-space free of a milling, noisy traffic; looking at the busy, vivid crowds moving around narrow unpaved streets, with small-scale retailers raucously selling a rich variety of goods and foodstuffs at their borders, itinerant merchants cheerfully calling their wares, her problem was not difficult to imagine. The *force-vitale* of the whole human pageant made shocking nonsense of her preconception of the misery of poverty. In such places, poverty in monetary terms is an ever-present reality, widespread enough to be the general rule. But we must be careful not to fall into the western trap of equating everything with money, and giving every form of worth and wealth a monetary value. Thus absolute poverty, at the level of a threat to immediate survival, is happily rare. Even the most hideously crippled beggar will not be allowed to starve to death, unless the whole community is so destitute that the personal survival of everyone in it is threatened by want.

In the cities this never happens. The rulers of such impoverished masses as congregate in and around 'Third World' cities are susceptible, in the last resort, to pressure which such masses can *in extremis* be aroused to apply. However much they may be shored up and sustained in office by external powers and interests – through provision of arms and of credit – those in power in the 'Third World' are obliged by this vulnerability to urban mass pressure to ensure adequate supplies of food and shelter, at lest above the survival minimum, if they intend to remain in office. Dispersed rural populations, on the other hand, can be – and usually are – exploited and drained of any wealth they produce at rates amounting to piracy, in the interest of maintaining a tolerably low level of civil strife in the city slums. They can do little about it – except in rare cases where nomadism is still possible, and when they can 'vote with their feet'.

In the case of our ILO study, my German colleagues determined on the necessity of carrying out a survey of a sample slum population, complete with questionnaires running to several pages – the data so gleaned to be processed by computer back at their head office in Germany. Their African 'counterpart' colleagues rarely set foot in any of the 'spontaneous settlement' quarters, about which they produced a constant stream of learned dissertations. And when they did, then only if accompanied by an armed policeman or two – for like 'Third World' slumdwellers all over the world, their subjects have an innate and well-founded distrust of any authority, and of its occasional attempts to register and count them, to regulate and restrict their lives.

In order to bypass this problem, I introduced two of the German team to an old Lagos friend, a shoeshine boy who performs his friendly and highly professional service under the *nom-de-guerre* of Bob Simba. On hearing that my companions wished to visit a slum, he beamed with delight. 'Come home with me to Apapa,' he promptly invited, 'the best slum in Lagos.' He reflected for a brief moment on the logistics of the proposal. 'I'll just close up my business . . . we'll have to go by taxi.' Closing up his business, we soon saw, meant packing and padlocking his shoeshine box, strapping this to his resplendent bicycle which was chained for safety to a nearby railing, and telling his few waiting clients that he would be back tomorrow. He hailed a passing Mercedes Benz taxi, and with the driver's help the bike and box were precariously laid half in, half out of the car's open luggage boot.

One of my German companions, on realizing that the four of us were expected to squeeze into the car's three passenger seats – which would habitually have accommodated six or seven Africans on such a foray – suddenly remembered an urgent appointment at the local reference library. The rest of us piled in, and drove some 15 kilometres to Bob's home, for although Apapa lies just across the neck of the lagoon, within sight of which we had first met in the commercial centre of Lagos, the ferry which nominally linked the two had broken down that day. It often did.

By the time we had completed the long detour, our stomachs began reminding us that we had not yet taken lunch. Bob evidently shared the feeling, and called on the driver to halt at a chopbar, as the unpretentious eating houses of the West Coast are called. He led us, joined by the driver, through a dingy front room from the streetside, out into a pleasant courtyard where long tables and benches were arranged under awnings of suspended reed matting to provide shade from the midday blaze. A lean-to at the far side with a verandah before it served as kitchen where several women busily tended a row of steaming pots, producing aromatic vapours to quicken the most jaded appetite.

Bob jovially ordered beer, and started catechizing the waiter about the cuisine's various offerings for the day, which were displayed on a chalk-board on the wall of the kitchen. Knowing nothing of the establishment's specialities, but confident from previous experience of Bob's discernment, I asked him to order for me too, from among the choice of spicy 'bushmeat' stews and grills on offer. My German companion was naturally more hesitant, amid such unfamiliar surroundings. He demanded explanation of each dish on the chalked-up menu, asked for a more familiar sandwich, which was not available, and finally settled upon an okra stew. When this arrived, however, he probed the rather mucous vegetable soup with a spoon, and decided to stick to beer for lunch. We enjoyed our own orders amid a continual exchange of greetings from customers at neighbouring tables, who gradually overcame their initial shyness at having white visitors sharing their local eating place, and joined our table one after another to order increasingly large rounds of beer. During all this, my colleague evidently became increasingly ill-at-ease, as the animated conversation and laughter extended to take in the surrounding tables. Finally, overwhelmed by his inability to contribute to the general affability, he announced that he would take the taxi back to the Ikoyi Hotel – the sumptuous and expensive establishment in the 'best' quarter of Lagos where we had made our headquarters, and from which we had sallied forth to study our slums. He left with our taxidriver, the latter somewhat disgruntled at being called away from a promising party. Later, as the sun had sunk some way towards a hazy horizon, Bob led the way to his room, wheeling the treasured bicycle beside us through unpaved, eroded alleyways and courtyards. The room opened, typically, off one of these. Unlocking the door revealed a clean, bare cell with cement walls and floor, a net-covered wooden louvre closing the single window, a large iron bed with immaculate mosquito net suspended above it, a simple wooden table and chair, and a cord strung overhead from wall to wall to accommodate Bob's drying laundry.

Having stowed the bicycle out of the way at the head of the bed, and seated me at the table, he opened one of the bottles of beer we had brought with us, collected a clean shirt and trousers from the washing line and suggested: 'While I go and get my bath, maybe you can have a look at my books. You might have some ideas for improving my business.' He pulled a large cardboard suitcase from under the bed, unlocked it and extracted with pride three foolscap-sized ledgers, and laid them before me. He explained that, three years before, he had decided to learn business accountancy, and with the help of EUP's 'Teach Yourself Accountancy' had begun plumbing the mysteries of double-entry book-keeping. These three tomes comprized an impeccable, and over the period continually refined, financial account of his shoe-shine business. Income was balanced monthly against costs ('dash' to the local police – or what we would more brutally call bribes – was one regular item carefully entered among the latter), balances brought forward to annual totals, and an effective general overview of the business given by carefully prepared graphs of income and net profits over the year. Monthly income hovered around 30–35 *naira* (the rough equivalent of the dollar at the time), although seasonal variations brought it down to 25 in the wettest months of the year. Annual income had been largely static over the three years of this unique record.

After Bob had returned shining from his bath and had routinely hung out the newly washed clothes he had worn that day, we pored over his accounts until late in the evening, searching for possible cuts in his costs or ways to increase income. An obvious item for cutting was the policeman's regular dash. He explained, however, that as a slumdweller he was illegally resident in Lagos, and thus lacked the residential qualification required for obtaining a street trader's licence. This left him vulnerable to police extortion, which is general throughout the land. It was cheaper, nevertheless, than the fines he would otherwise have to pay if he had refused to grease the palm of the law. And although even the difficulty of residence status could be overcome – with a suitable dash in the right quarter – and a licence obtained to keep the law at bay, the officials concerned were exorbitantly expensive, the dash they demanded never being less than 250 *naira*. Possession of a licence would not, in itself, open up any new earning opportunities, so it was obviously cheaper to continue dashing the policeman his ten *naira* per month. This had, too, some advantages, for the policeman then had a vested interest in seeing that Bob's earnings continued, and he often gave advance warning of planned police raids on the different districts where he worked.

As for expanding the business, he had already tried and found wanting every suggestion I was able to think up. Why, for example, did he not come to an agreement with the various resplendently-uniformed doormen at the biggest hotels and office buildings – whose functions included chasing away undesirable beggars and colporteurs – under which he would enjoy a monopoly of the shoe-shine business outside the establishment? The suitably dashed doorman would drive away any competition, and Bob could then put in his own 'apprentices' or subcontractors, provide them with their tools-of-the-trade and take a commission from their earnings. But he had already tried this. He sadly explained that the boys he had set up had simply run away with his equipment, to set up in business for themselves in areas beyond his reach in this sprawling city. Such a scheme would only work, he sighed, if the subcontractors were family members. Unhappily, his family lived far away, in a northern city.

Nothing that the World Bank – or any other bank for that

matter – can do would ever be of the slightest benefit to Bob and his like in the poor quarters around the world. Unique in his own way as a rich and warm-hearted individual, his enterprising spirit is, notwithstanding, to be found a thousand times over in every slum and deprived area – and not only of the so-called 'Third World' at that. His talents and innate drive to exploit and express them to the full represent, as Julian Simon has pointed out, the ultimate, inexhaustible natural resource of our earth, and thus our greatest wealth.

How, indeed, the Bank and the whole aid industry it heads harms, restricts and even destroys his chances of working out his own survival on the fringes of our money-mad system is the theme of the pages which follow. In the following chapter we will look in some detail at the activities of the agency most intimately connected with our daily bread, the Food and Agriculture Organization (FAO).

2. FAO spells famine, avarice and oppression

For when I was hungry, you gave me food.

Gospel according to St Matthew

And they feed, for love of Him, the poor,
the orphan and the prisoner.

The Holy Qur'an 76.9

All roads no longer lead to Rome as they did in ancient days when the Eternal City was centre of the universe. But all the major airlines do, many having daily flights into one or other of the two international airports, Fiumicino or Ciampino. For today, Rome's decaying splendours, its entrenched polyglot tradition and its easy airline connections attract the myriads of US and other foreign oilmen serving and surveying the oil-production industry of the Mediterranean Basin and Near East, who come in search of solace after the spartan rigours of oil's austere deserts and off-shore rigs, for a weekend stopover in one of Europe's more flagrant, fragrant fleshpots. But these facilities have also attracted a less ephemeral foreign community to settle in and around the city: the experts and administrators of the most important sector of the international aid industry – which concerns itself with food, fish, forests and fibres, and their production and sale. There is perhaps historical justice in this. For ancient Rome was the first to organize the world food trade, growing fat on plundering the 'bread baskets' of Egypt, the Near East and, in its later years, the northern countries embraced in its imperial grasp.

So today the city houses teeming thousands of employees of four major international organizations engaged in the business of promoting production and disposal of food and other agricultural products. These are UNO's Food and Agriculture Organization (FAO), the World Food Programme (WFP), the World Food

Council (WFC), and the International Fund for Agricultural Development (IFAD).

The *lingua franca* of this international population is transatlantic English, as it is for the airlines that fly you in. Indeed, you might get your first taste of this modern surrogate for the Latin of Rome's holy heyday while jetting in. For among the selection of newspapers the airlines hand out to help customers forget their fear of flying, is an English language daily published there, and otherwise distributed only around the Mediterranean, to the Gulf sheikdoms and, sparsely, to points as far north as Munich and Geneva. This is the *Daily American**, formerly the *Rome Daily American*. This small local paper (with a circulation of 17,000), modelled hopefully on its more prestigious Paris-based big brother the *International Herald Tribune*, is put together by a skeleton team of young professionals, aided by some enthusiastic local support from former or would-be journalists in the area. It is filled for the most part with international news agency reports and photos, US sports news, syndicated strip cartoons and local service advertisements aimed principally at visiting or resident Americans. Only its local coverage, mainly of events of interest to Americans, is original reporting by staffers. And yet, despite this low-budget profile, the *Daily American* has recently been making a deep and surprisingly far-reaching impact on the international political, financial and, more particularly, development aid scenes. A David among the several Goliaths of the multinational aid industry around it, the paper regularly and fearlessly takes to task the locally based aid agencies, which harbour the major part of its readership and make up the largest single sector of Rome's international community outside the Vatican. Chief among its targets is the FAO.

What is FAO?

This question puzzles many. The world at large is generally familiar with the acronym, but even a lot of 'insiders', who work for or live off this largest of UNO's proliferating 'family' of specialized agencies, know only what it was once supposed to be.

Housed in a six-storey white marble ministerial palace a short

---

* Since this was written, the *Daily American* has ceased publication.

distance from the Colosseum, its entrances are guarded by a private army of uniformed security guards. Visitors are admitted only by vetted appointment, and then only after depositing their passports with one of the 'heavies' entrenched behind bullet-proof glass, who carefully logs all contact persons – especially should the visitor be a journalist. Visitors are required to wear a coloured tag prominently displaying their status. Visiting journalists are further supplied with an official pressroom escort, to ensure that they do not enter offices other than those specified in their visitor's permits or talk, perhaps, to the wrong people. The press watchdog also has the evident function of ensuring that the receiving official will give the correct, officially approved answers to his or her questions.

With this 'high security' profile, the agency bears little resemblance to the 'institution for collection and dissemination of information', which was its founders' purpose some 40 years ago. The FAO issues a 'basic text' which includes some 17 pages devoted to the constitution, but the circulation of this booklet is confined to senior staff only. Yet the first clause of Article 1 of the constitution reads: 'The Organization shall collect, analyse, interpret and disseminate information relating to nutrition, food and agriculture.' Secrecy, in this context, seems more than usually bizarre. Even citizens of its host city know little or nothing about what goes on in the huge complex, which has its own Metro station, and even a private bus service to shuttle its 10,000 functionaries and messengers around Rome.

The FAO was conceived at a meeting of the Western Allies' ministers of agriculture and other leading figures of the farming world, in Canada in 1943, in the middle of the Second World War. It was formally constituted on 16 October 1945 in the immediate aftermath of the war, and shortly before UNO itself, its nominal 'parent' body. Its founders intended it as an international co-ordination centre and information exchange to serve in the struggle against world hunger, and for fostering world agriculture and food supplies. They laid special emphasis on feeding the poor and disinherited of the earth. Democratically constituted, with equal, single voting rights for each member nation, it was seen as a practical expression of idealism, and of human solidarity in confronting mankind's survival problems in an ever-more-crowded and devastated world. The perpetual scourges of famine and hunger were to be erased, and the Golden Age of Plenty was at hand.

Nearly four decades later, and after expenditure of tens of billions of dollars – 75 per cent of which were provided by the West, and 90 per cent of it spent there – the balance-sheet reads as follows: the West is, by and large, richer than ever; the technology which FAO and its allied organizations promote is in fewer and ever-more-powerful hands; the environments of many 'marginal' areas around the world have been damaged beyond all hope of repair, while those of the rest are threatened with impending collapse; the poor of the least endowed lands are greater in number and even poorer than at the start of the exercise, with thousands of people starving to death every year and many millions living constantly with inadequate nourishment, shelter and health care. Indeed, in both relative and absolute numbers, there are more hungry people in the world today – with an undue proportion of them in Africa – than there were before 'aid' was ever invented.

In contorted contrast to this, the 1983 world grain harvest – well over 1.5 billion tonnes (a tonne being equivalent to 1,000 kilograms) of it – was the biggest in human history. And at the time of writing, 1984's shows all the signs of being even bigger. With the average healthy human requiring around a quarter of a tonne per year of grain or grain equivalent, such world crops would seem ample to feed the four billion or so of us already on earth. What then has gone wrong? Why does development aid – and in particular food aid – not work?

Most people today, facing the glutted granaries and cold stores of the rich Western world – and the mountains of ever-less-valuable agricultural commodities produced by the poor tropical countries – have long since realized that the problem of hunger is not one of producing enough food. It is, rather, one of wealth, where wealth means either the right of access to land to produce food, or the money needed to buy it. For access to food is no longer the inalienable right – the most fundamental of 'human rights' – of everyone born on earth that it once was; while such a right remains for the water we drink, or the air we breath. And in the modern world, the land is no longer being farmed to grow food and other vital necessities. Farmers today – business farmers – are farming for money. The world's best land is being exploited solely for maximum profit, regardless of what is being grown. Today's agribusiness farmer will even prefer to grow nothing, if he can make more money that way, as indeed he often can in the United States, for example, where farmers are duly paid millions of dollars in government subsidies *not* to plant crops.

As the commodity producers and dealers take over the land, the earth is crowded by malnourished, landless and hopeless people suffering from hunger, and many dying of starvation or avoidable disease. In a world glutted with unsaleable agricultural surpluses, the prices of 'Third World' commodities have collapsed, and many poor countries face bankruptcy.

During this process, the FAO has grown from its modest early beginnings into a juggernaut bureaucracy, annually consuming hundreds of millions of dollars ($500 million at last count) and insatiable in its demands for more. Its role in this debacle had already begun to surface before the organization's tenth anniversary in 1955. While the political arm of UNO and its Security Council had amply demonstrated its disarray in a number of international outbreaks of armed conflict and many less violent manifestations of dissention, the FAO had grown, under strong Western leadership – the Soviet Union having refused to join – into the most powerful specialized supernational agency. Already at that time it was described by the conservative British financial weekly, the *Economist*, as 'a permanent institution devoted to proving that there is not enough food in the world'.

Today, 30 years later, serious critics both within and outside the agency have dubbed it 'an autonomous banana republic, run on the lines of a fascist state'.

What went wrong? The perversion of an ideal

The depraving of the original idealism which inspired the foundation of the FAO, resulting in today's disillusionment and the frustration of many capable and devoted public servants and technicians who have dedicated their professional lives to the service of this ideal, can be located in four concrete, identifiable events or factors.

Susan George, an American writer living in Paris, first drew wide public attention to the primary causes of FAO's failure. Publication of her seminal study, 'How the Other Half Dies', in

1976 largely exposed the fallacy of assuming the superiority of western agricultural technology for universal application, which was FAO's most fundamental error; equally important, it revealed and documented the invidious role played by agribusiness within the agency itself, and the methods by which the multinational giants of the agribusiness sector manipulate it for their own private purposes.

At the time she wrote her study, 120 of the largest multinational agribusiness firms – chemical fertilizer and pesticide producers and application contractors, farm machinery manufacturers, seeds and commodities dealers, food and fibre processers – had created a joint programme with the FAO, under the title of FAO/ Industry Co-operative Programme (ICP). Under this, these agribusiness firms sat with their feet under the FAO table – or perhaps it would be more exact to say with their snouts in the FAO trough – advising and consulting with suppliant governments seeking development aid. This gave these private companies privileged access to the most confidential areas of such governments' (and FAO's) affairs, and in particular of governmental spending plans and investment policies in general, crop-yield forecasts and projected needs. Such information, needless to say, is invaluable to those in a position to manipulate markets. Under these FAO auspices, the ICP promoted and sold to many 'Third World' governments a series of highly dubious – though highly profitable – projects and campaigns, invariably dependent on large 'high tech' western inputs. Since the costs of these were, in any case, beyond the reach of the poor 'recipient' countries, other international aid bodies such as the World Bank, or UNO's other main development agency the United Nations Development Programme (UNDP) stepped in with massive loans to pay for the operations.

A typical example of these projects, to be covered in detail in a later chapter, is the 'war' which an FAO/ICP 'task force' declared against the African tsetse fly. Like most of the long-term ICP programmes, this still continues today. As the vector of trypanosomiasis (human sleeping sickness or the often fatal 'nagana' in livestock), the African tsetse fly keeps large areas free from the destructive effects of cattle and their herders, as well as keeping many equivocal forms of development activity at bay. But the recent spread of deep-freezing technology to the remotest corners of the earth has transformed beef, among other things, into a profitable international commodity. In hand with this, the worldwide penetration of US-style hamburger chains with their massive 'hard-sell' demand-creation campaigns, has resulted in world demand for the low grade 'manufacturing' beef used in their products outstripping available supplies. Thus by the early 1970s the multinational beef-barons, having already stripped much of Central and South America of their forest cover in order to create short-lived hamburger farms, were searching the rest of the world for low-cost cattle lands.

ICP therefore set up its task force in 1974, its ruling committee jointly chaired by Fritz Bauer, a director of the huge German chemical concern Hoechst AG, and Reginald B. Griffiths, then chief of FAO's Animal Health Service (and since promoted to head of its Animal Products and Health Division). Their declared aim was to eradicate tsetse from most of Africa, using chemical poisons mainly sprayed by aircraft. They planned to spend $2,000 million in the process, the money to be borrowed by the African governments concerned, to be repaid in due course by the poor countries' taxpayers.

As we shall see later, many of FAO's own experts – as well as innumerable non-FAO specialists – criticized the programme from its inception, pointing out the futility, extreme hazards and the waste of public money it entailed. For in reality, not only is it impossible in practical terms to eradicate the tsetse – as was clear to many expert observers at the outset – or even effectively to contain it in many vast areas; but also, trypanosomiasis, the disease carried by the fly, the reason for trying to exterminate it, is in fact pandemic (or endemic worldwide), infecting millions of people and far more livestock in areas where no tsetse flies exist. Thus even if wiping out the fly were possible, it would ultimately make little difference to the problem – and could conceivably make it worse.

Despite all this, FAO carries on with its 'war'. After ten years of attack and the pollution of thousands of square miles of Africa with hundreds of thousands of tons of poison – and the expenditure of almost half a billion dollars so far – most experts now agree that more land in Africa is infested with tsetse fly than before the campaign began.

Susan George's revelations of ICP activities of this kind roused a caucus of 'Third World' members of FAO into action. Acting as a body, they forced the director general, whom they had been largely instrumental in electing, to oust the ICP from the FAO. Given six month's notice to quit, the agribusiness consortium reluctantly sought a new home, shopping around among the UNDP and other agencies – with the full-hearted support of UNO's secretary-general of the time, Kurt Waldheim of Austria – until finally settling in new offices at the UN Plaza in New York. As was pointed out earlier, however, the main ICP/FAO programmes are, like their 'tsetse war', still continuing today.

Singular resignation

The second cause of FAO's depravity was most clearly identified in an unremitting wave of outspoken and particularly well-informed criticism from within, or at least with the withdrawal from 'within', of one of the agency's longest serving divisional directors, Raymond Lloyd. An Englishman born in 1934 and educated at Oxford where he studied philosophy, politics and economics, he started working for the international community in 1956, first as a volunteer for the Red Cross refugee relief operations and later for the UN High Commission for Refugees (UNHCR). A man of ideas and acute moral sensitivity, his work soon brought him to realize that many of the 'Third World' hosts of the refugees he was concerned with were worse off than his charges.

His response was characteristic. He drew up what was to be the first of his 'round-robin' circular letters – later to become renowned, respected, and even feared – to legislators and leaders of governments and international bodies around the world, in seven languages. In this he originated the concept of the first 'Development Decade'. The idea was taken up by the White House in Washington in 1961, proposed to the US Congress, and in September of that year, to the United Nations. The idea survived; today we are in the middle of the Third Development Decade – though even Raymond Lloyd agrees that the world is worse off than ever.

On changing his unpaid volunteer status for that of an UNHCR employee, Lloyd also recognized the paradox of working for the poor and underprivileged from a position of wealth and privilege.

Consequently, he tried to resolve the problem, in a personal sense, in six different ways. The first was to give up the annual leave to which he was entitled, in order to work for Algerian and Congolese refugees on a volunteer basis during such periods; and later also for the FAO, the staff of which he joined in 1961. The second was to call upon his UNO colleagues to donate one day's pay to refugee funds – and to donate himself half of his own annual salary, anonymously, to the World Refugee Year. Thirdly, he set aside the price of one meal per day, during the Freedom from Hunger Campaign, to finance field work of the United Kingdom FFHC committee.

His next step was a self-imposed 'wage-freeze' on his own salary, devoting any increases to FAO's work – a YMCA farm school in Tanzania and similar projects. But by the beginning of the 1970s, this deeply reflective man realized that this approach was not enough. For he recognized a failure in FAO's thinking far more fundamental than its blind promotion of the 'technological fix'. The FAO's activities – and indeed those of the whole development aid industry – bypass and largely ignore the most productive primary producers. Women not only prepare most of the food eaten in this world, they also grow most of it. While the production of vast western surpluses of agricultural commodities is indisputably a 'macho' matter of machinery, marketing and money, the overwhelming proportion of food grown – most of it never appearing on the market – is produced largely, if not entirely, by women.

This hidden half of humanity not only feed their families and friends, they are also, over much of the earth, the 'hewers of wood and drawers of water' too. And yet as Lloyd pointed out, they are largely unaffected – or worse, disadvantaged – by the development process. His solution was, characteristically, a practical one. He began to make monthly contributions of $1,200 from his remaining 'take-home' pay to women's groups in the 'Third World'. This time he did it publicly, regularly publishing lists of the organizations to which he had contributed; not, however, in any spirit of immodesty, but rather in the hope that others would be inspired to follow his example.

It is a sad measure of Lloyd's idealism, and of the greedy world the rest of us live in, that few responded. For doing so demands a degree of altruism and magnanimity that few of his colleagues – or indeed any of us – could aspire to. But even the most canny of his colleagues could have aspired – or been inspired – to emulate his last solution to the paradox of 'rich living on the back of poverty'. In 1966, having taken a personal pledge that he would work within the UNO system only as long as his efforts financed his own salary and produced a surplus for the poor and hungry, Lloyd conceived and launched the FAO's 'Money and Medals' scheme. This was a subtle educational campaign, using the coins in their pockets and purses to remind ordinary people all over the world of the primary importance of food. Under it, the FAO received an allocation of the special coins minted by the participating countries, for sale to numismatists and museums in other countries.

The scheme developed into a major Money and Medals Programme, which Lloyd directed for the next 14 years, during which time it produced 5.5 billion 'Food for All' coins in 90 countries, with a total cash value of $240 million. The programme not only financed Lloyd's and his departmental colleagues' salaries in full during the period, but also by 1980 had produced a net profit of $2.8 million. Of this, $1.6 million was distributed among 43 projects in 92 lands. Watching meanwhile the growing depravity of the agency which he, and many others equally idealistic, had joined, Raymond Lloyd was not satisfied to leave his efforts to introduce a sense of dedication and probity at the level of exemplary personal gestures. Demonstrating an energy and initiative rare among full-time functionaries, he produced his incessant stream of circular letters and newsletters promoting the two causes dearest to his heart.

The first of these, which he continues to promote today, concerns the advancement of women, particularly into the top ranks of the international agencies. To this end he has founded, together with his Italian surgeon wife, an organization simply called 'Women and Men'. A private and entirely independent 'shoe-string' organization which he runs almost single handed, it aims to place the names of suitable women on the candidates' list of any of these international bodies when senior posts become vacant or subject to re-election of current intendants.

In furtherance of this, Lloyd has drawn up and put forward a series of lists naming suitable female candidates for top posts in the World Bank, UNO, FAO and several others. Producing these as concrete proposals, which are circulated by his round-robin service, he makes tellingly clear the extent to which women are under-represented in the higher administration of our affairs – as well as the extraordinary wealth of female talent which exists, largely unrecognized, in our male-dominated world.

The second of Lloyd's major campaigns, in some respects overlapping with the issue of promotion of women, concerns the constitutional morality of his own agency, the FAO. At the end of 1979, Raymond Lloyd resigned his divisional director's post at FAO. He explained that this was in protest against the methods its Director General, Edouard Saouma, employs to dominate and manipulate the organization which Lloyd had served so long and devotedly.

In a further circular letter explaining his decision, he appealed to his former colleagues for at least 200 of them to follow his example, in a mass protest aimed at convincing the organization's delegates to replace Saouma with a more suitable head. Not one responded. Lloyd's letter of resignation – circulated likewise as a 'round robin', and later published in full over two pages of the *Daily American* – makes moving reading. The steps which led him to this unprecedented public severance will be examined in more detail later in this chapter.

Power and profits of poverty

The usurpation of power by international agribusiness – first announced by Henry Kissinger and Earl Butz in 1973, in speeches to the effect that 'Food in US hands is a more powerful weapon than the H-bomb' – converted the FAO in great measure into a well-accredited sales organization, selling multinational agribusiness's 'high tech' food systems. This was a major factor in the third source of FAO's depravity.

International business's universal method of bribery and corruption, in the promotion of sales of its wares, first became institutionalized (to the point of becoming officially deductible from taxes, in many western countries) during the 1960s and early 1970s – the heyday of the Lockheed and many similar affairs. This pervasive venality led to the whole UNO system, and particularly the FAO, becoming seen by 'Third World' candidates for office or professional posting, as a source of easy pickings beyond the legal emoluments with which such posts are generously endowed.

Influence there is also a saleable commodity, as we shall see later.

In the world of supranational official bodies, the only safeguard of probity lies in the quality and ethical sense of their functionaries – and only in a minor way, in the degree to which they are answerable to some independent and effective inspecting authority. Accountability has become such a contentious issue between the 'North' (which generally demands it) and the 'South' (which rejects it), that on several occasions Saouma has felt himself so invulnerable with his 'Third World' backing that he has responded to suggestions of the introduction of the most restricted degree of accountability into FAO's conduct of its affairs with public personal insults and vituperative attacks on national delegates and western parliamentarians daring to propose this.

The problem with all such UNO bodies is that, unlike normal governmental agencies, they have no direct constituency. Their membership with voting powers consists of representatives' representatives. And as Raymond Lloyd succinctly says, 'a civil servant who is answerable only to another civil servant is, in effect, answerable to no one'.

If Lloyd's leanings are, in his own words, 'in the old-fashioned liberal tradition', his campaign to reform the FAO on moral and constitutional grounds is supported and strengthened by former colleagues of all political hues. Notable among them is Otto Matzke, a West German economist of an equally old, if rather more conservative school. Like Lloyd, a former divisional director, Dr Matzke spent his early career in the German foreign service. It culminated in the senior direction of the FAO/UN World Food Programme, from which he retired with honour in 1974, the year in which Saouma was first elected to FAO's top job. Long before his retirement, however – starting in fact with a journalistic debut in the West German press in 1966 – Matzke had overtly criticized many of the FAO's more bizarre financial and constitutional practices. Upon retirement, he settled in Rome to become correspondent for the highly conservative *Neue Zürcher Zeitung*.

From this position, he watched the degeneration of the FAO under Saouma – who until his election to absolute power had been, like himself and Lloyd, one of the agency's divisional directors – with growing dismay and critical hostility. His motive for joining Lloyd's campaign to restore a sense of constitutional morality into the organization's conduct of affairs is, he says, his interest in preserving an efficient world body which could promote effective development. His earlier, pre-retirement, published criticisms had received positive appreciation and even praise from Saouma's predecessor as Director General, A.H. Boerma of the Netherlands. Today, Matzke bitterly resents attempts by Saouma's chief spokesman, Colin MacKenzie, to brand him in the press as 'a disgruntled ex-employee of FAO'. In reality, he never belonged directly to that body, having served in the separate entity which the World Food Programme constitutes – even though WFP is housed in the FAO's building and co-operates closely with certain of its operations.

As another knowledgeable former 'insider', Matzke is a constant, considerable thorn in the flesh of the present FAO establishment. He sums up his reproaches directed at the latter under six main headings: the lack of external control over the efficiency and development impact of FAO's projects; inadequate independent evaluation of the agency's activities; violation of UNO's 1970 consensus on technical assistance, particularly through the establishment of Saouma's own Technical Co-operation Programme (TCP) in 1976; lack of or insufficient co-ordination with other UNO agencies, especially with the UNDP; political use of emergency food aid; and finally, the considerable waste of public funds resulting from the entirely unnecessary expansion of FAO's country and regional 'diplomatic' representation.

Matzke's critical contributions to the German and international press are among the most telling of the vast flood of critical appraisals of the agency published in recent years, in the eyes of our rulers and their 'decision makers'. For he concentrates, in true German style, on what they see as the essentials of economics and finance. Ethical and social problems rarely find place in his trenchant writings, while environmental or ecological issues might – for all the attention he devotes to them – never exist.

They are given as little importance by another prominent critic at the other extreme of the political spectrum. For if Matzke represents the far right of opinion, Ireland's Erna Bennett, as a self-proclaimed Marxist, is at the far left. A senior FAO 'seeds' expert and geneticist, she was squeezed out of her role as advisor to 'Third World' delegates at the 1981 biennial Conference, when the FAO debated a Mexican proposal to set up a 'gene bank' of seeds. This proposal, concerning an issue which will be discussed in more detail later, aimed at avoiding the danger of monopolies developing in the field of plant genetic resources, to ensure that they were used for the benefit of all humanity, and not just as political tools in the hands of the rich western powers. The latter, led by the United States, West Germany and Switzerland (and backed by Japan), objected to this proposal – as, indeed, they might well be expected to, being holders of the patent rights to all the so-called 'miracle' hybrids about which we have heard so much. In deference to this powerful western alliance, coupled with its clear threats to cut off funding should the proposal be accepted, Erna Bennett – FAO's most respected plant geneticist – was prevented from addressing the assembly on the issue. She could not be prevented, however, from personally briefing 'Third World' delegates who asked her to do so during the conference.

Squeezed off the conference floor, she was not so easily to be expelled from the organization entirely. With the solid backing of her 'Third World' friends, and her own qualities as a charismatic teacher and tenacious fighter, West German and British demands that she should be forced out of the agency's employment were of little avail. During her years with the FAO, Bennett not only became its most honoured seeds expert, but also one of its most effective trade union organizers. She organized some 1,500 Italian service staff into a union and brought them out on strike, in protest against their abominable working conditions.

Someone with a fighting spirit like this is obviously difficult to squeeze out. So her Belgian departmental chief, Robert J. Pichel, was ordered to buy her out – at any price. By this time she had realized that, with western opposition so adamantly united against her, she could easily be isolated within the organization, and thereby effectively neutralized. The better, therefore, to continue her deeply felt mission to serve the poor of the earth, she decided to accept the 'golden handshake'. She recounts, with some glee, the months of overtures and haggling which preceded her final acceptance and resignation, and claims that if she had known of the 'any price' tag, she would have extracted even more out of the deal, to facilitate the continuing fight for her ideals outside the organization. This she pursues from Trinity College, Dublin, where she has a fellowship, and from her home just outside Rome.

Like the majority of its more serious critics, Erna Bennett is committed to the necessity of FAO as an institution. The reforms she would suggest might, however, denote another set of priorities. As a Marxist, she retains a wary scepticism about the motives of the most vociferous right-wing FAO critics, and consequently of many other progressive reformers who find themselves in general alliance with the right-wing coalition. And they, in turn, in a saddening manifestation of the sort of international and political bickering which so frequently divides (so permitting authority rule) such heterogeneous movements, question the altruism of her own commitment – and even probity – by claiming that her acceptance of a 'golden handshake' has compromized any claims she may have had to idealism as grounds for resignation. For her part, she explains her position thus:

> The world is threatened by famine because governments, big seed and petroleum corporations – with FAO's literature behind them – have propagated the false miracle of the so-called 'Green Revolution'. FAO has pushed these high-producing new seeds, by-passing the fact – concealed by the companies – that they require huge amounts of capital. Farmers must increase cultivation and irrigation, and buy more fertilizer and pesticides to force two or even three crops a year out of the soil.
>
> Since these plants are genetically as alike as matchsticks, a nation's entire crop can be wiped out at a stroke if disease breaks out. Our only safety is to protect all the healthy natural variants in seed banks, so that we can call upon healthy strains to replace defective ones which might appear.

The extent of Erna Bennett's continuing personal influence on events and developments within the seeds sector is reflected in the bases of support and confidence she still enjoys – outside FAO as much as within – among 'Third World' country delegates and experts. Their countries, grouped together in an alliance known throughout the aid business as the 'G77', now control almost every aspect of this and other international agencies – except for control of the pure strings. This last is the only surviving function remaining in the hands of the West, which can and does employ it to dislodge such indomitable and embarrassing opponents despite their enjoyment, as in Bennett's case, of the solid support of the G77.

What is the G77?

The 'Group of 77' (G77) has been called many things, and resents most of them. It was first formed by 77 poorer countries – usually called, in today's patronizing jargon, by that other misnomer, 'Third World' – as a bargaining counterweight to the West's rich man's club, the Organization for Economic Co-operation and Development (OECD), as well as to the common market and other rich-world power blocs assembled at the 1964 UNCTAD Conference. The last is, of course, a further offspring of the UNO family, concerning itself with 'Trade, Aid and Development'.

Since that time, the G77 has acquired many more adherents, totalling 124 members by 1982. To further confuse the issue, they now include such dubiously 'Third World' countries as Yugoslavia, Rumania, Iran, Argentina, Brazil, Venezuela, both Koreas, Mexico, Kuwait, Lebanon and Qatar – the tiny population of the last statistically enjoying the highest *per capita* income in the world.

The greater proportion of the 'Third World' grouping were former colonies of the imperialist powers, and were initially called 'under-developed' in the aid industry terminology. Their universal objection to this denigratory term was met by converting them into 'developing' countries – until it became too abundantly clear that many of the poorest among them were rapidly becoming vastly poorer. These then became the 'Least Developed Countries' (or LDCs, for even poverty and immiseration must have its acronyms) as someone noticed the difference between, say, Taiwan, Argentina or Kuwait (all approaching western standards of affluence) and such countries as Haiti, Upper Volta or Tanzania – among the many of those suffering from rapid negative growth, in fact becoming more 'undeveloped' than ever.

Be this as it may, the G77 does indeed group the majority of economically poorest countries – and the economic qualifier is necessary, for we should bear in mind that very many of them are still far richer than much of the West in indigenous culture, social cohesiveness and even development potential – into a single caucus. It is indeed the only real voice with which they can make themselves heard in the halls of international power. Formation of the G77 brought these countries to realize the omnipotence of a united majority interest group, under the 'one-nation-one-vote' system enshrined in the constitutions of UNO bodies. Current FAO membership is 152 countries at the time of writing, and each has equal voting rights at decision-making conferences, regardless of size of the country or its population – or even its contribution to FAO funds. Thus G77's 124 membership, voting as a block, automatically represents a majority to support any measure or person enjoying the group's favour, or a blocking vote for any measure it disapproves. Voting rights are vested in country delegates appointed by each national government, who are supposed to guard their own country's best interests.

However, as Raymond Lloyd points out, many of these countries are ruled by dictatorships of one political colouring or another, maintained in power over their subjects by armed force (frequently backed by secret police terrorism) and sustained by one or other of the opposing world powers. In January 1983 he published a list of 83 G77 members, the governments of which rape, murder, torture or imprison political, religious or ethnic opponents who have neither committed nor advocated acts of violence.

These domestic abuses of citizens' rights raise serious questions about the democratic guise of any organization basing its constitution on such national government representation. On the other hand, any other form of representation – perhaps in proportional terms based on a free choice of the people represented – is difficult to envisage in practice. In any case FAO, like UNO, refuses adamantly to consider any such possibility.

Daily American's dossier of indictment

The embattled FAO has been subjected to continous sniping, with an occasional salvo of heavy gunfire from writers like Susan George, or English economist Colin Clarke's publication, 'Starvation or Plenty', since the time of the *Economist*'s first attack in 1955 mentioned above. The most savage onslaught – a veritable bombardment – struck home just before Christmas of 1982, with the publication by the *Daily American* of a 52-page 'FAO dossier'. This supplement to the regular edition of the paper laid out in detail the major issues upon which the agency's critics based their bitter complaints.

In this, FAO's Director General, Edouard Saouma, stands accused of a veritable catechism of sins: of squandering public money; of constitutional manipulation and political intrigue; of using bullying methods, intimidation and vindictiveness; of arrogance; and finally – worst of all – of failing the under-privileged and hungry in pursuit of glamorous agribusiness schemes which could only benefit the West or the politicians and senior functionaries of G77.

Publication of the *Daily American*'s 'FAO dossier' presented a damning indictment of the 'State of FAO' under Saouma. Within the agency the immediate effect, according to trustworthy informants in its information services (who demand anonymity, for fear of reprisals), was one of general panic in the upper echelons, and bemused wonderment, not unmixed with a certain secret and admiring joy, at subordinate and service levels. Nevertheless, Saouma's chief press spokesman, Colin MacKenzie, rapidly fired off a reply, which the paper duly published, full of invective and personal slander directed at the paper's publisher Robert Cunningham Jr and singling out three of the 15 authors involved.

Otto Matzke, a contributor to the dossier and one of MacKenzie's joint targets, pointed out subsequently that this was merely an attempt to use personal defamation in lieu of substantive argument. It made no pretence of commenting on any of the serious issues raised by the paper. Apart from this single, unfortunate response, nothing more was forthcoming as the agency battened down the hatches to await the storm's blowing over. There has been no official comment since, although Yugoslavia's Milan Zjalic, then current chairman of the G77, did write a short reproachful letter inferring that an attack on Saouma was an attack on his group, and expressing solidarity with the beleaguered Director General and his staff.

Privately, however, the press lines were soon at work. A well-trusted source within the pressroom of the FAO's Information Division, begged inquiring journalists to consider, in his own words, 'How a "two-bit" fascist rag like the *Daily American* could ever afford the luxury of a glossy 52-page production like the dossier . . . without a column-inch of advertising in it, to help pay for it.' He went on to claim that the CIA was behind it – recalling that the paper's forerunner, the *Rome Daily American*, formerly owned by Robert Cunningham's father, was once totally financed by the CIA, and subsidized long thereafter.

3. The CIA connection

As custodian of the bulk of the world's exportable grain, the USA might regain the primacy in world affairs.

CIA report

It is a sad reflection of the world we live in – and of the reporting of it which we are offered by the media today – that the extent to which the US Central Intelligence Agency (CIA) has a finger in every pie, has become a yawn-provoking banality. We forget the extent and depth of influence of such clandestine bodies. When Kissinger or Earl Butz make speeches glorifying the power of the American 'food weapon', they are merely quoting the researches and assessments of the CIA, which works intimately with the National Space Administration (NASA) in evaluating 'spy-in-the-sky' photographs of the world's croplands, and keeps a running check on world harvests and crop potentials. The intelligence agency is thus fascinated by food and agriculture, and the organizations which influence its production.

The FAO, in its campaign of calumny in response to the *Daily American*'s critical onslaught, touched on a tender nerve when it referred to a past CIA connection.

What is the *Daily American*?*

Even in Rome, long-standing local residents have·difficulty answering this one. Adding to their confusion, there are in fact two – and over time have been three or four, or perhaps five – newspapers of similar name, format and style of content.

To bring a little clarity into the matter, I went to see Robert Cunningham. He explained that, at the time of the 'CIA Connection', the paper was owned and published by his father, a one-time employee of the CIA. He later transferred from the intelligence agency to the US foreign service. On leaving

* See footnote, page 14

government service he settled in Rome, bought the newspaper, and ran it for several years. When he finally retired in 1972, Cunningham Senior returned with his family to the USA, having sold the *Rome Daily American* to Michele Sindona, a shady Italian financier and entrepreneur later involved in a series of international financial scandals, culminating in his buying and fraudulently bankrupting the Franklin Bank of Washington, for which peccadillo he served a sentence in a US jail. Sindona's Italian agent then sold the paper to an Italian printing firm.

About the time of Cunningham Senior's sale of the paper, a congressional inquiry in Washington was investigating the covert activities of the CIA. It heard – with the whole world listening in – about the wide range of western publications and radio services which were subsidized, or even entirely financed, by CIA funds. The *Rome Daily American* was one of them. As we then learned, it was originally set up entirely by the CIA, and first run by an editor appointed by the agency. As the paper became commercially viable, the CIA first handed over control, and eventually complete ownership. It was from this former CIA colleague that Cunningham Senior bought the paper in 1964.

Robert Cunningham Junior was 16 years old when he first arrived in Rome with his father. He first learnt journalism and newspaper publishing on the old *Rome Daily American*, and after returning to the US to study, he was quietly determined to buy the paper back and run it himself. On returning to Rome with this in mind, he was, however, immediately disenchanted with the idea, owing to the prospect of inheriting its million-dollar debts. Instead, he decided to await its imminent bankruptcy, indeed helping it along the road to collapse by setting up a new, competing English-language daily newspaper in the same limited market, calling this the *International Daily News*.

In a long and impressively frank interview, Robert Cunningham recalled that the *Rome Daily American*'s final collapse took far longer than he had expected. It was five years before he was able to buy the 'masthead' for a nominal sum, amalgamate it with his new paper and change the name to the *Daily American*. The paper is now entirely financed by sales and advertising income, and Cunningham categorically denied receiving outside financing of any sort from any source. He claimed in fact that, in printing all three daily newspapers and as 'third party' printer for 30 to 40 other periodicals, his printing business generates enough income for him not to need it anyway.

Asked what his motives were in publishing the FAO dossier, as the climax of a long series of investigations and exposures – which the FAO sees as a crusade against it – he repudiated the 'crusade' epithet, declaring firmly that all articles published in his paper are fair investigative reporting of matters of public concern and interest. He gave three main grounds for his paper's devotion of so much space to the FAO. The first might be summarized as 'duty-on-the-doorstep': because the *Daily American* is a permanent inhabitant of Rome, all main local issues and organizations – the Italian state, the Vatican, the FAO and other Rome-based international agencies – are in the legitimate publishing domain of the paper and require its special attention.

His second reason was humanitarian, rooted in his personal experience of living in some of the poorest countries in the world, on his father's various consular postings. After becoming well acquainted over the years with FAO's inside stories, he became thoroughly disgusted with the way the agency is run; projects never becoming reality, and the money destined for the poor being swallowed up by a luxury-living bureaucracy.

In explaining his third main motivation, Robert Cunningham made no secret of his personal political interests and ambitions. An active right-wing Republican, he was involved in the Republican National Committee which drew up the electoral platform with which Reagan successfully campaigned for the presidency. Thus during his examination of possibilities of 'streamlining' US government costs and contributions to international agencies, he was deeply shocked to find America contributing 25 per cent of the FAO budget, while the money goes mainly to countries which, in his words, 'unrelentingly knock the USA'.

He was not merely referring to 'Third World' countries, as he made clear. The dossier, quoting a 1982 article from *African Business*, graphically demonstrates that the FAO pays far more to the nationals of other donor countries than they themselves contribute to its funds. For every million lire the Italians allocate to FAO projects, they get 16 million back in the form of salaries and contracts. The ratio for Holland is 1:5; for Belgium, 1:7; the French, on the other hand, have to be satisfied with more modest returns – for each franc they contribute, they get only two back.

The British do much better. One of Mrs Thatcher's first economies upon taking office was to cut 'aid' spending, including that on FAO. But the businessmen's lobby, in the form of the British Chamber of Industry, soon put her right, and spending was once more increased. For every pound the UK allocates to FAO, British business interests get seven pounds back. And yet all these countries, said Cunningham, are among the foremost of those where carping about the United States – contributor of a quarter of all this money – is loudest and most widespread. He emphasized that this does not mean he believes that people in countries criticizing the US should not get food, but his main cause for anger is that only three cents out of every dollar actually reach the poor. He summed up his position thus: 'There is no such thing as hunger having any political colour, but the problem is that the US should have proper accountability for what happens to our money. One-country-one-vote is OK for whom it is to be used for. But there should be more proportional control on *how* it's spent'.

Accounting for sensitivities

Cunningham is far from alone in his concern for responsible spending. But accounting for where the money goes is one of several areas in which Saouma is most sensitive. As mentioned earlier, he adamantly abjures any attempt to investigate the subject. He sees a threat to FAO's sovereignty in any attempt to introduce effective measures of outside assessment of the agency's massive spending, even in terms of the development effect it has. Equally unwelcome are proposals that FAO should co-ordinate its efforts with those of the multitude of other UNO agencies also heavily engaged in the food sector. Apart from the World Bank – which is not part of the United Nations family, although it tends to arrogate a kind of 'honorary suzerainty' through its control of the development purse strings – these include the UNDP, the ILO, WFP, the World Health Organization (WHO), IFAD, the United Nations Children's Emergency Fund (UNICEF) and many more (to a total, according to the former Canadian Minister of Agriculture, Eugene Whelan, when speaking at the 1980 World Food Council meeting in Arusha, of at least 20 major organizations).

Indeed, Saouma violently over-reacted when a Swiss delegate to the 1979 conference proposed a limited external evaluation of the agency's performance based on spot checks. The Director General intervened in an open plenary session to subject the delegate concerned to a blistering attack, a personal onslaught which left other delegates breathless with astonishment. Saouma later apologized, in private, to the head of the Swiss delegation. The latter, however, insisted on reading into the session's record, the following day, his delegation's diplomatically worded protest: 'I must declare to the Conference that the Director General's intervention yesterday concerning Switzerland is unacceptable to my delegation. It is not the director general's right to make uncivil remarks to representatives of member states.'

In the event, the conference rejected the Swiss proposal, on the somewhat singular grounds that 'the results might not be commensurate with the costs involved'. This effectively endorsed Saouma's free hand with regard to disposal of vast resources for projects and their implementation.

Even the lists and locations of many FAO projects are kept in the 'top secret' classification. At the last biennial conference, delegates managed, after a considerable struggle, to force the Director General to produce a list of the 60 FAO 'embassies' he has opened around the world since taking office – the appointments of their 'envoys' and senior staff being at his personal discretion. (Previously, FAO shared the representative services these are supposed to perform with other UNO bodies, such as UNDP or ILO.) Nevertheless, a list of some 1,200 projects set up under his personally created and controlled TCP remained under a protective cover of secrecy, despite the most persistent donor country demands. We will examine the TCP, and Saouma's handling of it, in further detail in the following pages.

Stratagems for survival

Many observers of the FAO phenomenon legitimately wonder, not without some wry admiration, how Saouma succeeds in surviving in office, given the barrages of 'flak' fired in his direction ever since he came to power. His survival mechanisms have long been the subject of intensive study among his leading critics. To analyze them, it is necesssary to go back some way towards his origins.

Born in 1927 into a Maronite Christian family in Lebanon, Saouma studied modern agricultural technology at Beirut University's School of Engineering, graduating in agricultural chemistry in 1949. In 1952 he graduated in agricultural engineering at the Montpelier School of Agronomy in France. His present penchant for 'high-tech' agricultural systems and chemical pesticides thus appeared, or was inspired, at the outset of his career. He immediately entered the Lebanese public service, first to run a school of mechanized agriculture, and then as director of Lebanon's National Institute for Agricultural Research.

It was during this period in the late 1950s, that a popular left-wing movement appeared to have a good chance of democratically achieving power in Lebanon. In 1958 the United States, fearing that their interests in the region would be threatened by any such development, sent in the US marines. They then installed a puppet government, under Maronite President Gamayel Chamoun's successor, Fuad Chebab. Its members and all senior officials serving it were thoroughly vetted and approved by the CIA, then in its heyday.

Under this regime Saouma, then just over 30 years old, and whose assiduity and ambition were never in doubt, went from strength to strength. By 1961, as the Lebanon's delegate to the FAO Conference, he was largely instrumental in swinging six key Arab country votes – Beirut then being the oil sheikhs' favoured banking centre and playground – to support the contested re-election of India's Dr Sen, then incumbent Director General. Saouma's judicious interventions on Dr Sen's behalf during the election debate were promptly rewarded, upon its successful outcome, with a plum appointment to FAO's upper echelons. He became FAO's regional representative, a job with ambassadorial pretentions, for the western zone of Asia and the Pacific, based in India.

Saouma insisted that, before he took up the appointment, its grading in the UNO ranking system should be raised to 'D1'. This category, reserved for senior directors, placed it among the third highest non-elective appointments within the UNO system, carrying a pensionable remuneration (generous perks and allowances apart) of $77,000 a year. As Raymond Lloyd has wryly commented, this was an unusually favourable entry, in those uninflated days, for a 37-year-old Lebanese technician.

From there, his ascent to the top was no less fulminant. In 1970 he was briefly nominated as Lebanese Minister of Agriculture, but instead became FAO's divisional director of the powerful Land and Water Division. From this elevation he commenced a two-and-a-half year campaign, spending $1.5 million in the process – the money being provided by Saudi Arabia – for the top job in the agency. He took up office in November 1975, having defeated six other candidates, for a non-renewable term of office limited by the constitution of the organization to six years.

Once power was in his grasp he clearly had two immediate objectives. The first was to remove the constitutional barrier to his getting re-elected six years hence – a barrier which, ironically, he had played an influential part in creating ten years previously. He set in motion his campaign to achieve this within three months of taking up office. The second objective was, essentially, to find ways of obtaining a tight grip over the agency, thereby also fostering the first one.

Having some time earlier stigmatized FAO Headquarters staff as being '80 per cent superfluous', and 'an army of quarter-masters', he was troubled by little conflict of conscience when, in one of his first acts, he cancelled 155 meetings, axed several hundred budgeted but unfilled posts, and suppressed several hundred publications. The result of these economies was a saving of around $25 million in FAO's domestic budget.

The strategy was simple, if typically shrewd. Saouma's basic problem on taking over direction of the FAO, was essentially one of control of the money. At its founding, FAO was conceived as an advisory and executive body in the field of food production, with its household funding coming from direct, obligatory contributions from member states. Funding of field operations, undertaken at the request of suppliant member governments, was to come from other sources – either major funding bodies such as UNDP, the World Bank, voluntary bilateral aid and other special contributions to specific field projects, or in some cases, partly from the 'recipient' countries themselves.

This gave the FAO little or no control over funding of projects, or of the development aid purse strings, the household budget being fully allocated to administrative functions. Saouma therefore decided to achieve a measure of autonomy in project initiation. The FAO could then spend the money at its own discretion, and not be answerable to any outside body for its disposal. His $25 million in budgetary savings thus gave him the free hand he sought. With it he initiated his Technical Co-operation Programme of field projects, funded, despite all the founding fathers' intentions, out of FAO's compulsory 'regular' budget.

FAO initially presented TCP as a means of providing prompt small-scale action in short-term, unforeseen situations, or in other words as a means of 'crisis trouble-shooting'. By 1981 TCP had become an established item of the regular compulsory budget, the size of which is decided by the conference delegates upon recommendations by the Director General. The size of TCP funding has settled at around 12–13 per cent of FAO's domestic budget – some $50 million in the last biennium. Attribution of TCP projects is entirely at the Director General's personal discretion. In practice they rarely amount to more than $75,000 each, although there is no limit to the number of projects any country may be accorded. Examples of this 'emergency aid' range from industrial forest plantations in northern Greece, or the implementation of the Vistula project formulation mission in Poland, to a pre-investment study for processing tropical fruit in Upper Volta or a campaign for the prevention of African swine fever. Fifty per cent or more of TCP funds are spent on capital goods – vehicles, tractors and equipment. Such goods remain in the recipient country as free gifts on termination of the projects, a scale of generosity unmatched elsewhere in the international aid industry.

As was mentioned earlier, the FAO direction treats TCP project lists as 'top secret' internal documents. This is probably because, as the inevitable leak of some information about their contents has proved, they provide a wealth of ammunition for Saouma's critics. Although damage to recipient countries' own agricultural sectors frequently occurs as a result of ill-planned gifts of food – damage which has been widely recognized and publicized over the years by authoritative bodies and people engaged in the famine-relief field – Saouma nevertheless continues to instigate countries (such as, in recent years, Cameroon, Ghana and Upper Volta) to ask for such aid, frequently against the better judgement of the country's own experts.

Saouma's largesse is by no means restricted to that permitted under his TCP. In relative terms it even appears to be a minor source of 'handouts' when compared with the greatest supply sources. Two funds here – the Emergency Reserve Fund of the FAO-UN World Food Programme (amounting to $45 million in 1980), and the International Emergency Food Reserve (which aims to guarantee availability of 500,000 tonnes of grain a year through voluntary contributions) – allow him absolute discretion over the disposal of food worth some $200 million, including transport.

Craft of power

The second lever to power which Saouma grasped immediately on attaining office was control of staff appointments. Until his arrival, senior staff normally enjoyed the security of permanent appointments. On taking over, the new Director General restricted all new Assistant Director General, Senior Director and Director contracts to a period of five years – renewable at his own discretion. This could not be made retrospective, to affect existing incumbents of such posts, but many of these – especially from the western countries, which in the early days provided the majority of senior staff – were at the peak of their careers, and fairly shortly due for retirement.

Thus with a large number of such 'D1' and 'D2' posts within his gift or due for renewal, 167 of them carrying remunerations (without allowances) of $77,000 up to $117,000 a year, he not only holds the most powerful means of guaranteeing a complacent senior management, but also the most effective means of keeping them docilely in line once installed.

Apart from the fear and inertia induced in the 'tamed' FAO staff by such methods (and the agency has become rightly renowned, even in the world of international functionaries, as the world's leading centre of masterly inactivity), Raymond Lloyd traces another corrosive influence in staffing policies at the top. This relates to the fact that senior staff of such international organizations enjoy the privilege of tax-free diplomatic status. As a result, in many western civil services – particularly their foreign ministries and 'aid' departments – senior functionaries approaching retirement angle for a secondment to the FAO, in order to spend their last five working years there. If successful in obtaining such an appointment, this entitles them not only to an FAO pension on top of the pension rights they have already acquired in their home service, but also gives them the right, should they so wish, to retire in Italy with life-long tax-free status on the lot. A graceful retirement spent under the Italian sunshine is no inconsiderable incentive for such people to keep their greying heads down.

However this may be, another senior official, currently if belatedly arranging to resign in protest at the decline of the organization (he has not yet done so, and like many other informants requires anonymity until the process is completed), has also served for many years and has an intimate knowledge of US foreign policy as well as of the intrigues of FAO. He is convinced — and claims that his conviction is shared by several other knowledgable US insiders — that whatever power Saouma may hold, he could never have survived the massed antagonism of the major western donor countries without himself still enjoying the firm, if discreet, backing of the CIA. According to this official, who has established the reliability of his views over many years, Saouma is secretly favoured by the Americans simply because he has the G77 in his hand, buying up any dissenting voices as necessary, and steering them (and the FAO) in the directions most desired by US agribusiness.

A simpler, less dramatic if rather more cynical explanation is given by Paul Vaughan, formerly the 'French Desk' officer of FAO Information Division's pressroom. Asked why the wealthy western countries, currently almost unanimous in their criticism of FAO's policies and practices under Saouma, continue to finance an organization in which they will always be in a minority, despite their providing 75-80 per cent of the money, Vaughan suggests that FAO merely serves an inexpensive 'alibi function'. Western ministers of agriculture gain the right, through their countries' 'membership fee' contributions (paltry sums compared either with the turnover of their own national agricultural sectors, or with the needs of FAO's hungry 'clients'), to make a biennial descent to Rome, and have a guaranteed public platform there. The biennial conference allows them, each in turn, to trot out their tired old platitudes about solidarity with the 'Third World' and concern for the plight of the starving poor. Then they return home with good conscience, to get on with the business of plundering the earth's resources for the benefit of their own well-fed citizens, and the profit of their agribusiness interests which run the whole show.

Vaughan is able to express his criticisms openly, having left the FAO to return to his original field of journalism. But many people of moral stature and discerning conscience remain within the organization, and indeed throughout the UNO system, today chronically riddled with similar problems and abuses – and they stay not merely out of self-interest. But it is not easy for them to find the suitable vehicle for voicing their qualms. Some genuinely believe that they can still do much good and that, by staying with the agency, they might still serve in some small measure to preserve the lofty ideals which endowed its foundation. Some, again, believe that there is little point, in the situation in which their organization currently finds itself, in publicly exposing its lacunae – and thereby themselves. Immediate retribution, accompanied at least by isolation within the organization if not with rapid expulsion from it, would nullify any further usefulness and influence for good they may hope to have.

Publication of the *Daily American* dossier in itself produced a crop of new revelations from people with troubled consciences still inside the agency. As usual, these 'whistle-blowing' officials demanded the safeguard of anonymity, at least until the backing and protection of their own governments could be arranged. Such backing is by no means automatically assured. Most startling among them was a senior advisor in FAO's Investment Centre; he not only recounted details of how he and his colleagues were on occasion ordered to 'cook the books' in pre-investment studies, but even brought documentary proof of such practices, consisting of official correspondence and copies of internal memoranda.

FAO's investment advisory service was set up to advise both supplicant member governments and other non-technical aid bodies like the World Bank, on the feasibility of proposed projects. The agricultural agency also offers itself as technical executive for such of these projects as see the light of day, once the financing authority is satisfied with its pre-investment studies. The costs of FAO's experts and administrators are, in such cases, paid for by the funding authority. Thus success here further extends the reach of FAO's 'empire', at no cost to its own budgets.

It is obvious that 'recipient' governments – especially in the persons of their expert advisors who prepare such project proposals, and delegates who shepherd them through the complex selection processes – are keen to see their own projects accepted by the selectors and financiers. It follows that a great deal of lobbying and covert pressure is applied to ensure success in this. Even when the motives of such people are irreproachable, sadly not always the case, it is natural that they should see such success of favoured projects, to which they have often contributed great efforts, as a yardstick of their own professional value and advancement. Thus the door is open to much swapping of favours and influence during the process.

The Investment Centre 'whistle-blower' made it plain that many such projects, of dubious viability when examined objectively, receive the special favour and support of the Director General. He quoted a number of cases involving projects put up for World Bank financing, where he and other colleagues, having produced a first unfavourable report on their financial prospects, were ordered to think again, and to 'massage' the figures of their projected accountancy to produce an acceptable 'bottom line'. In practice the World Bank refuses in general to involve itself in projects offering a predicted return of under 10 per cent; this informant told of instances where the order came down from on high even specifying the precise, if entirely fictitious, percentage return to be forecast, usually around 11-12 per cent.

The possibility of any FAO projects achieving viability is even doubted by some experts. Dr Pietro Rava, an independent Italian consultant agronomist, worked for over 25 years on the preparation and realization of tropical agricultural projects for all the major aid agencies in the field. He defines FAO and similar aided projects as 'preselecting economic lunacy'.

In his view, any project which is at all likely to produce a reasonable return will find all the financing it requires in the normal commercial sector, either domestic or international. This leaves only such projects for the FAO as are – for a variety of possible reasons – of dubious viability and unlikely ever to produce any economic return. The point has not escaped the specialists of FAO's Investment Centre. However, political pressure from the top has resulted, in the cases revealed, in the abandonment of all the classical rules of financial caution, for the benefit of Edouard Saouma's friends.

4. Zapping Africa's flies

And in the earth are *diverse* tracts, adjoining one another, and gardens of vines, and corn-fields, and date-palms, growing together from one root and *others* not so growing; they are watered with the same water, yet We make some of them excel others in fruit. Therein are Signs for a people who understand.

The Holy Qur'an 13,5

We have dealt thus far with the more general themes of administrative policy and moral principle in the FAO. It offers an excellent proving ground for such basic ideas and ideals, in that it typifies the practices and problems of this nature which confront all international bodies so constituted, throughout the aid industry. While the FAO provides a paradigm of such organizations, a typical example of its own failures or false directions can best be illustrated by examining in depth one of its most extensive, enduring and most heatedly criticized field operations.

FAO's 'tsetse war', as has already been mentioned, is one such campaign which clearly shows its dangerous addiction to what its critics have called the 'technological fix'. Dependency of the poorer countries on highly sophisticated western technology is created, expanded and perpetuated in the course of such operations; and the future sales of western agro-industry thereby assured for years to come.

In itself this could be counted a minor blemish if the result was a majority of better-fed and healthier people in the lands affected. This is indeed claimed by the agribusiness salesmen and their FAO sponsors – who can hardly be expected to say otherwise. But the true situation brought about by such expensive activities looks very different to more objective or less interested observers, and the foreseeable future holds out worrying prospects of damaging environmental change and human disaster on a continental or even worldwide scale.

Surplus food in US hands might well be a more powerful weapon than the H-bomb; but its production through the universalization of a single western 'high-tech' food system promises to be more environmentally devastating than the nuclear holocaust. The horrific consequences of loosing off even a small proportion of our 'overkilling' arsenals of H-bombs are clear enough to all. Unfortunately, the menace of ecological collapse and its consequences are, in their complexity, more difficult to envisage or appreciate.

It was at the World Food Conference in Rome in 1973, scene of Kissinger's and Butz's rattling of the US 'sickle-sabre', that the FAO first formulated its 'declaration of war' on Africa's tsetse flies. A $2 billion 40-year eradication programme was drawn up by the pesticide producers, aerial spraying contractors and equipment manufacturers, in collaboration with the FAO, and the package then offered to over 40 African governments.

The aim of the campaign was initially to eradicate – though in the light of the realities on the ground, it was later reduced to the more modest ambition to 'control' – tsetse flies over 70 per cent of their African habitat, which in all encompasses some ten million square kilometres. These vast areas, greater in size than the United States or, for the total infested area, than China or Canada, were according to FAO's publicity at the time, 'almost all rainforest or woodland'. As this announcement went out, UN experts were estimating that the world could be losing as much as 245,000 square kilometres of tropical forests every year, and an increase in the rate didn't require this latest contribution from the FAO. Of a global total of around 9,350,000 square kilometres of tropical moist forest, some 22 per cent was in Africa; and losses of the most precious 'climax' areas were then estimated at 51.6 per cent per year.

The object of the exercise as declared by the FAO was to clear this land in order to introduce 120 million additional head of cattle for the production of some 1.5 million tonnes of low-grade beef a year. Who was actually to produce this meat was unspecified in the programme's preliminary publicity.

The tsetse fly is a small brown insect, more or less the size and shape of the common house-fly. Its innocuous appearance is belied by its vicious bite and vampire life style, for it feeds exclusively on the blood of other living creatures, at least in its adult winged form. It is only known in Africa. (An insignificant pocket reported in Asia Minor, which had probably migrated across the Red Sea, may now be extinct. Apart from this, fossil evidence shows the tsetse might once have lived in North America millions of years ago.)

Tsetse – keeping Africa green

Some 20 different species and subspecies of tsetse flies are classified collectively under the generic name *Glossina*. Of these, some become infected with and transmit the microbes (known to science as 'protozoa') which cause sleeping sickness. The disease is known to doctors in the tongue-twisting terminology of their profession as 'trypanosomiasis'. These, again, are divided into many, perhaps a hundred, species and subspecies – although there is still considerable doubt and contention among the specialists of the field as to which can be definitively placed in the various categories open to them. There is, however, general agreement that few tsetse species carry (or 'vector', in the technician's jargon) the type of sleeping sickness trypanosomes (called 'tryps' for short) which we need to fear. It is also thought that only two of the latter (or in the latest view, possibly two strains of a single species – *Trypanosoma brucei*) are implicated in sleeping sickness as it affects humans.

Animals, on the other hand, are susceptible to a far wider range of trypanosome species, which produce in them a disease known in Africa as 'nagana', deriving from the Zulu word for a familiar and often fatal disease in their cattle. The animal version of the disease takes its heaviest toll among domestic animals, nearly all of which are not among the original fauna of Africa, but 'exotic' imports of the last few thousand years. Longhorn and dwarf shorthorn cattle probably arrived in Africa some 4,000 years ago, and the Portuguese black pig only 500 years ago; these are now regarded as 'trypanotolerant'. The susceptibility of the zebu, which has probably been in Africa for about 3,000 years, relates rather to its capacity to be herded at the desert margin, rather than the length of time it has been in Africa. In contrast, natural selection means that local or 'indigenous' animals are obviously resistant to tsetse-borne disease, if not completely immune.

The tsetse is endemic – or more properly enzootic – in areas which scientists call the *Grenzwildnis*, the intermediate or frontier wilderness zones (often poorly watered uplands or watersheds between natural drainage systems, which in themselves form ecological units), or the 'interface' zones between conflicting tribes or peoples. These are areas, then, which are less suitable or desirable as human habitats, separating as they do the ecologically based communities which Edward Goldsmith has termed 'ethnocracies'.

Human settlement tends to drive out tsetse, by destroying the bush or forest cover which the fly needs as resting places. The better land, where people settle in first preference, is cleared of bush – the first step in traditional shifting or rotational agriculture as it has been practised in Africa for millennia, until the arrival of the slave traders, colonists and developers. Under the traditional system, the bush is chopped down flush with the soil, and burnt; but the roots of trees and bushes remain alive in the cropland, each year's regrowth being chopped back during hoeing as it appears. Rotational cycles are short – and under the pressure of development becoming very much shorter – so that the bush regenerates periodically. But when crop growing is disturbed by wars and other forms of unrest and mass migration, the same regrowth will occur throughout the abandoned area, which the tsetse then rapidly recolonizes. Indeed the fly appears to lurk in the marginal, uninhabited areas simply awaiting such opportunities to colonize the rest whenever suitable bush cover happens to offer it a habitat and the wild animals it lives on return to guarantee its food supply. With the constant turmoil of wars and insurrections blighting the stability of rural Africa today, this is a common occurrence.

In less troubled times, while it is kept at bay in its *Grenzwildnis* realm by established intensive human activity, the fly itself serves to protect these zones – and the wildlife they contain – by discouraging encroachment of pastoralists' herds which do not share wild animals' immunity to tsetse-borne disease to anything like the same extent. Thus many experts believe that over much of the continent, it is only the tsetse that is keeping Africa green.

As the *Grenzwildnis* concept implies, tsetse habitat is agriculturally marginal land, unstable as a human habitat. Even if cleared of tsetse flies, prospects of maintaining long-term, viable settlement without permanent outside aid are slim. On the other hand, those familiar with these regions view proposals to introduce uncontrollable numbers of livestock with foreboding; the primary cause of spreading desertification of such fragile areas – as for instance in the Sahel Zone which we will be looking at in a later chapter – is overstocking with cattle.

The only available management systems for running cattle in such uninhabited areas are either that of the nomadic (or seminomadic) pastoralist, or imported sophisticated 'high tech' systems on the western model. The nomads are renowned for a tendency to disappear over the distant hills with their herds whenever the census-taker or taxman makes his annual rounds, and are stubbornly deaf to suggestions that they should limit the size of their cattle herds, or stop cutting down trees to feed them during periods of drought and fodder shortage. The alternative, which in almost every case would require the importation of outside management and carry high overheads in terms of other imported inputs, is unlikely to be economic unless it can find markets for its products in the rich world. It is also subject to the dangers of overstocking, leading to erosion, in so far as the marginal economics of such undertakings would exert tremendous pressure to maximize returns in profit-motivated enterprises.

Our friends, the enemy

To appreciate the difficulties confronting FAO's attack force, it is necessary to look more closely at the tsetse fly's lifestyle and sex life. Both are unusual even among insects. For the female tsetse needs only to mate once in her short eight- to ten- week lifetime; unlike most other insects, she lays no eggs, but gives birth to single young, and not many of these. She produces on average less than one young per week, depositing them carefully on the ground in suitable places under logs or other protective vegetation litter. They then burrow into the soil, there to pupate and metamorphose into adult flies. This last process can take from three weeks to three months, depending on the weather, and particularly the temperature. During it, the immature insect lives on food absorbed from its parent before birth, so that it stays safely buried, out of reach of most predators and of its tsetse-exterminating human enemies.

Emerging from its chrysalis an almost fully formed adult, the young flies still have a soft carapace, which gives them the name 'tenerals', and their digestive tracts are not yet fully formed – a characteristic which has far-reaching consequences in relation to their subsequent role as possible disease vectors. Despite this, they first see the light of day with fully fledged mating and feeding appetites.

The flies feed in general once every two or three days. If undisturbed after they have sunk their hypodermic-like probiscus into the skin of their preferred victim – humans rate low on the list, although above zebra or impala it seems – they drink their fill. Newly born with a body weight greater than its mother's, the larval tsetse uses most of the nutrients she endowed it with during the metamorphosis from larva to teneral adult form. Thus it must find a blood meal within hours of emergence if it is to survive. In fact, scientists have found that the energy reserves of a teneral fly will suffice for only about 20 minutes' flight, giving it a range of around 200 metres.

While its feeding schedule might appear abstemious, the fly is a glutton once at its sanguinary banquet. Injecting saliva with its bite to keep the blood from congealing at the wound, it will consume as much as two or three times its own body weight, so engorging itself that it can only fly with difficulty. Such bloated flies, looking like ripe berries (or in one early observer's description, like red currants) with their distended translucent bellies, make for the nearest safe undergrowth, and spend the subsequent few hours digesting and dehydrating the blood meal, reducing its liquid content to a point where they can once again take nimbly to the air.

The sexual behaviour of male tsetse flies contrasts, like that of the females, with the sexual behaviour of many other species of insect, in which the male's testicles are ruptured, with fatal results, after a successful nuptial flight. A male tsetse can copulate repeatedly, and does so if the opportunity presents itself. So, after digesting his blood meal, he joins a swarm of like-minded males, and together they proceed to follow any likely looking animal in the neighbourhood, in the opportunistic hope that it will attract a hungry female. When the latter approaches her vital food source, a score or more of the following swarm of males will buzz wildly around her, and a nuptial dance ensues. The successful male mates with her, filling her internal semen storage sacs, known as spermathecae, with enough sperm to last for her lifetime. Then, if she is a newly hatched teneral, she is allowed to take her first fill of blood, and retire thereafter to digest and parturate.

As mentioned above, tsetse are viviparous, or more precisely larviparous; the fertilized female will give birth to her first offspring at about three weeks old (age measured from pupation), and thenceforth at regular intervals varying with weather and temperature – from as little as every eight days to as much as every three weeks or more.

A teneral female, urgently bent on her first life-saving blood meal, mates easily. Mature, semen-filled females, on the other hand, seem to spend most of their time in quiet retirement, discreetly gestating and bearing their young between meals. However the drain on their reserves caused by the production of larvae necessitates that they, too, may be obliged to run the male mob gauntlet from time to time. This can lead to their mating for a second time.

An interesting recent, though as yet unconfirmed, observation by one scientist is that the second successful male, in such cases, sometimes cleans out his predecessor's semen from the female's spermathecae before filling them with his own – a fascinating example of 'genetic jealousy', perhaps. If found to be a widespread practice, this might have important repercussions for a method of tsetse eradication which we will examine later.

. . . Bugs to bite 'em

The tsetse's vicious bite and vampirical lifestyle are not, however distasteful, the source of its bad reputation – nor the reason for FAO's declaring chemical war on the insect. As many big-game hunters have discovered, a degree of tolerance to its initially painful attacks develops in a relatively short time. The tsetse bite, on first intimate contact with this pest, raises a painful inflamed weal; but this is no more than a temporary irritation, unless the fly is infected or the wound becomes so through scratching. After a week or two of constant exposure, however, many human victims become less susceptible, the bites causing little pain and no visible mark. Perhaps our bodies produce some counteracting agent to neutralize or remove the tsetse's saliva injection that causes the angry weal to appear in 'fresh' victims.

The flies are otherwise usually harmless to healthy adults. The amount of blood they draw is normally so small in relation to the total in our bodies as to be insignificant. Real trouble only threatens when the flies themselves have their own 'bugs to bite 'em'. These, the trypanosomes, are minute, generally corkscrew-shaped organisms which live parasitically in both their insect hosts and the latter's blood-supplying victim. Unfortunately, they are not merely content to do this, but feel as compelled as any of God's creatures to follow the injunction, 'be fruitful and multiply'. They follow it explosively.

As in many vectored diseases which pass through an 'intermediate host' before reaching their human (or other vertibrate) victim – malaria is perhaps the most familiar example – trypanosomes lead a double life. The configuration of their life history can be represented schematically as a figure 8, one loop occurring in the body of the main host and the other in that of the intermediate host. (Point of view largely determines the definition of which is considered 'main' and which 'intermediate'. However, those who claim that opting for human or mammal as main host is a sympton of 'anthropocentrism' might well reflect that we are, after all, concerned with 'tryps' and tsetse primarily because we are interested in the sickness they produce in ourselves and in our cattle, being naturally obliged to give first priority to our own survival.) In each of these symbiotic loops the trypanosome reproduces itself madly, thereby causing illness in both of its hosts to a greater or lesser extent. But to keep the extent and overall impact of such sickness in perspective, it is worth looking first at some of the statistics involved.

There is general agreement that very few tsetse flies ever become infected by 'tryps', and very few people in Africa die of the disease. Of the former, all experts agree that – while cases vary in different areas at different times, and also among different species of *Glossina* – the average number of infected tsetse in any area is as small as one in every two or three thousand. The upper extreme is contested by some, but all agree with something of this order-of-size. However, while few of the six species of tsetse implicated in the transmission of sleeping sickness trypanosomiasis carry detectable infection with *T. brucei*, the latest research work suggests that this may be because the infection is hidden away in the fly's gut cells.

As for the number of human fatalities, WHO estimates that some 7,000 people suffer from the disease per 'normal' year (i.e. excluding exceptional outbreaks or epidemics which frequently result from civil unrest, warfare, or the mass deportations which accompany many major 'development' projects). Of these sufferers, some five per cent (or around 350 people) die of the disease. In comparison, WHO estimates that ten times as many people in Africa die of measles. The UNO agency is, however, properly cautious about giving too much weight to such estimates, which are based on consideration of the claim that, at the most, only a third of known cases are reported in locally assembled health authority statistics. Besides, as WHO points out, official statistics originating in Africa are so notoriously unreliable that, since 1978, sleeping sickness figures have not been included in its annually published review of the world's health and diseases.

In view of this low incidence of infection in flies, as well as a number of other limiting factors influenced by the flies' habitual behaviour, such a low rate of occurrence of the human version of trypanosomiasis seems entirely credible. Indeed considering the tsetse's feeding habits, it even seems surprising that the disease occurs more than rarely. As we have noted, the tsetse feeds every few days, and lives for only a few weeks. The flies can live without apparent harm for five days on the first urgent feed, while the female's life expectancy in the wild is about 8–10 weeks – rather longer than that of the male fly. Thus a healthy fly may bite no more than a dozen times in its whole lifetime.

The 'aging' of flies is not, incidentally, as difficult a matter as might be supposed. Their wings fray continuously at the rear or 'trailing' edge throughout their lives, and age can be assessed by measuring the amount of fraying against that of a standard fly of known age. The method works better with males than with females, mainly because they are easier to catch in their swarms than the more solitary females. This makes setting of age or fray ratios easier in males. For females, however, Russian scientists (working with mosquitoes) first developed a more accurate method, although this involves greater technical skill and equipment. It depends on the pattern of ovulation. Female tsetses have two ovaries (some creatures, like the ostrich, have only one), each containing two egg-producing ovarioles. The eggs develop in a definite, alternating sequence in capsules or 'follicles' which split to release the ripe egg, leaving a permanent remainder or scar. Counting these follicle remnants under a microscope can give a pretty accurate estimate of the fly's age if ovulation frequency is known.

In captivity, under artificially ideal conditions, females can be kept alive for longer than their natural life span in the wild. An English laboratory at Langford near Bristol has bred captive tsetse by the 1,000 over the last decade. By mating females at three days old (with males that have never mated more than four times) the scientists here keep them alive and productive for an average (or mean) of 120 days, producing during that time 9–10 pupae per female. Until recently, these 'battery' tsetse were fed on captive goats strapped to special trollies, for 15 minutes per day, although never on Sundays. (The goat's suffering was limited – to prevent excessive formation of scar tissue – to 500 bites per session, spaced to every third or fourth day.)

The same dedicated researchers discovered that the flies' output is even better if fed on the ears of floppy-eared rabbits. Average life span increases to 139 days, and average larva production up to 11.4 per female; but the rabbits need more care and attention than goats, and because of their size, fewer cages of voracious flies can be strapped to their ears than can be to the specially shaven flanks of the captive goats. Thus costs of the tsetses' 'bunny-banquets' are higher. However, such feeding routines at Langford have now been abandoned, and flies are fed on a tray of blood covered with a plastic membrane.

Another group of scientists, working this time in Basel in Switzerland, has been examining the effects of 'tryps' infection on the tsetse fly itself – research initiated at the University of Salford in the UK. They may have come up with one answer to the problem of why, given the wild tsetse's essentially modest feeding demands, sleeping sickness is as widespread as it is. Their findings, like the sexual behaviour studies mentioned above, might eventually have a far-reaching influence on approaches towards controlling the disease. They began by infecting a group of flies bred in the Langford laboratory, with trypanosomes imported from Tanzania years before, and preserved by deep-freezing until required. Twenty males and 20 females were infected by feeding them on mice previously injected with the thawed out trypanosomes, while 40 other flies were left uninfected, as controls. They then offered all the flies, starved for one or two days, a blood meal on laboratory mice. More humane than their English counterparts, they first anaesthetized the mice with Nembutal. Carefully counting the number of times each fly probed for a meal, they noted that, after 24 hours' starvation, while all 40 infected flies fed, only 28 of the non-infected ones did. After 48 hours' starvation, all 40 infected flies fed, and 38 of the 40 non-infected flies joined them. Perhaps more importantly, they also counted the number of 'exploratory' probes or bites each fly made before actually feeding; all the non-infected flies fed on the first or second probe, while the infected flies made an average of 4–5 stabs at it before feeding to the full.

The scientists' next step was to find the reason for this curious and ominous discrepancy. They knew that tsetse have a form of appetite control, based on the measurement of the flow of blood through the probiscus. This control function is performed by a number of sensitive organs within the tube of the probe, or *haustellum*, with which the fly pierces the skin and draws in blood. These minute organs, known in entomological jargon as LC1 mechanoreceptor sensillae of the labrum, are in effect flowmeters which tell the fly when it has had enough. With its almost infinitely distendible belly, it presumably needs something to give the message of a feeling of satiety to prevent its eating (or drinking) more than it can carry in flight.

The Basel group then dissected the flies' mouth parts – a delicate operation in itself, only possible since the development of electron microscopy. They found in the infected flies that close-packed colonies of trypanosomes had collected around these flowmeter organs, effectively blocking them off. They also partially blocked the tube itself, cutting down the rate of flow of blood through it. Thus an infected fly neither knows when it has had enough, nor is it able to consume an adequate supply during a normal feeding period. It therefore bites, spreading infection, more frequently than a healthy fly in similar conditions. This factor is of great advantage to the protozoon. Since any such parasitic organism risks killing off its host, and itself in consequence, if too successful in multiplying *in situ*, it has a natural imperative to spread the risk – and thus the infection – by colonizing as many fresh fields as opportunity offers. Trypanosomes do this by means of the fly's feeding habit of injecting saliva into its victim; the parasites around the fly's mouth-parts get a free ride into the next host. The more often the fly bites, the more opportunities the 'tryps' are given to conquer new empires. Scientists have a word for this opportunistic evolution: 'advantageous behavioural adaptation'.

A final factor in this symbiotic cycle of tsetse-trypanosome union is worthy of our attention for the understanding of how we ever catch the disease from so few infected flies; it relates to the incompleteness of the teneral fly's digestive equipment at emergence from the chrysalis. The tsetse, like many other insects, grows a protective lining for its mid-gut, called a peritrophic membrane. This starts to grow at emergence, and is formed of the same chitinous material which hardens the insect's outer carapace (likewise the hair, horns, hooves, beaks or scales of higher animals). It grows as a tube from secretion out of a ring of glandular cells around the gut immediately after the proventricle – the insect equivalent of a stomach – and after several days it has pushed backward down the gut, its upper end remaining attached to the ring of secreting cells. Thus it forms a protective sheath or inner-tube, which is virtually impenetrable to the trypanosome. (The latest work has shown that *T. brucei* can in fact penetrate the peritrophic membrane and develop hidden away in the cells of the mid-gut. This apparently offers the 'tryps' an alternative route to that around the bottom of the gut lining.)

The microbes come to infect tsetse by being ingested in the blood of the fly's food source. Various 'tryps' species behave in different ways once in the fly's digestive system, but the one which need concern us here, *T. brucei*, is perhaps the most complicated. It descends with the blood to the mid-gut, and then penetrates the wall of this to undergo its metamorphoses and reproduction in the space outside the gut. Later, in the infective elongated form known as metacyclic, it bores its way back and makes its way to the fly's salivary glands, to await re-injection into another host.

Once the chitinous sheath has formed, the trypanosomes are foiled unless they can find their way around the unattached end of the protective lining – which apparently rarely happens – or can penetrate the sheath's junction with the gut wall before it has time to harden properly. A field worker in Kenya, D.J.B. Wijers, showed in 1958 that in the case of the sort of 'tryps' infective to humans at least, the fly must take its first blood meal from an infected source. Otherwise, it is unlikely to become infected itself by later infected feeds, and so will remain harmless to all intents and purposes.

Wijers in fact drew up a set of five essential conditions, which must be satisfied before a fly (and it should be born in mind that only very few *Glossina* species are implicated here) can become a potential infectious menace to people: the fly must be ready to feed, and have the opportunity to do so, within 24 hours of emerging from its puparium; its first host must be a human being; that person has to be suffering from sleeping sickness; even then, the disease must be in the early stage, when sufficient 'tryps' are circulating in the peripheral bloodstream; the tsetse must live thereafter, surviving the many natural perils of predation, as well as the effects of its own sickness, for at least 18 days in order that the trypanosomes can go through their cycle of development and metamorphosis before returning to their infectious metacyclic form in the fly's salivary glands.

A further factor – which might cause some relief to anyone reading this account in the temperate zones of the world – is that the duration of the trypanosome's development cycle, a minimum of 17 days at high temperatures, is critically affected by temperature. It has proved difficult or even impossible to obtain infection in laboratory flies at low temperatures.

With all these delicate factors working against it, it becomes less surprising that sleeping sickness epidemics are as infrequent as they are – and infection from an occasional tsetse bite almost unknown.

Lines of attack

It will be seen from the foregoing that, in its attack on one of Africa's few remaining friends of the natural environment – and the vast resource this represents – the FAO has taken on a considerable enemy. Its task force's main function is to co-ordinate the campaign against the fly right across the continent.

While including some experimental work on more sophisticated techniques, which we will examine later, the weaponry overwhelmingly deployed consists of the 'hard' pesticides – DDT, lindane (BHC gamma isomer) and the deadly range of 'drins' (dieldrin, aldrin, endrin etc.), or the more recently developed Thiodan (endosulfan) – which are known to chemists as chlorinated hydrocarbons, or else organochlorines. The even more lethal organophosphates – malathion, parathion and dichlorvos – are also used, although not on any wide scale, and mainly for testing and comparative research purposes. Practically all of these pesticides are ordered and paid for (often with the aid of World Bank and other international loans) by the African governments concerned or agencies they employ, on the advice of the various task force and bilateral aid experts. The FAO, however, and all of the bilateral aiders it co-ordinates, deny any involvement in the choice of which pesticides are used.

All of these poisons are manufactured in the West. The first (and perhaps least deadly) of these, DDT, was banned or severely restricted for use in all western countries – and its manufacture or importation totally forbidden in many – following widespread acknowledgement of its dangers after Rachel Carson's publication in 1962 of *Silent Spring*. However, the Second International Conference on Environmental Futures in Reykjavik heard, in 1977, that more DDT was being manufactured in the West than before the prohibitions were imposed.

The 'drins' on the other hand are produced entirely in the West, exclusively by the Royal Dutch Shell company's plant at Pernis in Holland, and in small quantities at the Velsicol plant in the USA, the entire production being marketed by the London-based Shell International. Use of all these poisons, manufactured in their thousands of tonnes per year, is now totally banned throughout the advanced countries for all practical purposes, with the notable exception of endosulfan, produced by West Germany's Hoechst Company near Frankfurt on the Rhine. They are dumped in the poorer tropical countries which have not yet instituted such bans, the sales being paid for most often from money loaned under the title of 'aid'.

In this way the western chemical manufacturers have been able to overcome the embarrassment of surplus production capacity and, together with the application specialists with whom they work, to make considerable profits from this dubious trade. We will, again, be examining the profits of poison in a later chapter; suffice it to say here that the recipients of this poisonous 'aid' are left with an immediately poisoned environment which often leads to the rapid occurrence of dependence on these chemicals, a massive load of foreign debt and, especially in the case of the tsetse war, the disappearance of their traditional wildlife meat sources – either directly as a result of spraying, or indirectly through the effects of land-use change and competition.

According to the programme's advocates, tsetse eradication involves a far smaller order of magnitude of risk than does crop protection spraying; quantities of the active ingredient (the technician's euphemism for the pure poison, which is always used highly diluted in the field) employed in aerial spraying of tsetse habitat usually amount to about one kilogram per hectare (10,000 square metres), while land producing three crops of cotton a year may receive an annual drenching of over half-a-tonne per hectare. It should be borne in mind, however, that the use of hard chemical pesticides to open up new lands also opens the door to further, and much more intensive, deployment of chemicals to keep subsequent crops pest-free.

Eradication of the tsetse fly has long been the dream of Africa's colonial settlers and developers, even from the times of the early explorers. In 1858 David Livingstone was asked, on leaving Britain to explore the Zambezi, to carefully note the number of tsetse bites required to kill an ox – an inconvenience with which he became all-too-familiar, as tsetse killed off his riding animals and reduced the intrepid doctor to walking across Africa. And two years later, Sir Richard Burton, who knew the pest from his explorations further north, around the sources of the Nile, wrote: 'It is difficult to conceive the purpose for which this plague was placed in a land so eminently fitted for breeding cattle . . . Possibly at some future date, when the land becomes valuable, the tsetse may be exterminated by the introduction of some insectivorous bird, which will be the greatest benefactor that Central Africa ever knew.'

Although Burton's bird has not yet been discovered, battle really commenced in the early years of this century, the attack being aimed mainly at the fly's habitat and wild animal hosts. Wide-scale spraying only came into vogue after the Second World War, with its introduction of the organochlorine insecticides.

Traditionally, it was carried out by teams of locally trained semi-skilled African 'control assistants', using back-pack tanks of pesticide and hand pumps with manually operated spray nozzles. The method works well. The insecticide dosage can be accurately controlled, and the spray directed very precisely at the fly's resting places. The disadvantage is that it is very labour intensive, and with the rising expectations of the people capable of using it, it is becoming increasingly difficult to find labour prepared to suffer the hardship of life continuously in the bush for months, for small rewards.

This difficulty, plus the refinement of aerial spraying techniques and aircraft, created an opening for the technology-minded developers, to the obvious delight of the pesticide manufacturers. Their first campaigns were carried out by slow flying fixed-wing aircraft, deluging high concentrations of 'active ingredient' – usually DDT or dieldrin at the time – dissolved in petroleum-based solvents. The object was to leave the residues of sprayed droplets, after the solvent had evaporated, on the vegetation of trees and bushes where the tsetse sleeps at night. Spectacular killings of fish, birds and other animals as well as the 'target organism' tsetse, led to refinements of the method to reduce the quantities of poison distributed. This is now down to the point where operators refer to the technique as 'Ultra-Low-Volume (ULV)'.

To get enough pesticide down onto the fly's sleeping quarters still involves spraying as much as 800 grams to a kilogram of potent poison on each hectare, and the areas involved usually run to some thousands of square kilometres for each operation. Some areas have to be ULV sprayed several times, and as much as 25 per cent of the total area being cleared is sprayed at least once. The prime targets in any area are the streams, rivers and banks of water bodies (lakes, dams etc.).

Dieldrin is notorious for its effect on fish and other aquatic creatures, and those who live on them. Endosulfan, the still widely permitted Thiodan of West Germany, is reputed by its manufacturers to be even worse. But these and other chemicals do not knock out the tsetse entirely by this ULV method, because of the creature's habit of sleeping upside down, like a fly on the ceiling, on the underside of leaves where the poison cannot reach it. The droplets of pesticide only reach flies perching on the upper sides and vertical faces of twigs and branches.

A more advanced technique was developed to overcome this problem. Known as 'aerosol' or 'mist' spraying (or again, sometimes 'drift' spraying), the idea is to create a mist or cloud of molecular-sized droplets, to envelop completely the vegetation and the fly, catching, in effect, the fly on the wing. But here again, problems rapidly appeared. Today, much aerial spraying – both ULV and aerosol – is carried out by helicopter, and the first experiments at mist spraying were done by injecting the sprayed pesticide into the exhaust gases of a helicopter. The pesticide mixtures are of course highly inflammable, so it was found to be more practical to produce the mist by an electrically powered atomizer. The main problem, however, is to get such fine droplets to fall onto the ground.

Shell (and later, the Hoechst Company) hired a British meteorologist, Peter Coutts, to solve this, as it is essentially a problem of atmospheric movements. He found that in good weather, in the daytime the sun-heated ground produces upward air currents which prevent the pesticide cloud from ever reaching the ground, even if discharged at little more than treetop height. The gravitational pull on droplets so small that they have to be viewed under a microscope was so weak that even the slightest upward air movement foiled the sprayers. It also meant that traces of the poison were picked up 40 kilometres away from the zone being treated – while as Coutts says, more than 50 per cent of the pesticide simply disappears, no one having the least idea where it ends up.

He came up with the idea of using one of nature's own atmospheric tricks. This is known as a 'temperature inversion', when a reversal of the normal air movements occurs as the lower warm layer is trapped by an overlaying cooler layer. This frequently takes place in Africa just around dawn and at sunset. Thus by spraying just at dusk, the operators were able to get their deadly cloud to settle around the flies as they bedded down for the night.

Flying at treetop height is a hazardous enough business in favourable conditions; the need to do so at sundown or before dawn, under pressure to cover as much territory as possible while any light lasts or before the sun's heat starts to take effect, detracts immensely from the method's appeal. Mist spraying, while it works in the right conditions, is hardly a general answer if the spraying must be done from the air. The high cost of helicopter flying is a further disadvantage.

Wrong on all scores

Today, ten years after its declaration and with expenditures already approaching one billion dollars, FAO's tsetse war is arousing widespread and vociferous criticism from an ever-growing spectrum of people – experts and non-experts alike. Its overall impact on the tsetse and the diseases it vectors has been assessed, by many who know Africa, not merely as insignificant, but as positively harmful. According to one estimate by an expert within the agency, between 150,000 and 175,000 tonnes of active ingredient have been rained down on Africa's tsetse areas as a result of the decade's operation of this programme alone. And this, remember, means tonnes of stable, accumulative poisons so deadly that they are likely to prove fatal within hours to any adult person consuming as little as three grams of them.

Many specialists today believe that the tsetse now infests more territory than it did before the campaign began. Despite some small success in clearing limited parts, other larger areas have been invaded, or reinvaded by the fly. And this expansion is likely to continue until Africa achieves a considerably greater degree of stability. The tsetse eradication programme is criticized on three main levels; and at each of these, the FAO and its allied bilateral aiders have got it wrong.

First, the critics ask, why use 'hard' chemicals? If agreed that chemicals must be used to wipe out tsetse flies, why should such banned or restricted pesticides as dieldrin, dichlorvos or DDT be used? There are alternatives, such as the British-developed synthetic pyrethrins, or West Germany's endosulfan (which Hoechst say is now no longer under patent, and small quantities are also made in Israel and India). A number of 'chemical warfare' advocates agree that these are several degrees safer, in terms of long-term environmental damage at least.

Advocates of hard chemicals, on the other hand, say bluntly, 'we in the rich countries can afford the luxury of banning such cheap and effective crop-protection compounds. The developing countries cannot afford to do so.' Indeed, a Hoechst representative stated that while DDT probably costs around five German marks per kilo to produce, endosulfan costs at least five times as much; Shell International sells dieldrin in bulk at a price equivalent to roughly 15 German marks per kilo.

The danger to humans and environment inherent in such manufactured chemicals as these broad spectrum insecticides does not only lie in the fact that the right dosage can kill any living creature, apart from animals which the technicians refer to as their 'target species'. Nor do they only cause serious and ultimately fatal illnesses such as cancer. They are also generally reputed to cause sterility in both men and women, as well as causing impotence in men exposed to them. Nevertheless, an informant in FAO's Information Division insisted categorically that a less diplomatic – not to say more brutal – version of the opinion given above is frequently expressed privately by more cynical development aiders advocating hard pesticide use. In their confidential view, most of the poor countries affected are supposed to suffer from an overgrowth of population, so any such side-effects as help to reduce the fertility of Africans can only be beneficial. Any carcinogenic or mutagenic effects there may be constitute a rather long-term hazard, and the short life expectancy of the poorer inhabitants of these lands – those most intensively exposed to spraying – makes it likely that they will die of something else before any such effects can appear.

The double morality evident here epitomizes the attitude of the development aid industry and agribusiness. And the fallacies contained in such misanthropic 'doublethink' are also pointed out by the second group of critics, who are much more concerned by the social and environmental impacts of such ill-conceived campaigns. Before looking at this, however, we must examine the further objections of those who actively support tsetse eradication. For alternative methods of eradicating, or at least controlling, tsetse flies are available, some of them already well tried and proven.

Soft options

One alternative offered by tsetse eradication advocates who have doubts about the acceptability of pesticide chemicals, is known as the 'sterile-male technique'. It depends largely upon a highly technological and extremely expensive approach to disrupting the insect's fascinating sex life.

Scientists saw in this the possibility that any disturbance of the tsetse's breeding ecology could upset the fly population's balance. They therefore tried sterilizing captive males, by radiation or with chemicals, along lines already proven to work in North America with the screw worm fly and other insect pests, and then releasing them in areas where teneral females were ready for mating. The timing, location of release and prevailing weather conditions are all critical, but if correctly chosen, the copulatory success of such sterilized males can be so great that many females subsequently live out their lives without reproducing, their spermathecae filled with infertile sperm. The breeding success of the entire fly population can be so upset as to cause its local extinction.

Timing is all in any such enterprise. In the tsetse fly's case, problems are compounded by the fact that tsetse areas, almost by definition, are generally remote from human population centres, and that operations must be planned on a widespread scale to have any effect. These operations usually involve long cross-country trips through difficult terrain to reach areas far from the technical back-up laboratories, breeding and technicians' quarters, which are normally located at the centres. The operators have first to survey these bush areas minutely, on foot, to determine where within them the flies, of the right species, are breeding in sufficient numbers. This in itself demands a large number of reliable personnel skilled in tsetse spotting and identification. For the release operation, the flies must be carried into position as pupae through miles of deserted bush, and then only released when weather, wind and temperature are all suitable. Furthermore, the wild animals upon which the tsetse feed, and which play such a key role in their mating, must not be scared out of the country entirely, a frequent result of human movements in heavily hunted zones.

For these reasons, among others, the sterile male method is prohibitively slow and expensive. The returns on cattle ranching made possible by freeing areas of tsetse by this technique, which is in fact only applicable to finishing off populations of flies left over from major spraying campaigns, are likely to be so marginal as to banish any hopes of its commercial application. Indeed, in one of the two experimental stations set up in Africa to test the method, its American sponsors withdrew their aid support after deciding it had no real prospect of success. The second station, at Bobo-Dioulasso in Upper Volta, continues its development work on the technique, mainly with the aid of French and German funds.

But the fundamental weakness of the method, apart from its economics, is dependence on a high degree of technological skills not generally available in tsetse-infested areas, as well as research facilities to match. For instance, the British ODA is currently subsidizing part of the cost of an atomic power station which British contractors have sold to Nigeria, on the grounds that apart from power production it will also be able to produce radioactive isotopes for sterilizing tsetse flies.

Living with tsetse

A further soft option depends on living with the fly, rather than trying to eradicate it. Jan Rendel, the Swedish chief of FAO's Animal Production Service, is a staunch supporter of this approach. As he explains it, some old-established breeds of cattle have developed a degree of tolerance to nagana almost comparable to that enjoyed by Africa's indigenous fauna.

The difference between a 'trypanotolerant' and a non-tolerant breed is that the former acquire the ability to withstand the infection more rapidly than the latter; in other words, they are 'salted' more rapidly. There are ten different breeds of dwarf shorthorns in Africa that have this property, all except two, Tonga and Juba (the latter may no longer exist), being confined to West Africa. Early explorers noted them elsewhere, but unfortunately they are highly susceptible to rinderpest and have mostly been wiped out.

One such trypanotolerant breed, the dwarf shorthorns known as the Dahomey strains, can often be seen in European and American zoos, but as Rendel says, they have lost their tolerance. As indeed have all the other African animals there, of whatever species. Maintenance of this desirable characteristic depends entirely on the animal being under constant, heavy exposure to the disease. If the disease challenge is removed – by relocating the animal to a non-infected area, or by eliminating the disease along with the fly – any degree of tolerance will rapidly disappear. Animals born and bred in non-infected areas never acquire it without the necessary exposure.

On the other hand, the characteristic can be fostered by 'salting' livestock in a limited first exposure and then allowing it to recover from the disease which appeared – as the early explorers and settlers learnt to do – or by selective breeding. It is also passed on to the later generations of cross-bred offspring under conditions of exposure. Rendel advocates such cross-breeding, as well as improvement of the productivity of cattle already endowed with tolerance. This also entails, of course, letting the cattle live with the fly instead of trying to eradicate it. If the idea were to become generalized, it might even lead to tsetse conservation programmes.

The last method, dealt with here, for enabling cattle to live with the tsetse involves an alternative chemical prophylaxis technique. It was effectively demonstrated over 15 years ago by Frank Teubner, a Bavarian veterinary doctor then working in Somalia, and since returned to practise in his homeland. During a severe drought and consequent fodder shortage, he showed that even dairy cattle imported from Europe could be pastured in tsetse-infested zones, with suitable chemical protection.

Technical consultant to a large dairy-herd management near Mogadishu, Teubner and his colleagues were confronted with bare pastures and empty silos after three years of complete drought. A neighbouring tract of bush, however, offered a still edible area of grass, being protected from the native cattle by the presence of tsetse flies in large numbers. He ordered the cattle from the dairy farm to be driven into the infested bush, having first injected them with the drug Samorin, produced by May and Baker. He found that he was able to obtain complete resistance to two of the three types of 'tryps' present in the region – *Trypanosoma congolense* and *T. vivax* – while the third, *T. brucei*, although not counteracted by the drug-induced immunity, could be cured by another drug, Berenil, if spotted early enough. Regular weekly blood tests rapidly showed him which cows were infected, and prompt treatment assured their survival.

Today, however, drug resistance has appeared among the trypanosomes, making this at best a temporary solution in marginal areas on the fringes of fly zones, a situation which is likely to continue until better prophylactics are developed. Unfortunately, profit-motivated pharmaceutical companies are generally unwilling to invest in research for products purely for poor country markets – especially when their inhabitants are daily growing poorer despite, or perhaps because of, development aid. But in any case this solution also depends entirely on a high degree of technology – for example, a properly equipped blood-testing laboratory and technicians to run it – and the expensive products of the western pharmaceutical industry.

Incidentally, Teubner's 'trail blazing' into his strip of virgin bush – practically the last untouched piece of land in the whole of this arid desert country – had a sad ending. Ten years after his departure from Somalia, the British official aid agency ODA acceded to a Somalian request to spray this tract of land, to turn it into cattle pastures. What the ODA preferred to ignore – despite their senior officials being informed in unequivocal terms – was that it carried some of Somalia's last and most interesting species of wild animals, some so rare they are unknown elsewhere in the world.

Back in 1970, a Danish veterinary colleague of Teubner's, John Nielson, was working for the FAO in Mogadishu. (He is now back in Denmark, with the Danish aid agency DANIDA.) Apart from teaching in the local veterinary school, he was also a keen hunter. Shooting one day in the area in which Teubner later pastured his cows, Nielson bagged an antelope without first recognizing its species – an unpardonable sin and affront to any honourable hunting tradition. Only after taking the trophy home did he realize that he had killed a splendid specimen of the Hunter's antelope, an animal nominally totally protected under Somalia's rarely enforced conservation laws. Smuggling the trophy out via the 'diplomatic bag' – a facility available to FAO's field experts enjoying diplomatic status – he sent it to Rowland Wards of London for mounting. He then learnt that he was the proud owner of the world champion specimen of this rare and endangered species. Although one of the poorest lands on earth, Somalia is (or was) homeland of three of the rarest mammals; apart from the Hunter's antelope, the desert regions of Ogaden – their ecology shattered by a vast overpopulation of cattle and goats – harbour the dibatag, another gazelle which was believed to number no more than 1,500 specimens as long ago as 1967, long before the destructive Somali-Ethiopian war; the equally arid regions of the Upper Nogal Plain in the northern tip of Somalia shelter the few remaining and similarly unique Somali wild ass.

The Hunter's antelope population was estimated at 2,000 survivors in 1977, while a rather larger herd in neighbouring Kenya, on the Tana River, was thought to be even more vulnerable, because of its isolation, as with all surviving 'pockets' of rare animals, to many threats of disease and development. In such a threatening setting, Nielson's discovery of the antelope in the Webi Shebeli area, within 35 kilometres of the country's capital Mogadishu, might in a country caring about conservation of its wildlife resources, have been expected to produce some positive action to prevent any similar accidents. But Nielson, naturally enough, kept very quiet about it as far as local officials were concerned. And the tribesmen who occasionally hunt wild animals for food could hardly be expected to draw such subtle distinctions of animal identification, lacking any official guidance on the subject.

So it came about that the Hunter's gazelle's death warrant was signed, at least locally, by the British development agency, with British taxpayers footing the bill. ODA's response, on being informed by a member of the Fauna and Flora Preservation Society of the presence of these rare animals in the area of their Webi Shebeli project, was simply to speed up the departure of the technicians assigned to the scheme, to ensure that spraying was well under way before any possible delay or protest could surface.

The example of administrative bad faith shown here is but one of the manifold expressions of official ill will constantly met with by conservationists. As in so many other cases, it ensured that the next step will follow with almost majestic inevitability: the invasion of cattle herds into this last small relic of greenery in the dry, seared land of Somalia, and its consequent rapid destruction.

Ultimate futility

The third score on which environmentally conscious critics find grave fault with the tsetse campaign touches the roots of its ecological implications even more fundamentally. Such people ask why, if the project is designed to increase meat supplies to those in need, it should aim primarily at increasing production of beef – which the poor cannot afford at any price – while wiping out their existing game meat supplies in the process. This question, and the attendant problems of improving game meat production and distribution, will be examined in depth in a subsequent chapter. Before this, however, we must look at a last, more technical aspect of the tsetse-'tryps' symbiosis.

The final major objection to FAO's tsetse war is based on what 'tryps' experts see as its ultimate futility. The agency's standard claim is that by wiping out the fly vector, they will eliminate trypanosomes, the cause of the disease. In this the FAO turns a determinedly blind eye to the fact that trypanosomiasis has existed in Latin America, where tsetse flies do not occur, for nearly a century. Charles Darwin contracted the disease during his voyages in South America, and several million people, and many more cattle, continue to suffer today. The truth is that 'tryps' simply do not need the tsetse flies to go about their business. Indeed, if pressed on the subject, even FAO's own tsetse eradication experts will admit to cases of endemic or enzootic trypanosomiasis in regions of Africa where tsetse flies are unknown, for example in the Sahelian country of Chad.

In reality scientists are aware that, while the tsetse only exists in Africa (with a small pocket just across the Red Sea in Arabia, as already mentioned), trypanosomiasis is pandemic – i.e. a worldwide affliction – from Norway to New Zealand, and from Tahiti via Timbuktu to Trinidad. It exists in Europe in the (panzootic) form, among others, of venereal disease in horses and donkeys. Even FAO's most ardent pesticide pusher would hardly suggest wiping out tsetse flies there, for the disease is transmitted by sexual contact, without need of an 'intermediate host'. The recommended veterinary 'treatment', incidentally, is to slaughter the suffering horses.

A permanent problem confronting biological campaigns such as that undertaken by FAO is the genetic adaptability of the target organism. The weapons employed against it themselves foster any tendency to genetic shifts in directions that counteract their purpose. They thus create their own selective pressure towards resistance or avoidance of their intended effects. Thus in the case of tsetse, as we have seen earlier, the reported behaviour of some males in cleaning out the previous contents of the females' spermathecae before inseminating them, might possibly be fostered unwittingly by the 'sterile male' method of tsetse eradication; any male using this technique on a sterile-sperm carrying female will obviously have a better chance of perpetuating its genes than one which does not know the trick. If such behaviour should prove to be common and be linked in any way with the fly's genetic inheritance, this could conceivably result in such behaviour becoming generalized in regions where the method is applied, possibly nullifying its usefulness.

In the same way, and even more disquietingly, the theoretically credible prospect that the African trypanosome – a protozoon renowned for its nimble genetic adaptability – might switch to some other, wider-spread and less vulnerable carrier, and the resulting possibility of outbreaks of uncontrollable trypanosomiasis epidemics, brings a shudder of horror to more imaginative experts on the subject. As they point out, the Latin American version of 'tryps' was introduced to that tsetse-free continent during the eighteenth or nineteenth centuries in imported infected cattle. Today WHO estimates that some ten million people suffer from Chaga's Disease, as it is known there (the animal version, affecting cattle, horses and camels, being called 'surra'), and up to 50 million are at risk. The disease even affects animals as far as the 40th parallel of latitude in North America. This New World introduction has happily adapted to a wide number of alternative hosts; it can even be transmitted by the bite of a vampire bat. The most common host is a common household pest there – a bedbug, called locally the 'kissing bug' owing to its habit of leaving 'love bite' swellings on the faces of its sleeping victims.

5. The poison pushers

> Train up a child in the way he should go: and when he is old, he
> will not depart from it.
>
> Proverbs 22:6

Every year, hundreds of thousands of tonnes of quasi-indestructible poisons are deluged over the 'Third World', one tonne of most of them being powerful enough to poison a quarter of a million people lethally, if consumed directly. An estimate published in 1982 by David Bull of the respected British charitable aid agency Oxfam, declares that worldwide pesticide use was already 1.9 billion kilograms (4.1 billion pounds) per year – the equivalent of one pound weight for every man, woman and child of the four billion people then alive on earth. Production is growing constantly, at about 5 per cent per year, and is expected to total some 2.3 billion kilograms (five billion pounds) by 1985. Fifteen per cent of these totals are used in the 'Third World', the equivalent of 100 grams per person per year, while 'Third World' use of them is growing by a frightening 15 per cent per year. Out of the total of all pesticides, which include weed killers, fungicides and such things as rat poisons, 30 per cent of all insecticides are sprayed across the 'Third World'; sprayed not only across its country areas, but also across its towns and villages, or poured directly into its lakes and waterways.

Rather than reducing the totality of human suffering and disease, by eliminating hunger or such relatively minor diseases as sleeping sickness, this massive chemical use has contributed largely to the resurgence of much more virulent and widespread diseases which were once well under control. It has also contributed very largely to the development of hunger and poverty in the areas concerned.

It may well be asked why, in the face of all the publicized dangers and deficiencies of this terrifying trend, and the criticism amassed against such officially sponsored programmes, they are allowed to continue. As far as the FAO 'tsetse war' is concerned – and as remarked earlier, it is a classic example in this respect – FAO insiders suggest that the reason is the general impossibility of ever stopping the development aid juggernaut once it is rolling. Administrative inertia and the vested interests of those involved – contractors, suppliers, consultants, field technicians, officials – combine to overwhelm any dissenting voice, even when objections are based on the clearest and most urgent grounds.

In the particular case of the tsetse war, FAO officials are in no doubt that this is a specially favoured project of the agency's Director General, Edouard Saouma, and of his allies in African governments – not to mention his sponsors among the multinational chemical manufacturers and spraying contractors executing the project. It will be remembered, in this context, that Saouma's early training and first diplomas were in agrochemicals and the technological hardware of industrialized farming systems.

The interest of the agribusiness 'multis' hardly requires elaboration at this point. Their aims and methods have been exposed by many writers over recent years, and we will have occasion to return to this unsavoury topic shortly. The motivations of leading African officials, who might be expected to show a greater prudence in the matter – living as many of them do on top of the problem – bear closer examination. The reasons for supporting such questionable developments are twofold.

Before analyzing them in detail, it is necessary to introduce a note of warning. The reader must never assume, where specific examples of abuse are given in these pages as typifying negative trends or occurrences – however common these may be – that this is intended to suggest that all other people involved in similar activities or functions are likewise compromised or reprehensible. For example, many 'Third World' officials will accept or even demand bribes before deigning to render the services for which they are paid; yet despite this, there are still vast numbers, equally ill-paid, who perform their functions honourably, capably and with little reward. In the sectors we are dealing with in particular – agriculture, rural development, public health and environmental protection – many devoted people work unremittingly at their chosen tasks for modest rewards, and often in conditions so demanding and frustrating that many western readers would find their discomfort an intolerable hardship. Such worthy people can only solicit our constant admiration and, where possible, our support.

The first factor causing bias concerns the technical background and education of those currently controlling senior 'decision-making' levels of such technical departments as agriculture, invariably permeated by an absolute conviction of the superiority of western agricultural technology. Soviet 'high tech' systems also share the basic faults of the West.

Training in colonial or western agricultural schools and colleges enforces this bias. More recent, widespread doubts about massive mechanized and chemically blanketed monocultures, emerging amongst more thoughtful western agronomists, have not yet 'trickled up' through most 'Third World' administrations. In general the latter are at least 20 years behind the West in their awareness of such issues.

The factor described may be considered as an unavoidable hangover of former colonial influence, as well as of the neo-colonialist activities and attitudes of multinational agribusiness. In itself it can hardly constitute a basis for reproaching the hard-working, often over-extended and inadequately supported officials produced by the system. This apart, a second, more reprehensible complex of factors or interests all too often plays a decisive role in the initiation and execution of such projects as FAO's tsetse war. It is best illustrated by a concrete example. Space permits only one, although – lest this appear invidiously selected – it must be stressed that it is a particular illustration of, *mutatis mutandis* a quasi-universal temptation.

The value which accrues from converting 'bush' or traditional tribal lands into beef barons' hamburger farms – thereby turning undeveloped land into high-cost real estate – offers considerable temptation to those with the power to effect this. Government officials sometimes see in it a way of adding to their wealth, by acquiring title to the lands thus opened up.

In a Nigerian operation, jointly run by West German development aiders and the Nigerian government, several thousand square miles of Northern and Central Nigeria were drenched with poisonous sprays for over a decade in a largely successful attempt, initiated long before FAO's declaration of war, to eliminate tsetse flies. The chief of Nigeria's tsetse control operations was one of the first appointed consultants of the FAO-ICP tsetse eradication task force, and attended their frequent meetings in Rome. He was, simultaneously, a full-time functionary of the Nigerian government. Three highly placed sources, who for reasons already given must remain anonymous here, connected with the programme management at different times (one is a former Nigerian cabinet minister, now a prominent businessman in Lagos, while the others are both still tsetse eradication consultants to the FAO), have, independently of each other, provided the information that the chief of operations has now also branched out into farming. They each estimated that he controls, either directly or through family 'nominees', at least one third of the area cleared of tsetse under his programme.

The people of the area affected, living for generations at the extremes of rural poverty in a region not 50 miles south of the regional capital Kaduna, had long held a traditional belief that one day the millennium would arrive, in the form of a messianic 'saviour' who would descend from heaven to bring them all the riches they aspired to. Upon hearing of this mythology, one official ordered the German project leader in charge of spraying operations to place the unit's helicopter at his disposal for a day. Overruling objections that the aircraft, which was paid for out of German aid funds, was only supposed to fly on spraying operations, he had himself and his entourage shuttled in in relays, to arrive resplendently on the main village square, bringing promises of munificent bounty to follow – if only the local population would agree to collaborate, and allow their lands to be sprayed . . .

Shell's soft sell

The 'pesticide mafia' deploys the whole panoply of modern advertising techniques in pursuit of what admen see as their legitimate function – creating demand where none exists. With their richest markets restricted by legislation or saturation at the beginning of the 1970s, they turned their greedy eyes to the more vulnerable public of the 'Third World'. And in this campaign, ranging from the more obvious 'point-of-sale' publicity to the most insidious infiltration of government and supra-governmental bodies, no effort is spared in promoting sales of their poisonous wares, and planting in the potential consumer's mind an idea of the advantages of such chemicals. No chance is missed to refute or belittle the fears (even those firmly based on objective proof) of those who see these products as an unnecessary hazard to life.

It should be noted that pesticides must not be seen in isolation in this context. Their advocates are part of a systematic bid to take control of the world's agricultural sector in all its aspects – from production, through all stages of harvesting, storage, processing and distribution, to marketing and even actual consumption. This is most evident in the lateral expansion of agribusiness through its take-over of related sectors. The classic example is Shell's recent buying up of the international 'seeds' business, as amply documented in Pat Mooney's *Seeds of the Earth*. This huge Anglo-Dutch petroleum company today controls the greatest number of seeds merchants held by any single interest – Shell is in fact the largest seed-corn merchant in the world. A company which started out life mining and refining petrol and lubricants for car or heating fuel, it is today among the leading multinational agribusinesses which control the production of the bread you eat.

'Point-of-sale' advertising, much of it of the most dubious nature, is widely practised by all pesticide manufacturers selling in the 'Third World'. More sophisticated 'developed'-world customers have, despite every repressive countermeasure by the industry and its allies, been exposed to a great deal of publicity about the hazards of these products, especially via the more responsible western media. The case of the 'Third World' customer is very different.

The keynote is sounded by a US magazine giving advice to exporters wishing to sell products in developing countries:

> Use the visual and colourful; seek and achieve product identification and brand loyalty through non-verbal means, especially when illiteracy is widespread [i.e. where a credulous customer cannot read warning labels and instructions]; a pictorial or symbolic trade mark can be a great advantage.
>
> *Business International*, August 1978

Agribusiness goes further in such 'micropromotion'. Often adapting brand names for the same product to the local dialect in different countries (or even different regions of the same country), it makes inflated claims about their efficacy, safety and cheapness. This technique creates and spreads confusion amongst an illiterate clientele, and avoids possible identification of recognized hazards – word of which has penetrated even to the remotest corner of the agricultural world. Misleading labelling, absence of warning about dangers and lack of clear instructions for safe use and remedies, are currently matters of international public outcry – though few governments at either end of the evil trade seem prepared to take effective action to protect the public.

While many countries are slowly beginning to consider legislation to curb such visible excesses, none are even attempting to tackle problems created by salespeople's more clandestine methods of 'demand creation'. On the contrary, many governments actively foster them. We must consider the practices of 'macropromotion'. An effective medium for this kind of sales promotion is often offered by official 'unbiased' radio and TV networks; in particular, local or international radio broadcasting stations. The model for these is the British Broadcasting Corporation. The BBC is an autonomous, government-owned and subsidized body, constitutionally prohibited under the legislation which founded it from advertising commercial products or services in any form. Mention even of famous brand names which have entered the language as household words – Guinness, or perhaps Rolls Royce – is frowned upon.

It was the BBC which first inaugurated a public service of sound broadcasting. Its roles today range from book, magazine and audiovisual publishing to sponsorship of sport and the arts – and are now dominated by television. But 'Auntie Beeb' still maintains a key world position in sound radio, with the most polyglot, widereaching and powerful transmissions in the world, and a network of international correspondents second to none. Despite the innovations introduced ten years ago in local stations, it still maintains its tradition of lofty detachment and prides itself on 'impartiality'.

Radio services are divided between two separate administrations, domestic and overseas. The former, with its various national, regional and local subdivisions, maintains a measure of political detachment. Regardless of which of the two main UK parties is in government, the Home Service 'Beeb' stoutly continues to present its own broadly conservative view of what is happening in the world. The overseas-aimed BBC World Service, on the other hand, makes no bones about its role as official 'mouthpiece', narrowly reflecting government policies, and as promoter of British interests – though not, one would fondly imagine, those of private UK companies. One would be wrong. For in this last role, the BBC is assiduous – if often quite subtle – in its selling of British and allied agribusiness goods and services. One of the more blatant examples of recent times concerned Anglo-Dutch Shell.

The World Service's weekly 'Farming World' is a topical programme covering latest developments in agriculture. It is beamed primarily to the English-speaking 'Third World', each programme being repeated several times during the week. The service can easily be picked up in Europe, but is difficult for listeners in the UK to find owing to the selection of wavelengths and directional aerials used at the transmitter.

In June 1982 one 'Farming World' programme included an item about a Nigerian agricultural development. This involved construction of a small dam, growing rice under irrigation below it and fish-farming in the trapped waters above it. The rice growing was carried out by a co-operative of small-holders, each working his own plot. A very reasonable intermediate-scale project, one might think, its success being described during an interview with its English 'extension worker' who advised and managed it, in glowing terms. Only when he explained the workings of the Uboma co-operative did a seed of suspicion begin to germinate in the critical listener's mind. Co-operative membership amongst plot holders was voluntary. The project manager described, however, how one man first refused to join, and tried growing his crop without chemical weed killers and pesticides which were an integral part of the exercise. Social pressures from his neighbours – pointing the finger of scorn at the weeds growing in his plot alongside their own 'blemish-free' fields, or complaining that his plot was a breeding ground for bugs which invaded their adjoining plots despite the chemicals used – forced him to conform. He finally succumbed to the pressure, and joined in the chemically blanketed monoculture.

At the start of the broadcast, the project manager had been introduced merely as Mr T.D. Ross. Only in signing off did the presenter mention that Mr Ross is an employee of the Shell company. A letter to the BBC requesting a transcript of the broadcast – to ensure accuracy of quotation – met with the surprising reply that it was not possible 'for reasons of copyright'. (The BBC normally responds very generously and promptly to such requests, and has provided a dozen transcripts of other broadcasts – often stamped with a reminder of copyright holder's embargoes – over the past year.) For further information the programme's producer recommended applying to Mr Ross at London's Shell Centre. Ross replied, in turn, that although he 'had been connected with the project during the 1960s, [he] had no recent information', and that this could only be supplied by Basil Fox, Shell's chief PRO.

So much, then, for the programme's much-vaunted topicality, as the 'latest in world farming developments'. The former adviser to the 20-year-old project did not even know whether it was still running, although a report from an independent specialist familiar with Nigeria indicates that the Uboma co-operative disintegrated in bitterness and disarray more than ten years ago. More tellingly, this project received no BBC publicity whatever in the late 1960s and early 1970s, when the petrochemical industry first switched its main sales thrust from the chemically saturated markets of the western farming world to the more promising fields of the 'Third World'. They evidently felt that such publicity was unnecessary, or might even have proved counterproductive. More recently, however, the negative effects of this chemical onslaught, in terms of poisoned, impoverished people and environments, have provoked growing protest among the western public and its more responsive media. This has incited the chemical firms' managers and the business-supportive media to attempt to create a fresh 'image' for their products and activities.

The latest propaganda clearly demonstrates a double tendency. Most obvious is the dearth of actual 'integrated' small-scale projects on the ground, with which to back up the aid industry's tedious lip-service to their desirability: clearly they had to dig back 20 years to find one – and that possibly defunct. Shell's Basil Fox was unable to confirm or deny this, and the Nigerian representative approached in London was 'still informing himself' at the time of writing.

The second tendency illustrated in this joint propagation of the 'technological fix' by the BBC and Shell, is of a more subtle and insidious nature. It concerns clever selling or promotion at the macro- as well as the micro-levels. In general, agribusiness use of the BBC and similar media to push its wares may be defined as 'macro-promotion'; but the particular project described on the air is itself a good example of one method of 'point-of-sale' micro-promotion. Using personal relationships and social pressures, Shell is employing the same basic forces of 'conformity' selling as does in its own way the 'Tupperware party'. The poison pushers are driven by their desire for professional advancement and expanding influence. For example, the Shell company, apart from sending out its own training and extension workers as project managers and advisers, also runs regular courses, seminars and conferences for key people in the consuming countries. One major series of Shell courses in this area goes under the indicative title 'Training the Trainers'. Organized and run for Shell by Geoffrey Wilkinson, a Scots technical instructor from Wolverhampton Polytechnic, it is held each year in a different 'Third World' country (Zambia in 1981 and Indonesia in 1982). Courses last for three weeks and include 15 days of instruction on the uses, techniques and advantages of agrochemicals. For its 1982 course, Shell took over the Ciawi School of Environmental Conservation Management. This was first founded – with considerable financial and technical support from the Dutch government and the World Wildlife Fund (WWF) – in around 1979, and its purpose was the training of those government departments' local staff and services concerned with wildlife and forest resource conservation, fisheries and water resource management and other environmental protection matters in the region.

Shell's students, in contrast, were senior functionaries and extension workers up to ministerial level in rank – the 'decision-makers' – from various South-East Asian Ministries of Agriculture and related authorities. Not only were the Ciawi School's normal students excluded from the course, but the staff of the school themselves were denied entry to any of its lectures and working groups. They were, however, offered the option of telling the visitors of the dangers and disadvantages of chemical use during the first day of the course. The remaining three weeks were devoted, in privacy, to the agrochemical manufacturers and advocates. Wilkinson gave as reason for their 'closed door' policy,

that the course was one of a continuing series – and that the
teaching staff of SECM would be unable to gain any benefit from
it, not having followed the rest of the series.

A better example of 'advertising' to key consumers would be
hard to find, although the Shell company is by no means operating
in isolation in this. Most other petrochemical firms employ similar
methods of making friends of and influencing the people who
make the purchasing decisions. The latter become in effect their
most efficient and loyal salesforce in the field. Agricultural
extension agents are the peasants' prime source of 'impartial'
advice – and are seen in the 'Third World' as experts speaking with
the voice of the government which normally pays them.

It is not only industry that engages in this promotional field of
extension training and advice. In fact the whole development aid
industry – led by such international juggernauts as the FAO,
UNDP, the World Bank, the Common Market's Euro-
Development Fund (EDF), USAID and the whole gamut of
other bilateral aiders disposing of their own agrochemical export
industries – spends hundreds of millions of taxpayers' dollars on
such 'rural animation' programmes. Under these, many projects
are labelled 'crop protection' or 'post-harvest loss prevention'
campaigns. They are invariably based upon the use of pesticides
and, equally without exception, they point their attack at training
the trainers, whose subsequent careers depend on assiduously
passing on the knowledge and wisdom thus handed down.

Dining with the Borgias

The results of the advice described are sometimes unexpected –
and even horrifying. An example from the much-'aided' Sahelian
country of Upper Volta starkly illustrates the dangers inherent in
promoting dangerous poisons among poor peasants unable to
read or to otherwise heed the hazard warnings which should, but
rarely do, accompany them.

A multimillion dollar 'post-harvest loss prevention' scheme
there was financed by the EDF. It was run for many years by an
Italian agricultural consultancy firm, which at the project's high
point employed over 100 Italian, French and English field experts
all over the country, teaching the Voltaic peasants how to avoid
losing 10-15 per cent of their annual grain supply, which is stored

after drying, to the various vermin which share with them the contents of their household granaries. The traditional Sahelian granary is a work of art. It basically consists of a huge domed pot or 'urn', and is built by each family under the guidance of an artisanal 'expert'. Big enough to hold the whole year's crop of millet or maize, it will feed the family until the next harvest. Moulded out of packed laterite mud mixed with cattle dung to bind it, the granary sets brick-hard when dry. Its domed top is capped with a cone of reed or straw thatch, like the rooves of the circular village huts, to keep the rain off. Inside and out, the surface is smoothly polished to the finish of a terra-cotta flowerpot. The elegant curves of walls and dome are designed to prevent rats and other rodents from gaining the least toehold, and thus deny them access to the single 'porthole' opening near the top, sometimes three metres above the ground. This entrance is tightly plugged with a lid of wood or wickerwork, and is barely large enough for the passage of a slim person. Access is provided by a primitive stepladder – often the crooked trunk of a small tree – which can be set aside when not in use. As the level of the year's corn stock sinks, towards the end of the dry season, it is a common sight to see a pair of feet waving upsidedown to heaven, as mother or daughter scoops up supplies for the family's supper.

The structure is effectively ratproof, unless the user forgets to remove the ladder; but any rat so gaining access would be unable to climb out up the polished interior wall, and would be caught by the next user, making a welcome addition to the supper. But such refined structures are not proof against insects, which find access through the porthole, and some corn has always been lost to moths and weevils, whose larvae grow fat among the stored grain. Their excrement and fermentation products can cause development of harmful substances – as indeed in granaries around the world. Losses however are insignificant compared with those increasingly suffered in the fields, as a result of the concentration of wild creatures attacking field crops. Be this as it may, the EDF team set out to combat these storage losses, and undertook to show the villagers how to mix pesticide powders in with the grain they were due to eat. (This is a far more dubious procedure even than the US practice of treating seed corn for planting with mercury, which killed 6,000 Iraqis through mis-direction of the grain into their local bakeries.) The experts designed and had printed thousands of colourful 'strip cartoon' posters, and had them stuck on walls or nailed to trees at every village assembly point, store, school and administrative building.

The poster showed in close-up the brightly coloured plastic packets of pesticide, and an array of familiar local bugs – all clearly at their last gasp as they turned their toes skyward. This was surrounded by a sequential series of pictures, the order indicated by bright arrows for those unable to read numbers. First showed a peasant in local costume handing over money, and receiving a couple of the packets shown in the central display. He is then shown at home, with an empty 'calabash' or dried-gourd bowl the size of a large salad bowl, cutting open the packet like a ready-mixed dried soup, emptying its contents into the calabash, and filling this with corn. The two are then seen to be carefully mixed together by hand, to dilute and distribute the 'active ingredient' – a technique similar to that used by gardeners in mixing particularly fine seeds with a handful of sand to get a better distribution. The cartoon continues with instructions on how to fill the empty granary in layers by spreading 20–30 centimetres of grain over the bottom, scattering a cupful of poisoned seeds across it, adding a second layer of grain and another cupful, until the granary is full, the cup empty – and the family's whole year's food supply thoroughly polluted.

The 'active ingredient' recommended is lindane, although other organochlorines have been tried, including Shell's dieldrin. It is sold openly without restriction in half-kilogram packages (at 5–6 times the price of the same product in bulk) by a French-controlled firm in Abidjan in Ivory Coast, which imports it from Europe where sales are tightly controlled and most uses banned completely.

The operation was deemed such a success in terms of sales that the Voltaic health authority asked the rural animation team to tackle another pest-problem while they were about it. A constant irritation – and indeed cause of illness – in the rudimentary mud-built dwellings of such villages is a range of crawling and hopping bugs and fleas which enter huts through door and window openings, and feed on the blood of sleeping occupants. Efforts at cleanliness, sweeping and dusting out any possible hiding-place or cranny within, are of little avail, as the bugs lie in wait outside, and enter in the dark. One effective way to combat these ancient scourges is to surround the whole hut with a band of poisoned ground. The health authority recommended the deadly dichlorvos for the purpose, and asked the animation team to run a concurrent campaign to explain to villagers how to do this. In this case the 'active ingredient' was to be sprinkled in a continuous trail around the hut, choosing a windless day to do so. Severe warnings were given that in no circumstances should the powerful poison be allowed to enter the hut itself, or be used inside it in any way.

However, as the EDF consultants' team leader explained: 'The natives weren't stupid! They soon noted the large numbers of dead bugs produced by this new product. Since it was so much "better" than the "tolerable" lindane, they took to mixing it with their food; it must be better for that too.' He found them abandoning the organochlorine pesticide they had been taught to use in their granaries, and substituting this 100 times more toxic organophosphate instead. Unsurprisingly perhaps, neither the EDF nor the health staff thought to look for any subsequent effects of this malevolent 'development aid', either then or later.

Spoils of cotton

More direct macro-marketing is practised by other agrochemical manufacturers – often with equally horrifying results. The third largest in the field (after Germany's Bayer, and Shell in second place), Ciba-Geigy of Switzerland, prefers marketing through direct contracting of pest eradication programmes. Most other manufacturers prefer using middlemen or subcontractors in the application of their poisonous products. (Some, like Shell at Pernis, even prefer subcontracting the actual *making* of them. They also subcontract dumping the inevitable wastes produced, which end up poisoning our own fish and water supplies.) They all, however, maintain the closest relations with the major spraying contractors. Air Lloyd of Frankfurt and Hunting Air of Canada are two of the biggest. Ciba-Geigy, in contrast, owns its own fleet of aircraft, through its majority shareholding in Ciba-Pilatus Aerial Spraying, and undertakes large aerial spraying operations world-wide. Since 1967, it has carried out more than 100 regional spraying contracts in over 40 different countries of Africa, South East Asia and America. The company's action in the Sudan is typical, if among its biggest. Sudan's largest single hard-currency earner is cotton. Since British colonial times it has supplied the finest 'long-staple' cotton to the industrialized world, much in demand at the textile mills of Lancashire and elsewhere. The colonial power sought to draw some profit from the huge and largely barren land, to pay the costs of its administration. Its main interest lay in the strategic position it occupies along the Gulf of Suez and straddling the sources of the Nile. 'Foreign' occupation of either could have threatened Britain's trade routes with Imperial India and the Far East through the newly opened Suez Canal.

The British dammed the Blue Nile at Sennar in 1925, to irrigate some 2,000 square kilometres of land lying in the fork of the two Nile tributaries (the Blue and White Nile) below Khartoum, where they join to form Africa's mightiest and most historic river. They created thereby the largest single agricultural enterprise, or 'farm', in the world, in the Province of Gezira. Gezira grows the cotton upon which Sudan's economy depends. Up to 40 per cent of the huge 'farm' is planted with the crop, which brings the country some 60 per cent of its entire foreign currency income. Wheat, barley and groundnuts are also grown – mainly as rotational crops to feed Saudi Arabia – and the whole area of around 220,000 hectares is divided into plots which are laboured by 100,000 tenant farmers and their families and serfs. At harvest time migrant workers from elsewhere in Sudan, and pilgrims on their way to and from Mecca, join them in thousands for the two or three months this requires, working in the blazing sun for pitiful wages, and living in conditions of squalid misery that would have provoked revolt among the slave gangs which raised the temples and nearby pyramids of the ancient Pharaohs 5,000 years ago.

Tenant farmers are forced to plant cotton by decree. Many other crops will grow fruitfully there, given the plentiful, unfailing water supply, well-drained site and rich soil – and the insatiable neighbouring Arabian market ready to absorb any produce which could be exported. But the government has inherited the colonial tradition, and problems, of using the land and exploiting the peasants to pay the overheads of its power structure. It needs hard currency to pay for western imports, especially military hardware, and cotton is the most rewarding source of this, or was until recently. In 1970 Ciba-Geigy moved in.

The main problem facing such monoculture (where erosion and salification can be controlled) is in the build-up of pests. Pest control in Gezira is the responsibility of the Gezira Management Board, which sprays peasants' crops and decrees rotations over the whole area. In the early days, the main problem insect was the cotton bollworm, the caterpillar of a nocturnal moth which bores into the immature cotton pod and eats the contents of seeds and lint, moving from pod to pod as it grows. It was initially controlled by seasonal spraying with DDT or dieldrin, and when resistance to these built up later, with parathion, an organophosphate. Although these keep bollworm damage down, they produced a vast and rapid increase in numbers of whitefly, a tiny white insect which causes leaves to curl and wrinkle, plant growth to become stunted, and which covers leaves and cotton bolls with a sticky honeydew which reduces the value of the lint, even making it unworkable. Before the chemical onslaught on the bollworm, whitefly had always been present, but never at a level to cause appreciable loss.

By 1970 the whitefly was out of hand, and resistant bollworm making a massive reappearance. Ciba-Geigy undertook aerial spraying, at first on an experimental basis. Taking on board Vernon Joyce, well-connected with the Sudanese authorities through his former influential role as Director of UN's international locust control organization, they acquired a contract to control cotton pests for a fixed annual fee. Under this contract, the firm itself decided which chemicals to use, how much of them and how often.

Two years later the Swiss company made an even more valuable acquisition. Nur al-Hada, Managing Director of the Gezira Board, took an early retirement (with pension), and also took on the job of Ciba-Geigy's project manager, at five times his former salary – £10,000 sterling a year. Through the good offices of these 'friends in high places', the Swiss rapidly extended their exclusive contract to cover one third of the entire Gezira Scheme area, giving them a field of action of over 650 square kilometres of cultivation.

After a decade of operation, the Swiss company was as effectively in the saddle over this vast region as any colonial power. They brought in administrators, planners, logistics experts, agronomists, biologists, pesticide-application specialists, pilots, mechanics, and maintenance engineers. In the firm's Basel headquarters, their project area was officially referred to as 'Ciba-Geigy Territory'. A Sudanese entomologist on the Gezira Board, on the other hand, spoke of the operation as 'an impenetrable colony – a foreign body which wraps itself in a mantle of secrecy'. Indeed, the Board was only able to extract the sparsest details of what the Swiss firm was doing to its lands and people with the utmost difficulty, despite contracted training programmes and 'transfer of technology' agreements which never saw the light of day. Nor were only technical 'know-how' and insecticides imported; aircraft, vehicles, fuel and European food and drink for the expatriate personnel and their highly paid Sudanese counterparts all added to the foreign exchange bill. In a single season, this 'high-tech' operation consumed 384,000 litres of aviation spirit, 341,000 litres of automobile fuel and 750 *tonnes* of pesticides.

Ten years after Ciba-Geigy's entrance into Gezira, an FAO advisory commission reported: 'Cotton production in the Sudan is in a state of crisis, and is rapidly approaching catastrophe.' The Swiss Christoph Eckenstein Foundation, set up to study Swiss-'Third World' relationships, commissioned Silvo Bertolami, a freelance writer now with Swiss Radio in Zurich, to investigate.

After an initial year or two of success following Ciba-Geigy's entering the fray, the pests had returned with massive reinforcements – immune to any Ciba-Geigy chemicals the air-circus could throw at them. At that time, West German Hoechst's endosulfan was still being effectively used on the remaining Gezira plots, but the Swiss firm stoutly refused to consider employing anything but their own products on 'Ciba-Geigy Territory' – however ineffective they soon became.

Before the Swiss took over, spraying had been carried out once a year and pests remained at tolerable levels. When Bertolami visited the area, the Gezira authorities told him Ciba-Pilatus was blasting their area on average from 10.5 to 11.7 times *per season*. In 1980 Ciba-Geigy received £280 (Sudanese pounds) per hectare of cotton, more money than the average reaching the hands of the peasant farmers actually growing it. He discovered that the firm regularly sprayed fields – and indeed, peasants' homes, gardens, livestock, the slum dwellings of migrant harvesters and even people working in the fields – without warning or heed to the fact that people and animals living there have, for the most part, no other source of drinking and household water than the open irrigation canals under their attack. As a sole precaution, the flying operators would sometimes warn inhabitants not to drink water in the region for three days after spraying – difficult advice to follow in the Sudanian heat where nothing else to drink is on offer.

During the Ciba-Geigy period up to 1980, the total cost of pesticides mounted from £1.5 million in 1966–67 to £25 million in 1980–81 – a 14-fold increase (over the same period when cotton-picking costs rose by a mere two and a half times, in line with universal inflation). Because of this enormous rise, costs of production rocketed so high that poorer peasants have been forced into borrowing, from dealers and richer farmers, on their next crop on a '50–50' sharecropping basis. The result has been massive impoverishment of the peasant farmers in general, in a scheme which was previously a model of prosperous development unique in the 'Third World'.

Impoverishment has also resulted on a national level. Lack of incentive caused many indebted peasants to neglect the cotton they were obliged to plant. Production has fallen as well as quality. As a result Sudan's income from cotton is no longer sufficient to pay Ciba-Geigy's bills in hard currency. The country's Treasury was faced with defaulting on its mounting international debts, and Sudan faced economic collapse. On April Fools' Day 1980, however, the Swiss banks, true to form, stepped in to save the day. The Swiss government agreed to guarantee a bank loan of 16 million Swiss francs to bridge the gap, the money going directly to Ciba-Geigy. The loan is to be repaid, with 6 per cent interest per year, between 1983 and 1990 – though no one in Sudan knows quite how, and the likelihood is that the Swiss taxpayer will be landed with most of the bill.

Positions of power

All western banks work closely with the agrochemical industry in promoting and financing such poisonous 'aid'. None of them compares in influence or arrogance, however, with the US-dominated World Bank and its affiliates. Much has already been written about the devastating power-game played by this mighty capitalist institution, and space precludes going into much detail here. But those wishing to learn more about the Bank's ramificating grasp on global power, and its deliberate attack on the poor peasantry of the earth, cannot do better than to study Cheryl Payter's absorbing account of the subject, published in 1983.

It is merely worth adding a footnote in this context. Robert McNamara, with his debut as 'godfather' of the US Strategic Airforce Bomber Command during the Second World War, and having been defeated as US Secretary of Defence in a malevolent six-year attempt at 'zapping Charlie Cong' in Vietnam, spent the next ten years at the helm of the World Bank zapping the 'Third World' with destructive western technology and calling it 'aid'. Upon his retirement from the Bank in 1981 he joined the Board of Directors of the Royal Dutch Shell Company.

The scandal of pesticide pushing lies not only in the tonnages of poisons strewn around our environment. Greater or lesser usage means little in terms of long-term effect, given the longevity of the substances – and the speed of impoverishment of the prime recipients. As Wolf von Stephani, formerly head of Hoechst's agrochemical exports has pointed out, the scandal is not so much to be located in FAO's spreading a tonne of poison over every ten square kilometres of a seven million square kilometre swathe of Africa to wipe out tsetse flies (and to grow hamburgers); nor yet in cotton growers using half a tonne *per hectare* each season on their crop; but in the fact that these areas of Africa already produce a large quantity of meat, and could produce much more if left chemically unsoiled; and that, while cotton growers might get 400 kilograms of cotton per hectare with the aid of massive inputs of pesticides, they are as likely to get around 380 kilograms of cotton per hectare *without using any pesticides at all* – other than those which nature provides.

In Egyptian peasant cotton growing – a profitable sector of that country's economy since the days of the Pharaohs – pests are kept down by sending children into the fields to pick off insect eggs and larvae before they can do much harm. This cheap, labour-intensive and environmentally harmless method not only creates employment, but also saves the disproportionate costs of 'high-tech' inputs while avoiding destruction of the agricultural ecology.

While Gezira's cotton production is on the point of collapse, and Sudan on the verge of bankruptcy as result of the 'pesticide mafia's' assiduous attention, they are not alone in this predicament. Already by the mid-1950s, in the rich Peruvian cotton-growing area of the Canete Valley, pesticide-induced cotton pests had reached such proportions that even spraying *every three days* failed to control them. The Peruvians saved their cotton-growing industry from total collapse by abandoning chemical pesticides, and turning to natural control methods. More recently in Mexico, cotton growing did collapse, and has been abandoned over wide areas. Costs of chemical inputs to counter the ever-growing plagues of resistant cotton pests which have appeared, mounted to far more than the crop was worth, and the peasant industry was bankrupted.

Mexico also provides a chilling example of the danger of such pesticide use. In 1978 the US Department of Agriculture totally banned imports of beef from Mexican cattle breeders raising slaughter-cattle for the US market, for it contained residues of several forbidden chemicals way over tolerances permitted by US authorities. Mexican breeders were in the habit of pasturing their cattle on crop wastes and weeds, after the harvest was picked, or on grassland *alongside* chemically treated areas. Drift was sufficient to poison the latter to the point where the meat of cattle grazing there was unacceptably polluted. (Drift from aerial spraying has been found, in remote and previously uncontaminated areas of Africa, 40 kilometres away from the points of spraying – on a day with the slightest of breezes.) A further source of cattle poisoning was cotton-seed cake from treated crops, which not only supplemented the fodder of local cattle, but was also exported to other areas for the purpose. Similar problems of polluted beef have occurred in many areas. At the same period as the US ban on Mexican beef imports, the Department of Agriculture also banned imports from E1 Salvador and Guatemala, beef contamination deriving from the same sources amounting to 90 times US-permitted levels. Nicaraguan and Honduran beef suffered the same fate between 1973–76.

Technological fixing

Pesticide use – indeed, use of agrochemicals in general, including artificial fertilizers – is essentially addictive. The farmer becomes as 'hooked' on chemicals as the heroin addict on the 'fix'. The degenerative pattern of addiction is also apparent in this 'technological fix'. Alleviation of a relatively minor problem is rapidly followed by the need for ever-greater dosage subject to the law of diminishing returns, and exacerbation of the problem. Final collapse occurs as a result of massive overdose. This danger confronts monocultural, chemically-dependent agriculture worldwide – not merely in poorer tropical countries. The fragility of the latter's environments, however, and limited range of resources available to deal with such occurrences, make the problem there critically urgent, and demand immediate policy changes. Pesticide misuse can actually produce problems which did not previously exist, or reproduce those previously cured. Two examples among many available will suffice here.

The first arose in malaria control, and has appeared in so many different parts of the world, from Tahiti and the US to Turkey and Romania – including practically every tropical country suffering from this pest – that it can be considered pandemic. With the first widespread introduction of DDT after the Second World War, scientists began to believe that malaria could be eradicated from the earth. It is vectored mainly by mosquitoes, then highly susceptible to pesticides. By 1955 WHO had set up an ambitious eight-year programme to largely eliminate them, and with them the disease. Spraying house walls internally with DDT formed the main line of attack. It was initially effective, due to the chemical's persistence and the female mosquito's habit of resting on walls between feeds on the inhabitants' blood. Only females feed in this way – males die after serving their breeding function on the brief flight immediately after emergence from the water in which they are born. Pesticide application to human habitations has to be very carefully controlled, of course, and chemical dosages very small. Agricultural use, on the other hand, is practically uncontrolled, and usually massive. Particularly in paddy rice-growing or other irrigated farming, water channels and flooded fields make excellent mosquito breeding grounds, and similarly for innumerable fish, frogs, shrimps, crabs and other predators which eat mosquito eggs and larvae. In Africa, the killy fish eats nothing else. It lives, for a season as brief as the mosquito's, in the puddles on soaked forest ground left by tropical rain. As the puddles dry after the rains, the fish lays its eggs in the mud and then dies. The eggs survive the baking heat in the brick-dry mud, to hatch immediately with the next fall of rain. Their food supply is almost exclusively water-breeding insect larvae – predominantly mosquitoes.

These predators are widely eradicated by crop-spraying run-off, or by pesticide drifting directly into the water. Since most mosquitoes are also killed, any surviving predators die of starvation. The few surviving insects – selected resistant specimens – then have a field-day, free of predation, to expand uncontested throughout the habitat, and into pesticide-sprayed homes of human members of the ecosystem.

Malaria, the incidence of which at first fell remarkably, is now back in greater strength. Mosquito resistance to an increasing range of chemicals is observed worldwide, while the cause of the disease, a protozoon called plasmodium, is itself developing resistance to an ever-wider range of pharmaceutical chemicals formerly offering effective protection.

The second example of pesticide misuse occurred in Papua-New Guinea. The traditionally rural inhabitants live in communal 'long-houses' – impressive and beautiful structures constructed from local jungle materials, roofed with a thick thatch. Each long-house shelters a whole village community, every family occupying its own section. The thatched roof acquires its own biotic community of lizards, snakes, small rodents, bats and insects. The villagers' cats prey on these, and the whole complex develops a biological equilibrium. The inhabitants (probably also non-human – malaria affects even reptiles) suffer from chronic malaria, but have acquired a certain degree of tolerance, and mortalities are few.

WHO decided to spray the long-houses to wipe out mosquitoes. As a result lizards – a favoured cat-food – died of poisoning, and the cats in turn died of eating poisoned lizards. Malaria was checked for a while; but the cats also preyed on rats and mice in the peasants' fields, as well as in the thatch. Destruction of cats led to rodent numbers exploding. Within two or three years the people were not able to harvest enough of their crop to feed themselves, due to pest competition. Unchecked rodent damage also caused the thatched roofs to collapse.

Confronted with destitute, starving people, many living in inaccessible mountainous jungle, the colonial authorities appealed for help to the Royal Australian Air Force. The RAAF came to the rescue by parachuting in baskets full of cats to save the day, and put the whole 'development' back to square one.

Equally damaging rodent outbreaks resulting from pesticide cat-poisoning have occurred in several other parts of the world. This phenomenon is merely an illustration of the danger of wiping out any predator – or indeed, any living part of the complex biosphere.

Poisoning people

More direct and equally widespread damage to 'Third World' inhabitants is caused by directly poisoning people themselves. By 1972, WHO reckoned there were half a million accidental pesticide poisoning cases each year, half of them in the 'Third World', which then consumed only 15 per cent of total world pesticide production. In rich countries, equipped with proper medical facilities and emergency 'poison centres', only one per cent of cases were fatal. In poor countries accidental pesticide poisoning was calculated, on a purposely conservative basis, to result on average in 6,700 fatalities, over two and a half per cent.

Dave Bull of Oxfam made an exhaustive study of the problem. His results, just published at the time of writing, reveal that with pesticide use up 50 per cent in the years since WHO's figures came out, the annual accidental poisoning rate mounted to 750,000 cases, with some 13,800 deaths. Again calculating conservatively – making full allowance for dearth or unreliability of 'Third World' statistics – Bull estimates poor country fatalities at a rate of 10,000 per year out of 375,000 recognized cases of acute pesticide poisoning. He gives detailed figures:

> On the basis of limits of error at the time (1972), the current estimate for the Third World could be as low as 187,000 with 5,025 deaths, or as high as 1,089,750 with 29,205 deaths.

These, like WHO figures, take no account of longer-term effects or fatalities – cancers, birth defects, sterility – nor of suicide attempts, a frequent element in pesticide poisoning death. The pesticide industry invariably and unanimously contests these figures as 'unsupported hypotheses', some hard-liners even going so far as to publish claims that 'no certain cases of death directly and indisputably attributable to pesticide poisoning are known'. Such arguments are unworthy of serious attention. For whatever margins of error there may be in WHO's or Dave Bull's calculations, it is abundantly clear there is a poisoning problem of pandemic proportions, resulting in many thousands of unnecessary deaths and hundreds of thousands of people severely injured as a result of the industry's practices.

Forty per cent of such poisonings are occupational – workers mixing, decanting or spraying the chemicals, or cleaning equipment, all without proper protection, or working (or merely walking) in fields just sprayed. Other common causes are drinking pesticides by mistake (they are often sold in Coca Cola bottles and the like), using empty pesticide containers for food or water storage, and contamination of food during storage or transport. Bull explains:

> The Third World farmer is usually denied access to the protective clothing which in rich countries is accepted as essential for the safe use of pesticides. Even where protective clothing is available, the poor cannot afford to buy it and the heat makes it almost impossible to wear, except for short periods in the cooler part of the day, or at altitudes where temperatures are milder.

Effects of the poverty factor in increasing pesticide hazards to intolerable limits can be illustrated by a few typical examples. In a single district, Kegalle, of Sri Lanka during the five-month 1978 season, 1,021 poisoning cases occurred, the epidemic coinciding with an outbreak of the brownplant hopper which infests rice fields. Dr J. Jeyeratuam, head of Colombo Medical Faculty's Department of Community Medicine, studied 23 cases in detail. Nineteen of these were spraymen without protective clothing who had used pesticides with leaky sprayers, and had sprayed against the wind. At least seven of them had used Endrex 20, a formulation produced in Sri Lanka by Shell, through its subsidiary company Lankem.

Prior to 1976/7 Shell had used the Endrex trademark for a formulation containing the organochlorine endrin, totally banned here. Subsequently the same name was used for at least two different formulations, containing different poisons. The poison causing the 1978 cases contained Shell's aldrin (equally banned) and ethyl parathion, an organophosphate. Jeyeratuam points out that such a mixture – in which one compound can have inhibitory or activating effects on the other – 'may cause problems in providing appropriate therapy'. For any treatment, the ingredients to be countered must at least be known. To confuse the issue further, and mystify the medicos, Shell changed Endrex ingredients yet again, to a mixture of diazinon and methyl parathion. Furthermore, both doctors' and farmers' confusion was compounded by the failure of Shell's associate company to alter the medical advice given on Endrex labels until months after the changed formulation was marketed.

According to Dave Bull, Shell have since promised not to use the brand name Endrex on any future insecticide products in Sri Lanka (neither he nor they say where else they use it), and 'are satisfied that such an incident could not happen again'. Grounds for their satisfaction are not however clear.

Lack of worker protection is not limited to 'Third World' agricultural workers. An ILO seminar in Sri Lanka in 1980 heard that in local pesticide formulation factories associated with Shell, ICI and Bayer, safety practices were not observed by management, exhaust ventilation devices were wrongly installed, defeating their purpose, and adequate protective clothing was not provided to production workers. The report states:

> The workers of two formulation factories are biologically monitored once a week. The exposure level of workers to organophosphate pesticides is such that about 50 per cent of them show pronounced reduction of blood cholinesterase activity. In this connection it is regrettable to note the following phrases from a letter addressed to an employee by an employer: 'The purpose of this letter is to advise you that unless we notice a remarkable improvement in your blood cholinesterase activity within the ensuing three-month period, the company will be left with no option but to terminate your services.'

Such examples of misuse are not peculiar to Sri Lanka. They could be repeated manifold from every corner of the 'Third World'. Pesticides are often mixed by hand and even, in powder form, applied by hand – sprinkled over the crop through the unprotected fingers. Few workers under the tropical sun even cover their mouths with a cloth, let alone a proper filtered breathing mask – which might cost them a year's pay should they decide to bear the discomfort. And there is little point in expecting workers too poor even to own a pair of sandals to provide themselves with rubber boots for this work, nor a man without a shirt to his back to wear plastic overalls. An Indian plantation workers' union official, Mr R.M.R. Singham, says:

> Workers using pesticides do not get any protective clothing.
> This Union has raised a demand (with the plantation-owner's association) for gloves and face-masks.

With, it hardly need be added, as little success as thousands of similar demands wherever poor labour is exploited. Indeed, India's plantation workers may consider themselves lucky at least to have the right to join together in a union – a right far from common in most of the poorer rural areas of the world.

India's general population is among the most contaminated in the world, the average Indian body (including urban dwellers far removed from agricultural application) containing four to five times the organochlorine levels of European citizens. India today is not only the largest gross user of DDT, but also the largest manufacturer and exporter – the industrialized countries having largely dropped production of this first organic pesticide in favour of more powerful and profitable poisons. Leading the 'contamination league table', however, is probably Israel, whose thriving agricultural export industry is utterly addicted to massive chemical inputs, for the greater part homemade.

Misuse of this kind, and its ruinous consequences for poor countries, would seem sufficient grounds for all governments to agree to launching a major international campaign of prohibition and strict regulation of both production and commerce of these poisons. The aim should be to bring the poison-pushing industry under the tightest possible public control. The last examples of abuse of pesticides given below must surely be accepted even by the industry itself as demonstrating a crying need for such restrictive regulation.

We have already mentioned in passing the increasing frequency of pesticide use in suicide or even murder. The availability of these chemical weapons in itself constitutes an uncontrollable threat. The only defence against this is to treat them like the classic poisoner's weapons – arsenic, strychnine or cyanide – under the most stringent restrictions and safeguards. Pesticide use for other modern criminal purposes can only reinforce this view.

In a letter to USAID, a development worker tells the following story from Ghana:

> Market women travel to district market towns where they sell insecticides to local farmers and fishermen, and in turn buy their fish for exportation to larger market areas. The fishermen or farmers then use the insecticides by pouring them into the water of small shallow streams, following the flow downstream until the fish begin floating to the surface. They are collected for salting and smoking . . . Everyone agrees that fishing with poison is bad. Most don't realize how bad. The same fishermen who use the method complain that they are now in a vicious circle: they cannot catch enough using nets and hooks to pay for or maintain the very costly nets and fishing gear. Actually, poison represents the cheapest, easiest, most convenient and therefore most profitable method of fishing available . . . The fish population is dropping by about 20 per cent per year . . . People in fishing villages complain of blurred vision, dizziness and vomiting, but none makes the connection between these symptoms and the poison.

The effects of this evil practice – a sinister modern variant on the ancient African tradition of fishing with biodegradable vegetable poison – on fish consumers is unknown. But if profit-hungry Ghanaian fishermen and 'market mammies' limit their poisonous activities to fish, Zaire's greedy hunters aim at much bigger game. The results provoked parliamentary questions in Belgium's Senate in 1979. Senator R. Gillet, while asking for details of Belgian pesticide exports to Zaire and requesting stricter controls on Belgium's lucrative ivory trade, explained to the House:

> In Zaire, the traffic in ivory is massive and uncontrolled. It is practised by boat, aeroplane and lorry. The market is controlled by Europeans and by army officials and the Zaire government. In several provinces each village has been

ordered to produce 200 kilograms of ivory per year, the order being given by the provincial government.

Thousands of elephants have been poisoned in Zaire during 1978, particularly in the months of April and May . . . Twenty tonnes of pesticides were misappropriated from their normal use of protection of coffee plantations, for use in poisoning water-holes. Thousands of elephants died, some of them taking a week to die. Witnesses saw hundreds of tusks stacked in the town of Ngazi . . . each week during the massacre by poison. Some tusks were 20 centimetres long, indicating that baby elephants were victims.

The tusks were sent . . . to Kinshasa by plane. A DC3 (from the Presidential Flight) was so heavily loaded that (at first) it was unable to take off.

The ivory was, in fact, stacked in the grounds of President Mobutu's palace, under guard by the presidential bodyguard, until it was flown by Sabena to Belgium via Paris.

The Central African Republic – or 'Empire' as it then was – was the scene of similar massacres under the bloodthirsty Emperor Bokassa. Along with the rest of his land's resources, Bokassa kept the ivory traffic in his own hands. It did not cease with his downfall, however.

As recently as February 1982, the staff at the Garoua Wildlife School in north Cameroons were alerted by airport police that a massive shipment of ivory had arrived there by truck from RCA, for air-freighting to Douala International Airport, and thence to Europe. In view of Cameroons' total ban on the ivory trade, the director of the school, who estimated that the shipment represented some 2,000 elephants, appealed by telephone to his Minister in the distant capital of Yaoundé, who promptly ordered the shipment to be blocked. Two days later, the Provincial Governor of the area overrode the Minister's order, and directed airport officials to release the shipment. It was flown immediately to Douala, transferred to a waiting plane and left the same night.

Protective prohibition

Despite the aid industry's mythology to the contrary, pesticides produce no extra food for the poor of the world. They do produce out-of-season luxuries – and even ivory – for the healthy consumers of the rich countries, a contaminated global environment, and inflated profits for the petrochemical multinationals which run our lives out of reach of all public control or any democratic influence.

Only by totally prohibiting production of these dangerous substances anywhere in the world, reinforced by a similarly total ban on any produce at all from countries still found using them, can we ever have a chance of escaping from this vicious circle of poison which contaminates us all.

6. Aiding disaster

Since there's no help, come let us kiss and part.
                              Michael Drayton, Sonnets

Let us then question the whole concept of and need for development – its current style, its predictable future – and thereafter look at its possible alternatives. The harm caused by what is seen, by western or 'westernized' developers, as the imperative demands of poorer human communities for this style of progress, is in itself sufficient reason for taking a cool, detached look at any proposals for change, in so far as these are in the slightest degree dependent on exotic technologies, skills and inputs not already freely available in the region affected by the action.

The essential conflicts between aided development and local ecology, and between introduced, usually unnatural activities and the indigenous environment, come, mainly, from the dominance assumed in the process by two forces. These, once defined as separate but mutually counterbalancing interests, are multinational business (primarily agribusiness and commodity trading cartels, and their allies in the petrochemical industry) on the one hand; and on the other, the empire-building and in-fighting of the massive aid organizations – both governmental (or quasi-governmental) and supranational – which today constitute, worldwide, a self-propagating and practically autonomous industrial growth sector in itself. Although, formerly, these two massive groupings of interests might have been thought of as mutually exclusive and opposed in terms of their aims and responsibilities, the corruption of the aid ideal has gathered them together under one banner.

This unholy alliance is a public charge, but completely beyond any form of democratic control – beyond the reach or corrective influence of ordinary people at either end of the process. How this works, in terms of the damage done and the misplacement and distortion of the best and most generous intentions, can best be illustrated by a concrete example, taken this time from the Sahel. This region, its name synonymous – mainly through its misrepresentation by western media – with drought, hunger, poverty and potbellied 'starving' black babies, is home and habitat of over 30 million people from Dakar to Chad.

The story begins, though, many hundreds of miles away to the south, a couple of days' car-drive or more, according to the season and state of the roads. Ghana is the coastal land once renowned for its lush tropical forests and cocoa plantations, its rich gold and diamond mines (it was called the Gold Coast by the early colonialists), and above all for its people, in one of the gaiest, friendliest and most vivacious societies of all Africa. Ghana's heyday was its year of birth in 1957, when the republic was founded as an independent state, from the territories of the former colony and a part of the British-mandated territory of Togoland – a former German colony, split between Britain and France by League of Nations mandate after the Great War. The northern part of 'British' Togoland voted, during a plebiscite on whether or not to join the Gold Coast as an independent state, to remain mandated until the French half of the country was allowed its own independence by de Gaulle. The southern, mainly Ewe part, more impatient and distrustful of French colonial intentions (at the height of the Algerian war of independence), decided rather to link up with its Ewe brothers in the south-east corner of Gold Coast, and become part of Ghana. Trouble has continued there ever since.

We will examine reasons for this, and for Ghana's economic bankruptcy in another chapter. But in its heyday, Ghana was also justly famous – at least among those fortunate enough to have been there at that period – for its cuisine. Among its more memorable offerings was a ground-nut flavoured stew (or chop, in the local pidgin) of akrante, or 'grass cutter' (also called 'cutting grass', further along the coast in Nigeria). Akrante (*Thyronomys swinderiamus*) is a spineless cousin of the porcupine, and looks like an overgrown (up to 20 pound) brown guineapig. In 1957, this delicacy was readily available on demand, even in Accra – an urban sprawl far removed from any of its remaining wild habitats in the rural areas, where it was a standard item on any country 'chop-house' menu. A favourite eating place to enjoy this speciality then was Comfort's Corner Café, run by an imposing and hospitable Shai woman, the best cook in West Africa. One merely needed to tell Comfort that hungry friends were coming on a particular day, and she would send her 'small boy' to market for an akrante, and anything else she might require to cook with it.

Today, life is not so simple. Whenever I stay in Accra nowadays (and in truth I avoid it as far as possible, conditions there having deteriorated to such an extent in the meanwhile), I have a standing arrangement with my regular driver's ex-wife (Comfort having tragically died some years since, her café no longer even a memory) to prepare a ground-nut chop of grass cutter at least once a week, with the difference that she now tells me what day this will be, for often she cannot find the animals for love nor money.

The connection between these gustatory reminiscences and the dying land and suffering people of the Sahel is very direct. Ghana's wildlife has been almost completely wiped out beyond game reserve and national park boundaries, and will be even within them, if the crunch really comes within the next few years. The greatest threat to survivors is posed by two factors: the exorbitant rate of exploitation of wild animals by commercial hunting; and, more importantly, the immoderate rate of destruction of wildlife habitats by development and the extension of ecologically unviable agriculture and forestry. This latter factor derives mainly from excessive exploitation of forests, combined with opening these up to human encroachment, and the constantly growing pressure to clear new land as existing agricultural areas are exhausted by unsuitable farming methods, or by producing unsuitable export crops.

Over the last decade, the first of these two dangers, over-hunting, has increased tenfold as a result of increased demand throughout the country for meat, coupled with reduced meat supplies from traditional external sources, a shortage which directly increases hunting pressure on remaining wildlife stocks. Again, two factors are at work here. First the cattle died off (up to 80 per cent in some areas) as a result of drought in neighbouring northern countries of the Sahel, which traditionally supplied the coast with a large part of its meat requirements. In more recent years this has been aggravated by the trend, in countries like

Upper Volta, Niger and Mali, to build slaughterhouses with funds loaned by the international aid industry – especially the Common Market – with the aim of diverting formerly exported slaughter cattle from the coastal abattoirs they once supplied, to meat packing and processing plants for the production of conserves and deep-frozen meat for shipping to overseas 'hard-currency' markets. Secondly, the increase of human populations of the coastal and forest belts – through both natural reproduction and immigration – and the simultaneous growth in wealth (or at least, in expectations) of these people, combined with the galloping inflation which the western monetary system and terms-of-trade impose on their economies, have brought about major shifts in consumption patterns and distribution of demand.

This process is most clearly reflected in the sky-high prices of 'bushmeat' (compared with 20 years ago), when it is to be found on the market; in the diminishing success of the 'Sunday hunters' – groups of migrant workers, mostly northerners, who get together after finishing their week's work on a Saturday, hire a 'mammy lorry' and travel miles out into the bush to hunt during the night, to return on Sunday to offer their booty on the special Accra Sunday markets which have grown up around their activities; and in my own difficulties in finding an akrante ground-nut chop.

Deserts of vast eternity

Drought in the Sahel is a recurring natural phenomenon. The disaster that it often, more recently, becomes is largely man-made. At this point, it should be made absolutely clear that nothing said here should be interpreted as suggesting that 'normal', recurring droughts are any less of a hardship for people living in this region; nor is any disparagement intended of the goodwill and worthy purposes of those who donate the funds used in development aid. But the problems get out of hand, and hardship reaches disastrous proportions, when people, and the land itself, start dying as the result of aid planners' misdirected development efforts, and when their livestock – their main, if not only, form of wealth – dies off at the rates we have witnessed during the last drought crisis.

The effects of drought, of course, go far deeper than shortage of meat on coastal dinner tables or increased hunting pressure on wild animals. It destroys not only the Sahelian inhabitants' wealth, but also their social structures and traditions – and finally, even the independence of the proud pastoralists living in this harsh, unforgiving region. Once the 'capital-on-the-hoof' which their livestock represents has gone, the traditional pastoralist way of life is irretrievably lost for the majority, who then face a dispiriting future of rural or urban slum misery, unemployment for the greater part, and little better than survival in servitude for the rest.

During the worst of the drought, the *Observer* publicized one of the latest Oxfam 'Food for Work' programmes (called by some 'slave or starve' programmes) in the Sahel. Under this, Tuareg herdsmen – whose traditional activity is tending cattle, and who from time immemorial have employed another tribe to plant and cultivate their crops, rarely deigning themselves so much as to touch a hoe – were set to digging half a million holes in the desert and planting therein goat dung. The theory was that goat dung contains viable seeds of the scrub the goats have eaten, and these would grow into a bush cover for the bare ground, should it rain long enough to germinate them. Although Oxfam cannot be faulted for wanting to replant bush, the project typifies the 'man was born to work' philosophy of the productivity-worshipping development aiders. As for the inherent problems of 'Food for Work' programmes, these will be dealt with in detail in another chapter.

As far as Ghana's meat supply problems are concerned, however, these could not be solved for many years by the fortunate few herdsmen who managed to bring through any small breeding nucleus of their herds. They were, and still are, hard pressed to build these up again over the next decade or more. Fertility rates of their cattle are fairly high – especially in comparison to those of exotic imported strains of cattle under most African conditions – but the survival rate of calves in their first year is under 25 per cent in many areas *in normal years*. This means that three quarters of the year's crop of calves will not survive the seven- to eight- month dry season to the next rains – when they do come. When they fail, the effects on herd numbers are usually further influenced by the accompanying failure of cereal crops grown in the area – sorghum and millet. This happened in 1972–74, when the herdsmen were forced by dry wells and empty granaries to sell their livestock to the point where the market became glutted, and prices slumped to nothing. Many cases were seen of cattle simply being abandoned to starve, having become a liability rather than an asset, and as noted above, losses of 80 per cent of the entire herd were not uncommon. But the 'normal' loss of calves is a form of natural selection – perhaps the most dramatic form in nature – and has produced a strain of drought-resistant local cattle ideally suited to this semi-arid habitat, while at the same time allowing a very slow build-up of herd numbers. The cyclically recurring failures of the rains tend to keep these within some reasonable balance with the natural carrying capacity of the environment by further thinning out the herds, and by motivating herd owners to sell off some of the surplus, an activity they usually engage in with the greatest unwillingness.

These natural environmental restraints limiting livestock numbers until recently also influenced human population levels in a similar way, by the brutal natural process of limiting what the naturalist would call breeding success. What this means, in the unadorned language of human tragedy, is that babies and small children die – as many as half of them before reaching the age of five years, in very many areas. Under such circumstances, it is not only natural (in the truest sense of the word) for parents to have as many children as possible in order that some at least will attain adulthood; but in these poor lands, where old age pensions and social security are non-existent (for the poorer peasants and pastoralists, at any rate), it is only through the blessing of some surviving progeny that the parents' support and survival can be assured during their latter years. A result of these limiting environmental factors was, however, generally a stable equilibrium of human population in relation to the environment and the food supplies it produced.

There can be no one who would not give thanks for the fact that aid, in its various forms, did a great deal to soften the impact when catastrophe loomed large. The latest news from the Sahel is somewhat more hopeful, in terms of immediate danger and the suffering of its hardy inhabitants. Food aid programmes, health campaigns, agricultural improvement schemes and charitable relief operations have done much – though still vastly less than is needed – to alleviate the worst extremes. The survival rates of the people have been measurably increased and, in biologists' language, breeding success has been improved.

But the manifest failure of these aid operations, and of administration's development policies, lies elsewhere – not, obviously, in temporary successes in achieving the praiseworthy objective of palliating immediate human suffering and tragedy, but in the blind refusal on the part of the authorities and aiders to count the cost implicit in this very success. This means their refusal to confront the implications of interfering with the 'balance of nature', and to prepare to meet the consequences. The result is an ecological disaster which is rapidly destroying the southern Saharan belt as a human habitat. Put at its simplest, the aiders failed to ask themselves, 'If we are going to ensure that more people survive (as we must), what are we going to provide them with to live on?' To interfere with an ecological balance, which populations have built up over millennia with their inhospitable environment, *without providing for the consequences*, is to invite catastrophe and extend and perpetuate human misery, and at best is irresponsible sentimentality gone wild.

It may seem strange to those only familiar with the West African image of the coastal plains' burgeoning cities or the rich humid forest of the 'cocoa belt', to hear the sparsely inhabited near-desert of the Sahel being described as over-populated. However, the ideal (or optimum) population level of any habitable part of our increasingly crowded planet, theoretically at least, is the greatest number of people that can inhabit and utilize it without producing negative interaction either among themselves or between themselves and the environment – in other words, without undue strife or irreversible ecological damage. The 'theoretical' qualification is mentioned because, in practice, any two specialists in this field are rarely able to agree on the level, or threshold, at which such negative effects – visible in deterioration of the quality of life, as well as in more obvious pollution and other ecological failures – begin to appear. Definitions aside, however, the pre-aid situation of the Sahelian belt might almost have been paralleled with what ecologists call a 'climax community'. This is not entirely true, in that a climax community (undisturbed rainforest, the tundra, certain grasslands, deserts or certain alpine ecosystems) constitutes a permanently stable 'closed circuit' system of inter-dependence between the various plant and animal forms with the various non-living elements (minerals, air, water, energy), under more or less stable meteorological and other environmental influences. But the carrying capacity of the Sahel as habitat, and the impact of its environmental, and more especially, meteorological, influences on its various life-forms, including people in their traditional role, has always been cyclically variable.

Latest studies, interpolating from flow data recorded since the beginning of the century for the four greatest Sahelian rivers – the Senegal, Dagana, Niger and Chari – indicate a periodicity of 31 years (with a variation limit of three years) for extreme drought periods lasting more than ten years. These dry spells are interspersed with equally long periods of fairly high rainfall. In fact, the median figures for these maxima and minima work out at 10.3 years – surprisingly close to that of peaks of sun-spot activity, established at 10.4 years. It is anyone's guess at present whether this is mere coincidence, or whether in fact outbursts of sun-spot activity, with their accompanying increase in radiation reaching the earth, has any direct effect on such detailed meteorological phenomena; predictions have been made, however, that the current period of extreme drought will be ended by 1985, to be followed by far wetter seasons in the Sahel. The drought will then reoccur, according to these scientists, around the year 2005.

The fact that these cycles affected human mortality rates appeared to no one there as unjust, until western Christian ethics and the social philosophy of growth-oriented consumerism were introduced to the region. Before that, you died, 'Inshallah', or your children died, and such was the will of God – the law of nature. For there is no natural law which ordains that the span of human life (the 'average expectation of life' in the actuaries' jargon) should be 70 years or more. The predominantly judaeo-christian societies which comprise the richest, most highly developed group of nations of today's world, in their resistance to the concept of death as a part of life (witness heart and other organ transplanting, deep-freezing of cadavers, etc) have tried, with a considerable degree of success, to impose their cult of longevity as a fundamental part of the consumerist system (more is better – even in years of misery) on poorer lands which can ill afford such thinking. As Alistair Graham has written: 'Death, after all, is as common as birth, and at the point of discontinuity will even prevail.'

Modern humanity, however, is convinced that discontinuity is not inevitable and has built a series of defences against nature. In this way, we have learnt to interfere with natural selection processes and with nature's way of controlling populations – both euphemisms for dying earlier than we might. But in applying these defences to marginal areas – marginal as human habitat, that is (they can be defined, for present purposes, as areas having very little elasticity in carrying capacity) – we are inescapably confronted by the need for effective measures to accommodate the 'surplus' people thus produced. Lack of such planning, and the ensuing consequences of this shortcoming, constitute the culpable failure of aid. Local administrations can be exonerated in this, to the very large extent to which they were – and still are today – dependent on outside development planners and ideas, acting often upon western recommendations, the force of which is backed up by 'aid' packages, which as often as not comprise provision of such advisers.

But whatever the latest scientific studies may show regarding the longer-term drought and rainfall cycles of the Sahel, no one dares forecast for any coming year, as a basis for immediate planning, whether the region is likely to receive enough precipitation, adequately distributed over the growing season, to alleviate distress or even ensure survival of the people living there. And yet even the optimum rainfall (and it is not widely appreciated that countries like Upper Volta usually enjoy as much, or even more, precipitation over the normal years as parts, say, of France; but with the difference that it falls, at best, over a period of a little more than four months, at worst, in several weeks, rather than nine months), permitting maximum production of food and fodder crops, would only solve the immediate survival problems of the people, or free them at least from the need for outside charity. It would not solve the underlying problem. The process of habitat degradation has already gone too far for any short-term planning palliatives to work in the long run, short of a draconian depopulation programme. How this might be achieved will be examined later.

Make a desert – call it peace

The process of degradation of abused land in marginal, dry country is well enough known, in general terms, but some fundamental details, applying especially to the Sahel, may be worth repeating here. First of these is that when rain falls on ground covered by vegetation it penetrates many metres into the subsoil, while rainfall on bare ground generally penetrates no more than a few centimetres, and most of it runs off the surface almost as fast as it falls. The vegetation cover, with its root system, acts rather like a giant sponge, breaking the force of impact of the falling raindrops, impeding and thus moderating the rate of surface run-off, and allowing penetration of the soil surface by seepage through cracks and fissures produced by the plants' growth and root systems – as well as by a host of boring or burrowing creatures (from worms, ants and termites to moles, rats, foxes and aardvarks) which live off and with the vegetation. Thus soil carrying such a 'biotic community' acts as a reservoir of seasonal rainfall, ensuring that it penetrates into the subsoil strata to replenish ground-water tables, which enable plant life to survive through the dry season. It can be said that the soil/organic complex acts as a natural regulatory device, distributing seasonal rainfall over time.

Underground water also flows, in patterns related to the surface topography and subterranean formations, and this slow subterranean flow, seeping through to lower-lying surface areas of the catchment basin, is what keeps the upper branches of rivers like the Niger, Volta or Senegal flowing throughout the long dry season. Or did, until we recently interfered with the system.

Vegetation cover also holds together the delicate topsoil of semi-arid regions, as well as supplying it with humus and other essential components. When it is eaten and trampled away by excessive cattle grazing, wind erosion soon begins its rapid and decisively damaging action. Then, when rain does fall, surface run-off is accelerated, and the flow carries with it the finer particles, vegetable matter and soluble salts of the topsoil, leaving exposed the sterile subsoil of newly created desert. Raindrops themselves can also further compact bare soil surface, further increasing its impermeability and increasing surface run-off rates. The classic sequence then begins: deteriorating soil, diminishing agricultural returns, falling water tables, silting of streams and rivers (resulting in seasonal flooding downstream, and the drying up of formerly permanent watercourses). The last effect, seasonal disappearance of streams and rivers, results in turn in the death of formerly permanent vegetation of grass, bush and trees along the watercourse, together with the majority of aquatic creatures living in it – the latter constituting much of the protein ration of the people living in its neighbourhood.

That this process is well under way can be seen in every Sahelian river system; in the upper basin of the Volta River, for instance, it is evident in the increased burden of silt washing down as far as Lake Volta, the huge artificial inland sea created behind the Akosombo hydro-electric dam, second largest in Africa. This enormously expensive installation, built on loaned credits tied to a fixed price for electricity supplied to the North American aluminium concerns exploiting Ghana's rich bauxite reserves, was planned to silt up over 25–30 years, and the amortization of its costs was foreseen as an economic proposition spread over such a period. They have had to be revised – for the worse – several times since the proud opening of this grandiose complex under the late Kwame Nkrumah, largely due to planners' miscalculations of the rate of silting. This, and the rocketing world prices for energy, have direct and most serious impacts on the price of power to the Ghanaian consumer, although the international aluminium giants, sheltered behind their contracted fixed price of electricity, are unaffected. In effect, the dam mainly serves to subsidize American aluminium production, at the expense of the Ghanaians, today one of the poorest peoples of Africa. The effects induced by such hydro-electric and irrigation dam projects will be examined more fully later.

In the Sahel, on the other hand, when the land is in good health, the ground is normally covered with a litter of dried-up grasses, leaves etc., even at the end of the dry season. This unpromising vegetable matter in fact provides adequate forage for indigenous vegetarian species of animals to survive the dry season while awaiting the lusher feed of regrowth during the rains and post-rains period. Domestic livestock, which includes sheep, goats, horses, camels, donkeys and poultry, as well as cattle (all of them 'exotic', introduced species in the area – even the donkeys have no close relationship to the once-indigenous wild asses there, although there may once have been some interbreeding), can also survive on such sparse fare. The main distinction to be made between wild and domestic animals, in these terms, lies in their water requirements. Most local wild species have evolved the ability to live for longer periods without surface water. Their water requirements are supplied by residual moisture content in the seemingly tinder-dry litter, supplemented by dewfall, which in some seasons increases the moisture content of such fodder appreciably, for nocturnal and early-morning feeders. Their water needs are also often minimized by highly adapted metabolic systems which enable them to use available water with greatest efficiency. Some other species, although not so highly adapted, have developed habitual migratory patterns, which take them every few days to the next of a series of permanent water-points.

Domestic cattle, in contrast, need to drink at least once daily. During drought periods they can survive for some time if given water every other day, and in an emergency can sustain periods of several days without water, for example, when driven by lack of pasture to move from one distant water-point to another. But an extreme regime like this involves weight losses and deterioration of condition, and such a high rate of loss of weaker animals (a cow suckling a calf, for instance, cannot produce milk without a minimum water intake) that the cattle's survival is barely marginal. This unceasing water requirement imposes absolute limits on the grazing range open to the cattle. The hardy livestock can walk 10-15 kilometres a day between water and pasture, in extreme situations often 20 kilometres or more. However, at this farthest reach, they are unlikely to survive for long. Time spent walking interrupts the hours of grazing and cud-chewing they need to stay alive on such a meagre diet. Thus the number of cattle a water-point can support is set by availability of dry season grazing within the animals' walking range, i.e. a maximum of 20, or at the outside 25 kilometres.

Strict control of cattle numbers could theoretically permit maintenance, in the affected neighbourhood of each water-point (an area covering anything between 700 and 1,200 square kilometres), of herds of cattle below a threshold level of stocking at which range deterioration begins, thus conforming to the carrying capacity of the range. This could permit production of a sustained yield of surplus livestock for the market, instead of the current wild fluctuations of peaks (during dry periods when the market is flooded with emaciated, out-of-condition beasts of little or no commercial value) and troughs (when constant market demand pushes prices up, but no slaughter cattle are available). But harsh reality has taught, or should have, that in a society where family wealth and status is measured in numbers of cattle owned (often regardless of the quality of the cattle in the commercial, European sense), regulation of herd size, and thus of the pastoralists' wealth, is for practical purposes impossible.

Infrastructures of administrative and technical services, and above all, the political will – essential prerequisites of any regulation programme – are today conspicuously lacking in all the countries concerned. Apart from which, the theoretical carrying capacity for cattle, as was mentioned earlier in connection with human populations, although an idea infatuating some ecologists and conservationists, is extremely difficult to define, let alone determine for a given area, and is, moreover, rarely constant. Consequently experts can rarely agree among themselves – and even less with administrators having other priorities and interests – on where to set levels of permitted utilization, supposing the last should ever be enforceable.

On the other hand, empirical methods of trial and error, allowing for natural fluctuations of the environment and adjusting herd-sizes from year to year to correct errors or imbalances, come up against the problem that human populations, under the circumstances created by outside aid, inevitably increase. Their expectations and aspirations are equally inevitably increasing, intensifying demands for more livestock. The problem of human overpopulation, however, cannot be solved by sending the surplus to the slaughterhouse, as is possible with cattle. Apart from this, any attempt to deal forcibly with the people's surplus cattle by such means could lead to politically explosive conflicts.

Development aid agencies and administrators failed miserably to foresee these problems; and what is less understandable, they turned a determinedly deaf ear to many who did – often acknowledged experts with intimate understanding of the region which, at the outset of aid efforts there, was little known to the outside world. How many of us knew even where the Sahel was before drought and disaster hit the headlines? This may have been due, in part, to a problem specific to our modern, technological world, and one which is an especial malady of aid industry – the 'compartmentalization' of expertise. An illustration from personal experience is typical: while living for several years in Rome, home of FAO headquarters, I received much useful help and advice from FAO experts in the Wildlife Section of the agency's Forestry Division in a series of wildlife utilization projects designed for Africa; after three years of close, regular contact with these people I discovered, quite by chance, another Wildlife Section – an equally rewarding source of information – in FAO's Animal Production Division on the floor above Forestry. No one downstairs appeared to have heard of this 'competition'.

Planning for people

Apart from such cases of the organizations' left hand not knowing – not wanting to know – what the right hand is doing, a second major factor in the decision to ignore clear warnings of impending disaster can be defined as administrative expediency. Once the juggernaut administration is rolling, rational argument can do little or nothing to halt, or even deflect, the thrust of the development imperative.

More concrete proposals for remedying these deficiencies will be made in the final chapter, but it should be quite clear, here, that proper planning and population policies, based on the realities of the particular environment and the needs and wishes of the people living there (and not on office-bound western technocrats' theories and prejudices), should be absolute determining factors in any interruption in the delicate natural equilibrium of these marginal areas. Far from plunging in once an obvious crisis has been allowed to develop – in the hope of relieving acute hardship and suffering (in a crisis, of course, we have no choice but to try to do whatever we can) but too often causing permanent, more widespread harm – the remaining or renewable natural resources of these regions must be employed to the best advantage of the people inhabiting them, as well as their neighbours in other zones. Although the planners and developers will deny this, the latter usually know themselves what they want and the best ways to achieve it, when allowed to do so. Any external aid to these zones must be made conditional upon establishing and implementing policies designed to improve the lives of the people, and the state of the land, rather than to exploit both and, *in extremis*, to deploy aid merely to maintain the *status quo*. This is, naturally, a touchy political issue; but only the most despairing cynic would find it a hopeless one.

Nevertheless, the development imperative maintains its momentum. To take but one example from the threatened region, development aid of the kind Upper Volta receives goes mainly into agriculture and water resources development – even though much of it may in reality go to subsidize the public service composed of the ruling elite. In these countries agriculture depends on availability of water (to a far greater extent than in temperate zone 'water-surplus' regions). Development of water resources there takes the form of constructing small dams (Upper Volta, part of Africa's inland plateau, has no mountain ranges which would make big dams possible), and also of wells or boreholes tapping subterranean water tables.

Following the fiasco of the Common Market's EDF multi-million-dollar dam-building programme in the 1960s (a country-wide complex of some 60 dams was first planned; although it regally enriched its French, German and Italian consultants and contractors it failed to provide, or conserve, much additional water, since most of the half dozen dams which were finally built were not water-tight), the main thrust of water-development efforts has been to sink new tube wells, or deepen existing ones, throughout the land. The last years of drought crisis witnessed an acceleration of this activity, as each of the charitable emergency relief funds embarked on its own programme of sinking new wells by the hundred, ever deeper in the hope of catching up with falling water tables. All of them thus added their mite to the more massive, longer-term borehole programmes of a multitude of multilateral and bilateral aid agencies.

The dangers of introducing new, hastily and inadequately planned, water-points in such regions have been repeatedly pointed out over many years by ecologists and range management specialists. Results of such aberrant developments can be quite spectacular. Often within two to three years of installation of water-points, domestic livestock will have stripped off every trace of edible vegetation (and there is little a camel or a goat cannot eat) over a radius of 20 kilometres or more around the well.

Recovery rates of these pastures are extremely slow; and they are destroyed almost as much by trampling hooves as by over-grazing itself. In a frighteningly short time another roughly circular area of up to 1,000 square kilometres or more is added to the spreading desert. The effect can be clearly observed from the air, and the degraded patches have long since been recognized as 'germ cells', nuclei which tend to join up with one another, eventually eliminating the areas of bush cover untouched by the 'commuting' herds of livestock. A contributory factor in this may be overuse by surviving stocks of wild creatures migrating into untouched areas as their former habitats are eaten out, thus concentrating in higher densities than the natural bush can support.

In relation to Upper Volta's total area of some 275,000 square kilometres, it obviously does not require many such 'developments' for the whole of the country's top-soil to wash down into the lake behind Ghana's Akosombo Dam. Yet even today, despite rates of destruction well beyond the limits of folly, some parts of Upper Volta still carry impressive numbers of wild animals. Most of these are to be found in the sparsely populated area immediately north of Ghana's northern frontier, a zone largely denied to human habitation by tsetse flies and the evil African blackfly (*Simulium damnosum*). The African species, breeding only in the fast-flowing water of shallow streams and rivers or the spillways of dams, serves together with the tsetse fly effectively to protect the zone against the predations of pastoralists' cattle and other human influence. While tsetse is the carrier of sleeping sickness in humans, and nagana in domestic livestock, the blackfly vectors one of the nastier nematodes – a filarian worm which infests human (and some animal) bodies, with an especial preference for the inside of the eyeball. The long-term result of such infestation is, inevitably, blindness, called locally 'river blindness', or in medical terms, onchocerciasis. It is still possible to find whole villages of riverside dwellers afflicted by this appalling parasite along the upper reaches of the Volta River – and many other African rivers.

Game stocks in the area, however, have been severely reduced over the last 15 years, primarily by the seasonal drying-up of formerly permanent stretches of the Red and White Voltas which traverse it. This might be thought to have a slight counterbalancing effect, in that the distribution of blackfly, with its disease, may well be affected by lack of available running water to breed in; on the other hand, snail-vectored bilharzia only thrives in still or stagnant water, and quickly appears where this is present. Lake Volta, formed over a stretch of the lower Volta once riddled with river blindness, is now infested with bilharzia, while the blackfly is mainly restricted to the dam overspill and sluiceway zones, and the last free-flowing stretch down to the sea.

Following an initial build-up under strict protection of herds of the larger herbivores (bubal hartebeast, topi, defassa waterbuck, kob, buffalo and even elephant), as well as the numbers of less gregarious species (roan antelope, warthog and many smaller antelope), a rationally planned and well managed programme for utilizing these remaining Voltaic wildlife stocks would permit the culling of a regular crop of game meat for both the Voltaic and the Ghanaian markets. With regard to the latter, the proximity of the Bolgatanga meat-packing plant in northern Ghana suggests the possibility of processing Voltaic game-meat there, as a substitute for the non-existent beef for which its planners intended it.

This meat-packing plant, incidentally, is a symbol of development planning at its worst. It was conceived in the early 1960s to process slaughter cattle brought across the border from Upper Volta. Traditionally, the cattle were driven, either on foot or in trucks, to Accra and Kumasi for slaughter, but their loss of weight and condition on the way was so great as to make the siting of a proper slaughterhouse in the north an attractive proposition. However, the planners omitted to take into account a fundamental weakness in their plan. In normal times Upper Volta has no surplus of cattle, and the less so with the growth of Voltaic consumption in the meantime. What surplus cattle Upper Volta used to export originated mainly elsewhere, in Mali and beyond. The Voltaic authorities, seeing their land and pastures being used merely for the transit of livestock for the benefit of relatively far richer Ghanaians, imposed a tax on cattle passing through the country, thus effectively upsetting the rentability calculations of the abattoir's planners. Indeed, even during the short periods when the plant functioned at all, it rarely ever did so at more than 10 per cent of its potential capacity.

Even so, the experience of a restaurant owner – also a passionate big-game hunter – in Ouagadougou, capital of Upper Volta, gives at least some indication that a game-meat packing project may not be a complete 'pipe-dream', if the necessary inter-state co-operation and proper controls could be effectively ensured. He regularly (and quite illegally) supplies his restaurant's larders with meat from his weekend hunting in this border area, often returning to the capital on a Sunday evening with a pick-up truck full of antelope carcasses, or occasionally a buffalo. It is incidental to the theme that this practice is somewhat more wasteful of the country's wildlife stocks than it should be, owing to the frequent failures of Ouagadougou's municipal electricity supply. These have regularly resulted in his having a cold store full of de-frozen, rotting meat which could only be thrown away.

From the point of view of logistics, hunting areas along the Red and White Voltas are twice as near to Bolgatanga as to Ouagadougou – and Ghana, enjoying the fruits of Nkrumah's grandiose hydro-electric dam, has more reliable electricity supplies. A properly run cropping programme there could produce income for Upper Volta – a country largely dependent on tax revenues and external subsidies to keep even the public administration going – and also much needed meat for Ghana. It could also create an irresistible economic incentive to bring under control both present over-exploitation of these remaining wildlife stocks through unregulated sport-hunting (also, undoubtedly, a profitable attraction to a certain group of tourists, which could produce considerably more revenue for the country, if properly managed), and the sort of profiteering exploitation described above, which has little to do with true hunting 'sport' in the eyes of more dedicated hunters. Rationally planned and carefully controlled utilization of this renewable natural resource means keeping these wild herds in balance with their human-disturbed habitat – with the natural carrying capacity of the land – and, *per se*, limiting human occupancy and disturbance of their habitat to tolerable levels. This on the assumption that humans are meat-eaters, and that their requirements in this respect will be met, either from free-living game or from artificially raised and manipulated domesticants.

The juggernaut development aid industry rolls on its course, unhindered even by the fact that awareness of the damage it brings has filtered up to the highest establishment levels of agencies and governments involved. Two of these, at least, are worth quoting here at some length – both of them conservative, acknowledged expert officials or bodies – to illustrate the kind of outspoken criticism the establishment is hearing from within, and ignoring.

The first comes from Swedish Professor Kai Curry-Lindahl, a member of the Executive Board of the International Union for Conservation of Nature and Natural Resources (IUCN), since 1956 Vice-President of the Fauna and Flora Preservation Society based in London Zoo, and member of or adviser to a number of other governmental and non-governmental bodies. He was for many years an international official within the UN system, special consultant to UNESCO and UNPD, and until 1977, Senior Adviser to UNEP, the Nairobi-based UN Environment Programme, as well as adviser to African states. Hardly, then, a wild revolutionary out to smash the system or overturn the world.

Curry-Lindahl is now based at the Royal Swedish Ministry for Foreign Affairs, the department responsible for Sweden's aid programme. This authority charged him with the examination of aid's environmental impacts – defined elsewhere as 'the net change in human well-being resulting from an environmental effect, or change resulting from human action; the environmental impact of a development scheme is the difference in well-being between its implementation and its non-implementation'. His cool, damning, 500-page report in 1979 is perhaps the most-ignored classic on the subject. He begins fairly cautiously:

> So far efforts to promote development have taken little or no account of the functions of the eco-system or of environmental management as a whole. Policy-makers often seem to have been little aware of the environment in their decisions on development assistance. In the long run, therefore, results have turned out to be unfavourable and caused environmental deterioration.

He rapidly warms to his theme, however, and in reviewing today's environmental hazards confronting the 'Third World', writes:

> Since all the[ir] renewable natural resources are at the same time and in various ways deteriorating and in some places even being eliminated, the aggregate effects on the eco-system, particularly in the tropics and sub-tropics, are of catastrophic dimensions.

He continues (emphasis in original):

> Environmental problems are so grave there that it is understandable that governments give up in despair and relapse into a laissez-faire attitude, but it is unforgivable that multilateral and bilateral development assistance organizations are so hidebound or unenlightened that they do not try to counteract this state of affairs.
>
> This lack of rationale and environmental awareness when it comes to advisory services, planning and the carrying out of development projects, means that the *assistance organizations themselves are an environmental hazard*.

The second 'establishment' authority to be quoted here also has something to say on the subject of 'hidebound' aid organizations, though the authors' comment, written in the mellifluous prose of transatlantic functionaries, lacks something of the dauntless Swede's forthright 'de-development impact'. Brian Johnson, writing in 1980 with Robert O. Blake for the International Institute of Environment and Development (IIED) of Washington and London (founded by the late Barbara Ward, who was for many years Chairman of the Council, among whose members are Robert McNamara and Lord Solly Zuckerman), studied the environmental performance of six bilateral aid-donors. They tell of aid agencies becoming dominated by economists and planners whose training and experience in judging ecological and sociological consequences of their activities 'are (often) inadequate', of the 'trend for responsibility for environmental assessment to fall through the cracks', and of 'determined bureaucratic resistance'. On the process of damage to 'Third World' environments, and responsibility for preventing this, they comment:

> Entire regions of the developing world are faced with appalling physical devastation of their mountains, forests, grasslands, and . . . their best agricultural lands . . . The horror stories of Nepal, Haiti, the Sahel and Northeast Brazil are well known. Less well known are the rapid and dangerous deterioration of soil and water everywhere.

They go on to say that although agencies are starting to recognize the limitations this destruction imposes:

What we did *not* find in any agency . . . was adequate recognition of, or programmic response to, the desperate need of so many developing countries to stop or control damage to their resource base, much less reverse these trends. Agencies either have many plausible-sounding reasons for inaction or simply ignore the problem.

On the same theme, Curry-Lindahl is again more forthright (emphasis added):

Abuse of the environment is taking place daily to an increasing extent in all tropical continents, in order to make way for agriculture or cattle breeding *on land which cannot stand the strain of such activities*. The ongoing deterioration of the environment which is the very foundation of these populations' existence is an ecological disaster, which undermines the future efforts of these peoples to support themselves in these areas.

In the preceding pages we have been looking at an exemplary case, naming the details, which typifies many aspects of aid's negative effects. This is not, of course, intended to pinpoint any particular country or aid agency as being exceptionally negligent or malicious – any one of hundreds of cases from every corner of the 'Third World' could have been chosen to make the same point. Curry-Lindahl, in contrast, deals in generalizations, intentionally avoiding precise details which would enable identification of specific countries or projects. He is frank about this, writing in his foreword to the report: 'This "neutrality" may perhaps have resulted in what can be called sweeping statements unsubstantiated by definite examples. This caution is a weakness, but the method permits candour.' Moreover, he is right in thinking, as an official, that naming any one set of projects would be irrelevant; the problems he describes are so widespread as to be general, in practical terms. Thus, pointing the critical finger in detail would indeed be discriminatory – while a list of all the failed aid projects or those taking negative effect would be practically as long as the story of aid itself.

For all that, Curry-Lindahl's massive report does not lack precision. Of the Sahel's problems discussed above, he writes (emphasis in original):

Setting up a network of boreholes for water in a semi-arid region which is already intensely grazed by cattle is one of the fastest means of desertification that exists.

This has unfortunately been demonstrated by several development projects in Africa, which in this form constitute an environmental threat to the developing countries.

Moreover, the phenomenon is not only unlimited with regard to country or region and aid agency. It also covers almost every type of economically oriented or inspired development project, including all other kinds of water-resources management, fisheries, forestry, service industries (such as tourism, examined in some detail later) – plus health and social services, education and information. Everything that aid touches, when based on self-interested advice of economists and technocrats selling the latest 'technological fix', turns out in the final analysis to be at the cost of people it was supposed to help, and of their living environment.

We touched earlier on the problem of high dams for the production of electric power or for irrigation. If space allowed, this could be the subject of a chapter of its own, or even a book. Here let it merely be mentioned that flood plains and river deltas – the Nile is a classic example – often require their periodic (usually annual) flooding to maintain or renew their fertility. The cultivated areas receive an annual baptism of silt and mud laden with dissolved nutrients, far better than any dosage of artificial fertilizers produced by the petrochemical industry. This phenomenon was, of course, the basis of Egypt's becoming the 'bread basket' of Rome, 2,000 and more years ago.

Damming disasters

Damming the rivers causes the water's burden of silt to be deposited behind the dam, and cuts off the supply of nutrients to lower-lying floodable areas. Not only does this impoverish the farmers living there by forcing them into the market for expensive 'artificials', it also cuts off the nutrient supply to fish stocks of the lower reaches, in delta areas and even out to sea.

On the other hand, while dams might reasonably be expected to create opportunities for developing new fishing industries above them in the new inland seas they form, the case of Akosombo once more illustrates the sort of problems upon which such hopes often founder. The Volta valley above the dam site lies through the forest belt, and although heavily farmed at the time of flooding as the dam closed, it was in large part still forested. Since felling the trees and bush clearing over the hundreds of square kilometres about to be inundated was prohibitively expensive, the dam's planners counted on the hope that once the trees were under the water they would die and rot rapidly, so that within a very few years, after fish stocks had been allowed to build up, a large-scale trawling industry could be installed. In the event, the trees died as expected, but the rot failed to set in. Instead the skeleton trees – many of them forest giants – petrified or 'fossilized', owing to the action of the water. This effect is perfectly familiar to the region's inhabitants even in the north, in the drier treeless parts of the river basin.

Here, indeed, since building timber is scarce locally and has to be imported from the far south, their domeshaped round huts – some of considerable size and beauty – are constructed with arches made of 'tresses' or bundles of thumb-thick twigs lashed together to form a flexible material four or five metres long. These are dug into the ground at the corners of a square, and bent together at the apex to form a dome. This lattice is then filled with laterite mud, which makes a waterproof covering and walls. The stability of the resulting structure depends more on the homogeneity of the plastered mass than of the bundles of twigs, which mainly serve to hold the whole together during the building process. They do, however, have a certain function as reinforcement (like the steel bars in a ferro-concrete structure), until the ubiquitous termites and wood-rotting fungi get to work.

These traditional builders learnt centuries ago that the action of river-water on the bundles of twigs could greatly impede the attack of these agents. Such timbers, dropped in the local river and weighted down with stones to keep them submerged, will acquire a resistance to rot and termites, making them durable for decades instead of the two or three years which untreated timbers can be expected to survive. Some months of submersion are desirable, although a few weeks will already have a notable effect in prolonging the life of this important traditional building material.

This gem of local knowledge was freely available to the highly skilled technicians who planned the Akosombo dam and its ancillary functions, had they taken the trouble to come out of their air-conditioned office to have a look around the environment they were about to destroy. Today, Lake Volta is an odd spectacle of petrified forest – tree skeletons poking up above the surface in the shallows, while in deep water the submerged skeletons await the unwary fisherman's nets or lines, and bring to nought hopes of using this vast body of water for large-scale production of much-needed protein. The only stretch easily 'fishable' is in fact the original trace of the stream bed of the river before flooding.

On the subject of this type of water resource development, Curry-Lindahl comments:

> A comparatively large number of development and other projects continue to eliminate natural floods which sustain fertility in river valleys at the same time as other projects pave the way for flooding disasters which in the long run have negative effects on the environment. 'Aid' of this kind constitutes an environmental threat to the countries concerned.

Another important aspect of such aid concerns the question of energy planning. Between 98 and 99.5 per cent of aid funds loaned by UNDP, the World Bank, the Inter-American Development Bank and the Asian Development Bank for energy projects between 1972 and 1977 went into environmentally harmful water-power projects; only a fraction of these billions of dollars is channelled into research and development of alternative energy sources, such as biogas and solar energy. Curry-Lindahl puts emphasis on the problem of diverted resources:

> *As a result of these enormous investments in power sources which are unsuitable for developing countries, the destruction of vegetation for household fuel and the impoverishment of soils (through the collection of tree and bush waste, roots and manure for the same purpose) has accelerated. This pressure, which is a threat to human existence, could have been reduced and in some, particularly vulnerable areas, perhaps even eradicated if 'energy aid' had been channelled to where it was most needed.*

It was channelled, in fact, to where the oil companies and giant civil engineering consortia thought it would do *them* most good.

All of the foregoing, however, is a criticism of the aided development process and its consequences. Both authors accept, endorse even, the need of some such sort of 'progress'. This of course conforms largely with the philosophies and policies of the institutions for which they are writing — the inevitability of the development imperative. This can be summed up in the developer's slogan, 'don't just stand there — *do* something'. The 'neo-imperialism' of the development imperative is one of its more unsavoury and least recognized aspects. Yet Curry-Lindahl does not fail to recognize the effects of this entirely (if this is also true of IIED, they keep very silent on the subject). Let us end with a further quotation, touching this theme (emphasis in original):

> *We must also get rid of the prevalent ruinous idea that an unexploited natural resource denotes mismanagement, and that it must therefore be exploited.*

And further, finally:

> We have reached the point where the vicious circle of accelerating desolation of land must be broken, before the destruction of resource capital reaches such dimensions that it is irreversible and makes the areas concerned uninhabitable.

7. Monkey business

Woodman, woodman, spare that tree
Touch not a single bough;
For years it has protected me
And I'll protect it now . . .

Phil Harris, song lyric

Chimpanzees are not in any real danger of extinction, or at least, they are in no more urgent danger than the rest of us. For one thing, they breed too easily in captivity. As a result there is such a huge stock of captive chimpanzees around the world that they have become an embarrassment to zoo managements and others keeping them; doubts about their continued survival are only as justified as are fears about our own future. More than 4,000 zoos and safari parks display troops of chimps, some of them running into dozens of the animal.

Much more dubious is the continued tolerance of *wild* chimpanzees by the future inhabitants of Africa, these great apes' natural home. For like all the larger non-human primates, they tend to compete with us in lands where they live wild, and their interests conflict with ours wherever these impinge on each other. At present the apes' 'Lebensraum' is subject to continuous and mounting pressure, due directly or indirectly to the increasingly intolerable demands of the consumerist world on this tropical environment. It was not so very long ago, and certainly within living memory, that the greatest danger threatening individual chimpanzees arose from their own delicate flavour when cooked. Indeed, wherever they still survive in any appreciable numbers in the wild, they are highly regarded and sought after as a delicacy for the cooking pot. Their fine-grained, tender flesh combines the aroma of lean pork with the more subtle flavour of fresh venison. At least I can vouch for the Gabonese variety, having had the good fortune to taste it there several times. According to friends there who claim to have once been cannibals, it is the nearest thing they can get these days to human flesh. (I never was able to discover how far this cannibalistic claim was based on fact, and how much on their pulling my leg; though their fathers or grandfathers were quite possibly anthropophagic. As my friends explained, their elders were assured so repeatedly and with such conviction by early colonial conquerors like Carl Woermann, Mary Kingsley and de Brazza that they must be cannibals, that they began to wonder if they were missing something – and decided to try it.)

Elsewhere in its remaining habitat, which stretches from coastal Senegal and Gambia in the west to the western parts of Tanzania in the east, and from southern Cameroons down to Zaire, the chimpanzee is generally much rarer than in Gabon – and much warier of human predators. In these other regions it is much more difficult for foreigners to find an opportunity to taste this (for western tastes) rather exotic meat. And although the animal is protected, nominally at least, by game and wildlife conservation laws throughout its range, the fact that it is appreciated by most Africans as a food means that those few chimps which are still illegally hunted as meat are rapidly and furtively eaten away from the public gaze. One only hears of it at second hand, and little evidence is left to show; the skin is eaten on the meat after the hair has been singed off, as with most animals in Africa (or as we do with pigs in the West), while the skull and other bones are prized for esoteric purposes of medicine or sorcery – making 'juju', in the local term. What evidence does come to light is usually to be found in the surreptitious traffic in baby chimpanzees. This trade, which at the most profitable dealer's end is almost entirely in the hands of Europeans and Levantines, continues throughout West and Central Africa – despite prohibitions on their capture, possession or export – in every country where they still exist in the wild, and even in some where they do not.

Initially this macabre trade was limited to dealing in a 'by-product' of subsistence hunting, (such as occasioned my own gourmandizing in Gabon). Young chimpanzees are captured by killing a female with dependent offspring. The small ape remains helpless and terrified beside its dead or dying mother, and can easily be caught. Since the female's cadaver represents up to 50lb of meat (adult females weigh up to 90lb alive, and since Africans eat more of the carcass and skin than we, with our domestically slaughtered animals, the 'dressing-out weight' is higher), the hunter would often spare the young ape from immediate slaughter, for the extra income it would bring if sold alive to a dealer. His earnings would be small, however, compared with those of a miserable chain of middlemen: itinerant dealers and smugglers; air-freight transporters and shipping lines; corrupt officials who will sometimes, if the price is right, produce a beautifully stamped and quite illegal export permit (usually describing the ape as of some other primate species); leaders of zoo-catching expeditions whose subsequent best-sellers make such endearing reading for animal lovers; and finally, the wholesale importers, zoo directors, circus managers and research scientists who complete the chain as 'end-users'. The hapless creatures pass through all of these avaricious hands. Few of them survive this purgatory of passage down the illicit 'pipeline' (not more than five per cent, according to some authorities), to end their days as displayed prisoners in foreign zoos, as victims of sadistic scientists, or to succumb to the usually inexpert care of some misguided private citizen on an ego trip.

Since its beginning as 'by-product' trading, the whole business of satisfying this strange lust has become so profitable that hunger-hunting, which first supplied the market, was surplanted by hunting for young apes as the prime target. Today the mother ape's cadaver is often left to rot. Hunting grounds are usually distant, in the remotest reaches of the forest, and lugging a 90lb carcass back to the village game-meat market is hard work – and unrewarding at today's price of around 20 pence a pound. The baby animal, in contrast, might bring the hunter £30–40, if he can get it back to the dealer alive.

However much one may frown on eating chimpanzees, this is a waste of much-needed protein. It is insignificant, however, compared to the wasteful destruction of breeding potential of wild chimpanzee stocks as a result of this demand for chimps and the methods used to satisfy it. Such discriminating hunting, selecting successfully breeding females (where subsistence hunters will kill either sex of any age, and indeed, are just as likely to bag a male covering the retreat of an alarmed troop), is purely a result of market demand. The havoc it wreaks among wild stocks hardly bears contemplation.

The average life-span of wild chimpanzees is unknown. They have been known to live in captivity for up to 50 years. Confronting all the hazards of nature, it is unlikely that many wild chimps attain 40 years of age. Females begin breeding at 8–9 years old. Few live long enough in nature to reach the ape equivalent of the menopause – the end of female fertility – should indeed this phenomenon occur, for some authorities think that the menstrual cycle (of 31–45 days) continues to the end of their lives. Young are produced on average every three years, and may stay with the mother for as long as three years, separating completely from her to join the troop's 'juvenile squad' at four. But many of the young do not survive so long. They are fair game for a variety of natural, non-human predators, from leopards and snakes to baboons and even cannibalistic members of their own kind, as well as being subject to other natural hazards of disease and accident.

In her reproductive life-span of maybe 20 years, a female chimpanzee will probably produce no more than seven or eight offspring, and perhaps even fewer. On the reasonable assumption that breeding females killed by hunters are, on the average, at mid-point of their reproductive lives (in reality they are likely to be younger, since age and experience would make older animals more wily), a mother chimp's death eliminates her future breeding potential, amounting to perhaps four more offspring, half of which would themselves have been female.

According to the Fauna and Flora Preservation Society's *Oryx* in 1982, transit casualty rates even among much hardier and easy-to-handle monkeys such as macaques, which are captured as adults and are thus far less vulnerable than young chimpanzees, are equally horrifying. Fourteen thousand captive animals died before some 10,000 arrived in the US, while an Indonesian dealer claimed that 43 per cent die before export. Of the arrivals (in 1978–9) in the US, 1,600 died in flight or within three months of arrival. As FFPS says: 'Some mortality is inevitable in the wildlife trade, but a rate of two monkeys dead for every one making its destination alive is quite unacceptable.'

Each young chimpanzee successfully brought home alive (with a 90 per cent loss rate in transit) involves the death by human action of ten breeding females and nine other young lost *en route*. Moreover, given the type of scrap-iron-loaded blunderbusses (or 'daneguns') most often used, an unknown, but probably large number of young animals, carried by the mother, are certain to be fatally wounded by the charge of nuts-and-bolts which brings her down. Or else the young may escape into the bush, avoiding capture only to die of starvation or at the fangs of some other predator. Such 'lost' animals cannot be taken into account in this attempt to assess the overall drain on wild stocks.

Breeding potential lost to the present generation for each live export amounts therefore to some 40 unborn apes. In terms of the next generation, the loss is the whole potential of at least five young females (assuming half the captives are female), in all between 35 and 40 future offspring. The breeding potential of survivors of the 'pipeline' is, of course, lost to wild stocks.

Calculation of total losses to wild stocks in terms of the present and immediately following generations becomes mind-boggling. For every wild chimpanzee reaching a zoo or circus, it can be reckoned that, projected over the following 30 years, the cost of each captive to wild chimpanzee stocks can be summed up as ten dead females; ten young apes; 40 yet unborn to the adult animals; and anything from 35–40 to the young females not yet in breeding: a grand, awful total of 95–100 wild creatures.

The traders and zoo-men may counter that such figures are 'theoretical', estimates, assumptions and interpolations. But the figures and assumptions given above are intentionally conservative, and based on research by several authorities. Whatever their value, they should at least give pause to any but the most hardened of the 'fluffy bunny' neurotics, cooing over the pathetic antics of degraded inmates of our most popular urban animal 'attraction' – our local zoo.

Science maintaining markets

One major influence on the economics of this trade was mentioned at the beginning of this chapter – the chimpanzees' adaptable breeding habits, allowing them to reproduce freely under the most execrable conditions of captivity. One German circus and fun-fair showman keeps seven or eight animals most of the year round in a caravan trailer, fitted out with heavy steel-barred individual cells. He breeds from the females regularly, removing the young a few days after birth and bottle-feeding them, in order to bring on the mother's next oestrus earlier and thus increase her 'productivity'. Owing to this breeding facility in the western zoo and circus trade chimpanzees are a glut on the market. Growth markets today are mainly in Japan and elsewhere in the Far East, Australia, and some of the richer Latin American countries – while the best and largest markets for buying a chimp are in Hong Kong and Florida.

This has had some depressing or stabilizing effect on prices, and reduced demand for wild chimpanzees. Counterbalancing this, however, is a continued growing demand from another large-scale ape consumer. Permanent exhibition in an animal penitentiary may be the kindest of miserable fates awaiting these animals, once they have been torn from their natural homeland.

Modern 'life sciences' – whose main research activity seems to consist of destroying living creatures in the hope of finding out what life is made of – are the most demanding and assiduous consumers of apes (and many other animals). Chimpanzees are used for gruesome and arcane methods of research into mysteries which, given the moral immaturity of civilized humankind and our unwillingness to deal responsibly with any resultant knowledge, might better be left unsolved. For some of such work, captive-bred specimens may be adequate, or even in some cases desired, but wild-born animals are normally preferred, if only on cost grounds. Centres for breeding primate 'experimental material' have been set up in Germany and the United States, but their products cost ten times the price of an ape bought on the free market in Hong Kong, Singapore or Bangkok.

To give but one example of these scientific horrors, when US war scientists developed the neutron bomb (that paradigm of human evil, destroying people while minimizing damage to property), they first tested it on chimpanzees. In this case they chose the rare dwarf sub-species, which is much more difficult to breed, and truly 'endangered'. Human test-subject volunteers were not available, even among the military heroes and politicians who want to build and deploy this obscenity.

Demand from such sources maintains market prices, despite zoo over-production; indeed, part of the 'scientific' market is supplied by zoos, often surreptitiously, helping to dispose of the glut. Other aspects of this zoo-induced animal glut, and the ways it is dealt with, will be examined later. But prices for wild animals from the illicit trade 'pipeline' are thus maintained to incite further predation.

An interesting sidelight here is contained in a remark by a West African animal dealer, commenting on IUCN's 'Washington Convention', an international agreement endorsed by many nations to control trade in species which IUCN considers particularly in danger of extinction. Speaking under promise of anonymity, he told me: 'These regulations are mainly for the rich countries. Our country has signed the agreement, but not ratified it. In any case, with this kind of regulation . . . there's always a way. But making difficulties at the other end, for the purchaser, only makes it more expensive to get the merchandise to him in good condition. More animals die on the way, or on coming back when they're refused entry. This means I have to charge more, and pay less for the animals, to cover the extra risk. The trappers must simply work harder for their bread.'

He also discussed current prices. In 1978, a chimpanzee in Germany (sales of animals there are perfectly legal – once the animal is in the country, or bred in it) cost around DM1,200, demand being mainly for immature apes. To stay competitive, and allow for the cost of transport and losses through abortive shipments, he could ask no more than DM800–900 for a young chimp. He reckoned to pay the trapper or dealer DM150–200. His pens and stinking cages were in a dismal state, some containing obviously dying creatures, while unkempt, lethargic apes and various other sick-looking animals were tethered individually in various parts of the bare, dusty compound. The whole scene was one of squalor and unthinking cruelty.

Exporting inflation

Despite the obvious waste and cruelty of this commercialization of a wildlife resource, the threat it represents to the future of wild-living chimpanzees pales to insignificance when compared with the menacing twin ogres our over-developed consumerist world has introduced into the chimpanzees' forest habitat in Africa, as indeed, elsewhere throughout the 'Third World'. We looked in the last chapter at one of these – the delusory imperative of 'development' or growth-at-any-price. The second has so far only been touched on in passing – the systematic exportation of our domestic inflation. We will examine further its effects on 'Third World' ecology.

The problem was aptly illustrated in conversation with a West African cocoa farmer. Critical remarks about government, in all of these countries, can have unpleasant consequences for anyone identifiable by the authoritarian regimes in power, so let us call him Kofi Mbanifu – he could come from either Ghana or Nigeria. He told this story: 'Twenty years ago, when we first achieved independence, I bought a new tractor for my cocoa plantation. It cost me the cash I got from selling three and a half tons of cocoa. The tractor is long since worn out – nobody can mend it any more. I need a new one. But today it will cost the cash earnings of selling 13–14 tons of cocoa. The same cocoa.'

Advocates of modern technological progress (and tractor salesmen) claim that today he gets a better tractor – that there have been great advances in tractor design and construction in the last 20 years. Taxed with this, Kofi replied: 'They paint it a different colour, maybe, and it'll have a rear-view mirror and windscreen and other gadgets I don't need. But tractors don't seem as strong as they used to be . . . they rust, and break down more quickly than they used to.'

His problem is general, covering the whole range of imported agricultural inputs, from machinery to chemicals. It affects all 'Third World' products, any of which provides similar examples. Bananas, for instance. In 1960 a West African banana grower had to sell three tons of produce to buy a tractor; by 1970, he was obliged to sell 11 tons. This amounts to a 33 per cent increase in real terms (real bananas) over ten years – or at compound rates (where the inflated increase per year itself inflates) between 12 and 13 per cent per year; this during a period when western inflation was kept down at home to well under single figures. Since 1970, these rates of exported inflation have rocketed, to keep ahead of our own galloping rates.

For the 'Third World' farmer and his family, the price of everything else rises too. If his land and energies are used for growing cocoa or bananas, they cannot be used to grow food. He has to buy most of this, as well as clothes, household requisites and his tools. The cash-crop farmer has evolved a long way from the quasi-self-sufficient subsistence farmer – who grows his family's food; whose wife cooks in a home-grown gourd 'calabash' or home-made clay pot over a traditional African fireplace made of three stones, fuelled by firewood cut by the family in the neighbouring forest; and who demands a new 'cloth' once a year – usually to wear at some traditional ceremony – which he barters for some of his surplus produce, or for what he caught or collected in the forest. Even locally produced commodities, traded in the cash economy, are subject to the same rocketing inflation. Today, a stick of yam no bigger than a maize-cob costs two dollars or more.

Commodity trading prices given regularly in the world's financial press are no indication of what the African farmer gets in return for his labour. Governments and multinational commodity cartels control agricultural export markets, and impose their own buying prices, through organizations such as cocoa, cotton or ground-nut marketing boards and other agencies. These bear little relationship to prices paid for such commodities, mainly set by the exchange manipulations of international commodity dealers and processing firms. The price of cocoa beans paid to African farmers, for instance, is ultimately controlled by firms like Nestlés, Cadbury Brothers or Unilever's United African Company.

In many countries where official agencies impose unrealistic producer prices and a neighbouring country does not, the farmers' only way to get a fair price for their cocoa crop is to smuggle the beans over the border, to sell on the free market. But ethical or social considerations aside, this offers no general or long-term solution. For those far from the border, trucking costs are high. Then they have to pay porters to carry the sacks making up a truck-load over the border – and can never be sure that some will not simply abscond with their burden, to sell on their own account. Alternatively they truck the crop openly across by lorry, bribing police and customs men. The latter, well aware of prices on both sides, exact half the profits and more – and the danger of being caught and jailed by some unbribed member of either force always remains.

A far more serious difficulty is that farm productivity has fallen alarmingly over the last 25 years. The trees are old, and many of them ravaged by a colourful list of diseases – swollen shoot, mealy pod, brown pod, warty pod – which fail to respond to any of the chemical pesticide treatments which government agricultural advisers and chemical salesmen recommend. These cost money, too, and the pests only get worse. Even producing, from old-established plantations, the quantity of cocoa-beans Kofi once needed for his tractor is most unlikely today – producing three or four times as much to catch up with today's inflated tractor price is unthinkable.

This is a typical cycle of cash-crop monoculture of an exotic commodity. Cocoa, which once produced two thirds of the foreign currency income of countries like Ghana or Ivory Coast, is an introduced species in Africa, coming from Mexico via Brazil. And for many of these endemic cocoa diseases, no effective treatment exists. The farmer's only recourse is to cut down his trees and replant. The trees represent his capital investment. New plantings take five years to start producing fruit, and come into maturity only after 12 years or more. Apart from this long, non-productive period when his investment is tied up, the ground itself is diseased, and mostly worn out. His only realistic solution, under the circumstances, is to clear and plant a new piece of forest, and try to hang on with the diminishing returns of his present degrading plantation until the new one comes to fruition.

Nor is it merely a question of planting three to four times his original plantation area if he wants to keep pace with inflation's depressing effect on his modest standard of living – or even his capacity to obtain the tools he needs to function as a farmer. For the most suitable and accessible cocoa lands were already planted under the colonial powers hungry for cheap raw materials. Land which might be cleared and planted today would be 'second-choice' land at best, less productive, in zones less favoured by climatic and other conditions, further from markets (so adding to transport costs in both directions – for bought-in inputs and for marketing the crop), and imposes added difficulties in finding seasonal labour. As Kofi says, 'it is a "no-win" situation'.

As we saw earlier, cocoa farmers are by no means alone in this. Similar problems confront, and impoverish, every primary producer of commodities based on renewable resources throughout the poorer lands of the earth. Wherever traditional systems of shifting agriculture with crop rotation and long forest fallow – sometimes recycling the land over decades – have been abandoned in favour of cash-crop production for export markets, the same agricultural and social degradation occurs. A corollary to export commodity production has always been, in colonial times and since, the apparent necessity to 'sedentarize' rural populations, that is to tie them to a particular limited area of land. This applies especially to the quasi-permanent, long-term tree or shrub crops most suitable for erstwhile forested zones – cocoa, coffee, tea, palm oil and rubber.

It is noteworthy that in addition to this practically every other cash-crop or even staple food in tropical Africa comes from introduced 'exotic' plants: yams, cassava (or manioc), bananas, maize, rice, groundnuts, oil, date and raffia palms, cotton, sisal, tobacco, pyrethrum, mangoes. The only major exceptions are millet, grown to the north of the forest zone in the savannah areas, and taro (seldom used today). Yet the natural forest offers a vast wealth of edible or otherwise useful products. Most of these are all but forgotten by the region's inhabitants of today; and indeed many thousands of potentially useful species are doomed to extinction as the forest disappears. The genetic resource these represent is irreplaceable, and its loss devastating not only for Africa but for all of us.

Deterioration of existing farm land, diminishing returns for ever greater farming efforts, the growing need for increasingly expensive chemical fertilizers, pesticides and agricultural machinery which these downward trends create, together with the constantly devaluing prices we pay for the produce of these lands, all combine to tempt farmers simply to break new ground, to strip new areas of forest cover and spread the degradation wider. For the last remaining land reserves are forest. In developers' cash-register eyes, these lands are relatively unproductive, and far higher economic yields could be wrung from them under agriculture.

Forest fantasies

It is perhaps useful here to look more closely at this tropical forest, about which so much has been written lately and so many 'crocodile tears' shed. Myths and illusions about it are legion; perhaps they always have been, for, difficult of access, guarded by disease and parasites and inhospitable as a human habitat, tropical forests were always places of unexplored mystery.

Ecologists and others have been sending alarm signals for more than a quarter of a century, warning that forest is disappearing at such-and-such a rate, and that by the year so-and-so there will be none left. But many intelligent people wonder if it is true, and if so whether it matters? Let us look, then, first into prehistory, at the story of the forest before the first historical records. That we can do so is largely due to one of the more beneficial wonders of modern technology – the interpretation of pollen diagrams. These show, through microscopically small fossil evidence, the extent to which certain species of trees (identifiable by remains of their pollen as certainly as we are by our fingerprints) were breeding at an equally identifiable period of the distant past.

A.C. Hamilton, of the New University of Ulster, has been studying tropical Africa's forest history in this way for many years, and has come to some surprising conclusions. All that we read today about the problems of tropical forest, and its disappearance, tends to begin with the belief – or at least create the impression – that until recently, Africa was covered in dense steaming jungle since time immemorial. Not so, says Hamilton. The forest today, diminishing and endangered as it is, is still vastly more extensive than it was 18,000 years ago. The popular image of 'tropical forest' is often confused and oversimplified, so it may be useful to describe briefly its range of variations. These extend from mangrove forest to rainforest (also called 'Selva' in Hispanic areas), through semi-deciduous and dry deciduous forest to transitional forest mosaic and wooden savannah, which in turn grades into shrub savannah or 'orchard bush', and then savannah grassland with occasional trees and shrubs and gallery forests along permanent water-courses. There is also a distinction to be made between lowland and montane forest types, though as with the categories above, lines between them are rarely hard and fast.

The type of forest covering any area is governed by a number of stochastic pedological and, perhaps more importantly, meteorological factors. Mangrove forest only grows where soil contains a large amount of salt, as in coastal marshes and lagoons. Rainfall volume and temporal distribution are decisive in the definition of other forest types. In fact a map of the limits of forest types of a region will usually match closely one of its isohets, or rainfall distribution curves.

Lowland rainforest, evergreen, closed canopy (i.e. the tree trunks rise bare of foliage for a greater part of their height, the crests of foliage, perhaps 40–50 metres above the ground, forming a continuous closed ceiling viewed from the forest floor where little or no sunlight penetrates to) is probably central to the image conjured up in most people's minds by the words 'tropical forest'. Many take them to be synonymous. But the conditions creating such an ecologically distinct system are restricted to certain parts of the tropics only: those with high and fairly constant rates of humidity and precipitation, and of temperature and its variations, and an altitude below 1,500 metres. These occur principally in a narrow belt less than 10° north and south of the equator.

Outside this, as far north and south as the tropics ($23^{1}/_{2}°$ either side of the equator), and also in patches within the lowland rainforest belt, the second form occurs – montane forest. This is distinguished by notably different species of trees and tree-associations; here predominate species demanding lower temperatures and lower evapo-transpiration rates. These conditions are created by the high-rainfall 'shadow' cast by mountains, even in otherwise semi-arid country, as for example in Kenya around Africa's second highest mountain.

Hamilton concluded that during the Quatenery Period (an era of exceptional climatic instability and environmental fluctuations which encompassed the Ice Ages, or 'glacials', and ended 10,000-12,000 years ago) the repeated millennia-long intermediate dry spells in the tropics, coinciding with (and probably resulting from) increased storage of the earth's water in the extending ice-caps of each glacial, reduced the forest stands of Africa to a series of 'refugia'. He presents a tentative picture of forest cover about 18,000 years ago, and comments:

> While little is known about the exact limits of the various forest refugia during this arid period, there is no doubt that, compared with the present, forest cover was fragmented and greatly reduced in extent.

Another effect of changing climate since then – and change appears likely to continue – is the isolation of ecological islands of montane forest, at considerably lower levels than they are normally to be found today. The theory here is that the lower temperatures prevalent during the glacials depressed the lowland montane forest boundary by reducing potential evapo-transpiration, thus permitting montane species to colonize vast areas which were formerly unsuitable for them. This spread of montane species did not, of course, take place instantaneously, or regularly. Some better-adapted species spread out first, to be followed with growing delay by less adaptable or slower-growing species. This leads to an effect, which is still visible – and thus still continues – of a gradient of species variety, from the highly complex or richest at the still existing forest refugia outwards to the simplest, poorest species at the forest limits. Hamilton claims that surveys and plotting of species-incidence and distribution can show this colonization (or recolonization) process quite clearly. But his main conclusion is that the vast extent of tropical forest, in Africa at any rate within living memory, is a comparatively 'young' phenomenon, dating back roughly 10–12 millennia. The influence of humans on these forests and their ecology is certainly far older.

Use or plunder

None of the above should be taken to mean that tropical forests, however extensive they may be, are not shrinking at an exorbitant rate; not that the current ridiculous levels of forest destruction can be justified, even on grounds of shortest-term emergency interest. The destruction is rapidly converting economic emergency into ecological disaster.

The extent of today's forests is variously assessed by different authorities, and is largely determined by definitions; obviously the figures given depend upon what is being measured. Curry-Lindahl says:

> At present, 50 acres (sic) of forest are being felled every month . . . forests are being cleared for settlements and cultivation, they are being burned down, devoured and trampled to death; they are cut down for household fuel or are felled for industrial purposes at random, and without a thought for their ecological importance.

He continues (emphasis in original):

> The total climatic area of the tropical rain forests, i.e. the area they would cover had they not been devastated, is about 1,600 million hectares (some 40,000 million acres). Of this area,

about 665 million hectares (some 1,662 million acres) has been destroyed by man up to 1973, an area twice as large as India . . .

In spite of the fact that the very existence of man is at stake, no government has tried to put a stop to this plunder.

IUCN, with UNEP and WWF, in their joint 'World Conservation Strategy', estimate the rate of tropical rainforest felling and burning at 110,000 square kilometres (1,000 million hectares) per year. At this rate all this type of forest will have disappeared within 85 years. The World Bank, on the other hand, estimates the existing forest stock of developing countries at 1,200 million hectares, currently being consumed at the rate of 15–20 million hectares a year. At which rate (assuming constant demand) the bank thinks 'remaining tropical forests will be consumed in about 60 to 80 years'.

J.P. Lanly, a French forester who co-ordinates an FAO–UNDP tropical forest assessment project, is more conservative, within the terms of his own defined classifications – a system based on commercial use rather than geographical or ecological types – and more precise. Using a simplified classification of commonly accepted concepts of woody vegetation types ('tree', 'scrub', 'closed forests', 'mixed forest-grassland formations', etc.) he has developed a coding system for each, taking into account the purpose to which it is put (or not, in the case of unproductive forests), comprising in all 22 categories of natural forests, and a further ten for industrial plantations. These range from 'natural closed hardwood forests productive (or operable) and not intensively managed' to 'high yielding industrial softwood plantations'.

For all tropical countries, he estimated their natural forests, both closed and open, at a total of 1,760 million hectares, broken down by zones and countries. He found, for 1980, that the average annual rate of deforestation of closed forests was slightly more than four million hectares, and expected this to increase slightly between then and the year 2000. In his view, the prospects for the 25 years between 1975 and 2000 are depletion of closed forests by 140 million hectares, the rate of loss slowing down over the period, and depletion of open woodlands by more than 70 million hectares, mainly in tropical America and tropical Africa. Rather less alarming, as he points out, than wild suggestions that 'net losses are 50,000 hectares every day', as is frequently bandied about.

On the other hand, since Lanly works for FAO, his survey is designed for the purposes of the timber extraction and processing industries, to provide them with reliable forecasts of the availability of fibre products for western processing. Further, 'given . . . the industrial objective of the study, it was decided that fuelwood (and charcoal) would not be considered among the fibre products, despite their importance in most developing countries and the possible effect on industrial wood supply'.

Some authorities estimate that 80–90 per cent of tropical wood consumption is for fuel, cooking and other household purposes. World Bank projections of wood and wood-product consumption from 1962–85 suggest a figure nearer to 50 per cent – 1.017 million cubic metres consumed as fuel in 1962, compared to 1.049 million cubic metres used for industrial purposes. The bank expects the figure of wood used as fuel to remain roughly constant up to 1985 (1.064 million cubic metres), while that for wood used for industrial purposes will, in its view, almost double to 1.995 million cubic metres.

These discrepancies, or 'variety of options', with a suitable figure for every purpose, leave lay people with a feeling of insecurity, or perplexity about the size and urgency of the problem. To confuse matters further, the fuelwood-using countries are also, to a large extent, traditional practitioners of rotational (usually called by developers by the more pejorative term 'shifting') agriculture. This involves clear-felling a patch of forest – generally less than a hectare at a time – burning off any wood and litter that cannot be used or extracted, and then farming the land for several years in succession until the nutrients in the soil (partly deriving from mineral salts, potash, etc. from the burnt material) are exhausted. The land is then abandoned to revert to forest (the roots of the former vegetation cover remain alive in the ground during farming with traditional hand tools, and rapidly sprout up again when hoeing ceases), and it renews its fertility over the subsequent decades.

This ecologically sound system, which worked for thousands of years while human populations remained in balance with the land and forest available, also produces large quantities of fuelwood or charcoal, especially in high-forest areas. This adds further confusion to the experts' calculations of forest losses or depletion, since such clear-felled patches, while not continuously under forest, are more often than not under forest fallow – perhaps five years or so under cultivation, and at least thirty or forty (in a balanced system) under forest fallow. This means that while the forests are certainly stripped, and while they certainly produce a great deal of useful firewood and timber in the process, they cannot be considered as 'depletion' of the forest cover unless they are permanently converted to non-forest uses. This latter only happens under the pressure of development.

More important still, the generalities and global figures given by both sides in the conflict over use or conservation of forest resources hide important, alarming discrepancies between areas and countries.

Raping the primaeval forest

The horror stories of abject poverty and famine, resulting from total deforestation of Haiti, for example, or areas of North-eastern Brazil, have been mentioned earlier. But another, more insidious example of how commercial interests and profit-oriented considerations destroy such ecologically balanced traditional systems of forest exploitation for human purposes, is well worth examining in some detail. This again comes from Africa – this time from Gabon, Albert Schweitzer's land 'on the edge of the primaeval forest'.

The looting of Gabon's forest estate is a tragic story, which began with the arrival there of such men as Alfred Aloyisius ('Trader') Horn, Carl Woermann (founder of the Woermann shipping line and African trading companies based in Hamburg), and de Brazza, the French explorer whose name is com-memorated in Brazzaville, capital of the Congo Republic (or 'Congo Brazza'), Gabon's southern neighbour. They looked with greedy eyes upon the riches of primaeval forest, and set about seizing for themselves and for their masters in Europe, as much as they could lay hands on. Trader Horn, incidentally, sent the first complete carcass of a gorilla to Europe, pickled in a large wine barrel, and later shipped to Hamburg the first live gorilla to reach Europe, both via Woermann. Their main objects of interest, however, were other, more easily obtained and transported forest products: rubber from latex trapped by slave labour from forest trees, ivory, mineral ores from the earth beneath the jungle, and above all, timber.

Gabon's population was probably even smaller in Woermann's time than today's half a million or so, living now over an area of some 267,000 square kilometres (somewhat larger than Great Britain's 230,000 square kilometres without Northern Ireland, or West Germany's 248,500 square kilometres). The country's present borders are of course a modern colonial invention. Previously, the smaller population was also more widely dispersed across the land – half or more today live in cities which did not then exist, except as trading posts and slavers' camps forming administrative centres. The land was riven by colonial and tribal wars, and slave raiding, and had a sinister reputation, causing widespread fear among natives and invaders alike, for cannibalism (which almost certainly did become a factor threatening life and limb at subsequent stages of colonial occupation, even if it were not so prior to this). It was also afflicted by an appalling variety of endemic and introduced diseases. It is said that the colonialists first introduced syphilis, along with alcoholism and the gamut of Christian neuroses to add to a range of already endemic tropical plagues, from leprosy, malaria and sleeping sickness to a horrific range of filarian worms and other endo and ectoparasites. The population was thinly distributed around a network of rivers and streams draining the well-watered country, with large concentrations on the coast and along the lower reaches of rivers, where trading posts were set up, initially to serve the slave trade.

Transport, both along the coast and in the interior, was by dug-out canoe or by raft – or head-loading porters travelling jungle paths between waterways. The land is drained from the Central African Plateau, rising abruptly to 1,000 metres above sea level along Gabon's eastern inland border, to the Atlantic coast by a series of river systems draining roughly east to west. The Ogoové River is the most important of these. As in much of coastal Africa, the change from coastal plain to inland plateau occurs with an abrupt escarpment, running here roughly north to south, physically dividing the country and effectively blocking river navigation into the far interior by a series of spectacular waterfalls. Nineteenth-century raiders and explorers were forced to recruit head-porters to make their way along forest tracks in the interior regions.

In the early days of forest exploitation there, felled timber could only be removed from the interior by river, floated in log rafts down to the coast and thence to the waiting ships. This naturally implied floatable timber. Okoumé, a softwood of low relative density, is one of the few commonly occurring local species of any commercial value which will float. As a result, the whole commerce of timber extraction in Gabon has grown up around exploitation of this one species.

The natural forest contains many dozens – perhaps even hundreds – of rare and valuable species which in other circumstances (with more rational or less avaricious development) could earn the country even more than okoumé. In the situation prevailing then, however, with an inadequate overland transport infrastructure, they all have the disadvantage of being high density hardwoods, which are incapable of floating.

Since independence, Gabon has made great efforts to develop road and rail transport. A capitalist 'satellite' state, it has remained a French colony to all intents and purposes since nominal political independence was granted by de Gaulle in 1961. The current president, Omar Bongo, has successfully outridden several populist attempts to overthrow him, largely because he enjoys the solid backing of the French army, a battalion of whose 'paras' is permanently stationed at Libreville Airport – key to control of the country.

In conformity with the capitalist political path chosen by Gabon's masters, road building (and the development of communications generally) is an essential first step in the looting of the native natural economy and the seizure of any remaining natural wealth the country still contains. Indeed Gabon is a treasure chest of valuable minerals including uranium – the main cause of the 'paras'' presence and Bongo's continued survival – industrial diamonds, manganese and offshore oil, to name but a few. As Rosa Luxemburg pointed out in *The Accumulation of Capital*: 'Where natural economy has formerly prevailed the introduction of means of transport – railways, navigation, canals [and since then, of course, road transport] – is vital for the spreading of the commodity economy.'

Within this capitalist framework the authorities have also tried hard to encourage timber dealers and shippers controlling the markets to commercialize other species now accessible to modern transport. With few exceptions the trade has refused such directives to rationalize utilization of the country's forest resources. Moreover, the Gabonese producer gets little out of the timber trade. The price paid to the small native concession holder for okoumé logs is at least equalled, and usually exceeded, by the cost of freighting them to Europe alone, at shipping rates charged by the western world's shipping lines. And both these cost elements, taken together, amount to a small fraction of the price of okoumé (much of it made into plywood) when marketed in Europe and elsewhere. Furthermore, to complete the picture of the piratical looting of Gabon's forest resources, around 75 per cent of the small fraction of okoumé's consumer price which does actually get paid into Gabon, is re-exported. It goes out as the profits of foreign timber concessionaires, salaries and emoluments of expatriate managerial staff, and as inflated payment for imported plant and equipment used in the large companies' capital intensive operations.

Academic voice of reason

The massive draining of the wealth produced by the forests of the 'Third World', and the sensitivity and resistance of expatriate loggers and timber dealers to any attempt to guide their operations into more rational directions – rational, that is, from the point of view of conserving the country's resource base – are not the only problems confronting countries seeking to expand their own forest industries with the help of outside capital. Kolade Adeyoju, Professor at the Department of Forest Resources Management of Nigeria's prestigious Ibadan University, put it thus:

> Obstacles to the flow of private investment to developing countries are born out of painful experience and continuing relationships of inequality on all fronts. It is important for foreign investors to realize that their objectives of maximum net profits do not always coincide with local efforts aimed at alleviating the chronic problem of underdevelopment. New

forest industrialists should plan their activities to coincide with the economic objectives of the countries in which they plan to invest.

Speaking before a group of distinguished business men – he was addressing a seminar accompanying Munich's forestry machinery trade fair, 'Interforst', in 1978 – Adeyoju looked at several aspects of the problem from a side rarely visible to westerners. He also suggested some reasonable parameters which should govern – as well as actual restrictions confronting – new investors in 'Third World' industries.

He also has his own estimates of the size of the problem. According to these, tropical forest covers around two billion hectares, representing 56 per cent of the world's forest land area and approximately 25 per cent of the tropical land surface. While this area produces over 40 per cent of total world production of wood and wood-based products, the overwhelming majority of tropical timber produced (over 80 per cent) is consumed as firewood. Industrial roundwood production from the region accounted for 15 per cent of world output in 1973, although this figure includes 39 per cent of world production of industrial hardwoods.

Adeyoju has estimated elsewhere that in a country like Nigeria, the greatest enemy of stable forest ecosystems is current short-cycle 'bush-fallow' or shifting cultivation, which destroys an average of 200 square kilometres of Nigerian forest every year. Indeed, in the present situation he redefines 'land-hunger' as 'forest-hunger', to describe the 'clamour for de-reservation' all over his country.

Another disastrous factor in Nigeria since 1961 has been forestry management policy. This is based on rapid conversion of natural forest to artificial forest, and has caused untold wastage of timber resources. Less than 25 per cent of the usable cellulose of the 20–22,000 hectares of forest being clear-felled annually in the country is in fact extracted. The remaining 75–80 per cent of the wood is either burnt on the ground or left to rot. The result of such destruction, combined with over-exploitation over the last 70 years, has converted Nigeria from a major forest products income earner into an insatiable importer of logs, plywood, flush doors and sawn timber from neighbouring Gabon, Ghana, Ivory Coast

– and even Europe.

This incredible turn of events has particularly dangerous implications in a land which, in spite of its petroleum income (which has fallen dramatically in recent years), is still rated by the World Bank as one of the 20 poorest countries in the world, with a per capita share of GDP of under $160 per year. Furthermore, Nigeria's oil resources have already introduced unmanageable distortions and inflation into the national economy – to the point where the simplest staple foods have been priced out of reach of the poorest. And the country's oil reserves will be exhausted within 15–17 years according to some estimates. At its present rate of destruction, forest resources which could have been self-regenerating virtually in perpetuity if properly managed, will also have been wiped out even before the oil wells run dry.

Apart from flamboyantly wasteful management practices, Adeyoju also identifies other obstacles to profitable development of tropical forest industries. The influence, still strong, of previous colonial administrators, 'who could not, and were not economically compelled to work long hours under the tropical weather', is one. Short working hours came into vogue during the colonial occupation and the fashion continues today, resulting in low productivity, high prices and monopolies. In such industries as pulp, paper and fireboard manufacture, where production operations are continuous, such constricting factors are of considerable importance.

Turning to more recent problems facing potential investors, countries without existing major forest industries have difficulty in providing staff familiar with the management and operation of modern processes employed in pulp and paper mills or in manufacturing wood-based panels. Foreign investors need to import foreign personnel until local 'counterpart' staff can be trained to take over. Restrictions on work permits, payment transfers and high personal taxation often make it difficult to find suitable expatriate staff. Yet in the absence of any such restrictions, foreign capital would generate job opportunities for high-level expatriate personnel indefinitely, without making the least contribution to the 'transfer of technology' so dear to the development aider. Some countries therefore insist on training programmes as part of any deal for new industrial establishments.

An investment proposal without a training scheme permitting definite and rapid transfer of technology has little attraction, whatever its potential profitability. As a general line of policy, Adeyoju recommends that 20–25 per cent of capital resources envisaged should be committed to training needs of new industries.

On the other side, an acute cause of disappointment and contention in the past has been the choice of equipment for such new enterprises. All too often equipment is being recommended which is obsolete in the supplying country, for which spares are no longer available and for which more efficient versions or substitutes are already in use at home. Such obsolete plant is frequently 'dressed up' with a quick spray of paint, and presented as reliable and the latest technology. What has, in effect, become scrap in its country of origin is sold at exorbitant prices under the title of 'development aid', with donor government or international agency guarantees to the supplier – though not to the buyer. On arrival in the developing country, the plant appears superficially new and usually functions for a short period, before breaking down completely and irrevocably.

Nigeria is a large importer of wood-working machinery, and Adeyoju believes the low technical efficiency of the country's wood-based industries is largely due to unfulfilled promises on the part of machinery manufacturers and suppliers. This is compounded by a general lack of back-up services.

But despite such difficulties, opportunities for profitable investment are widespread in the forestry sector in most tropical countries. And there is no doubt in the minds of developing countries' governments that they need foreign investors. Minimum guarantees ensure a favourable business climate, and they hope that fundamental conditions for industrial activity are created. But it is equally important for foreign industrialists to understand why and how their resources are needed. As Adeyoju sums up: 'A patently beneficial rather than an exploitive legacy in developing countries should be the sole and whole purpose of new foreign investment policies.' Such high ideals are rarely if ever in evidence in the practical results of development. Furthermore, Adeyoju's strictures and proposals are based entirely at the practical, economic or material level. He takes no account here (it was not in his brief for the occasion to do so) of the environmental and ecological consequences of such investments, either in Nigeria, or to return, in Gabon.

Happier hunting grounds

The effect of logging operations in opening up inaccessible forest to invasion by hunters and farmers is easy enough to grasp. From the most ancient times, as the evidence of our oldest fables and myths bears out, high forest was always a menacing, melancholy place in the eyes of most people. Its only permanent human inhabitants were – and still are – the rare and elusive 'little people', the pygmies. These aside, people tend to live on the forest fringes, or in extensive clearings within it. Their penetration into the deeper reaches is limited by difficulty of communication and orientation, and usually follows the course of streams large enough to be navigated by canoe. As with the extraction of felled timber by floatation, this is also limited to the lowland, or flatland reaches.

Opening up virgin forest to timber extraction today involves bulldozing tracks to get lifting and skidding equipment in, and the cut logs out. In some areas, actual damage done to forest stocks by felling is almost negligible compared to the havoc caused by these preparatory functions; under certain circumstances, the logger might find his commercially desirable trees at intervals of little more than one or two per square kilometre of concession. Obviously, cutting tracks and working space to get at them means wasting infinitely greater numbers of non-commercial trees. Experiments have been made in lifting logs out by captive 'barrage balloons', or even by helicopter in the USSR. But in practice neither proved economic.

The main attack follows later, after the loggers have extracted all they consider of value, and abandoned the tracks and clearings created by their operations. It is motivated by neighbouring people's search for food, collecting forest produce or hunting. As we saw earlier, in a naturally equilibrated system, subsistence hunting does little long-term or permanent harm to healthy wild stocks. Indeed, a self-regulatory process is built into hunting for food, which holds the balance between hunter-gatherer people and the ecosystem of which they form a small but influential part. When access to new hunting grounds is opened into a virgin climax ecosystem containing plentiful stocks of choice game (and subsistence hunters' choice of prey is vastly wider than that of western sport hunters), animals will at first require little effort on the part of the hunter to bring them down. They will be unwary of the unfamiliar danger humans represent – may even be curious about the approaching hunter instead of being afraid of him – and will be common enough for easy availability. (It is only the sado-masochistic neuroses of European sport hunters which make rarity and difficulty desirable.)

Numbers of game animals will decrease more or less rapidly, depending on the rate and intensity of hunting, from the climax maximum existing before the intrusion of hunters. As time goes by, however, and the animals become increasingly rare, hunting pressure itself exerts a 'natural' selection function. At first hunting tends to eliminate weaker, slower, less aggressive and – especially – less wary or adaptable individuals. This generates or reinforces behavioural tendencies (whether inherited or acquired) in the survivors, thus propagating evasiveness, timidity, extra-specific aggression, alertness, speed of flight and, in great measure, adaptability.

With the numbers of more easily attainable animals decreasing, the difficulties of hunting the remainder, and consequently the input of hunting effort required, increase proportionately. Moreover the situation is further aggravated (from the hunter's point of view) by the preferentially selective trends just mentioned. This means that only the most wary or elusive specimens or groups survive to breed – emphasizing these traits and thus reducing hunting success even more rapidly – over-proportionally in fact.

Eventually the point is reached, under the condition of moderate over-hunting of a given species, where the hunter's effort in tracking down, killing or trapping, and bringing home his prey far exceeds its value in terms of the needs of his family or tribe. At this point the subsistence hunter will most likely lose interest in this particular species, reckoning it 'unhuntable' or not worth the effort. He will then turn his attentions to other easier species. Where the food hunter finds no suitable alternative, he will seek other more productive hunting grounds.

When this happens, and hunting pressure is thereby relieved, surviving stocks will usually breed up again fairly rapidly to something like their former levels. We can see this effect in the modern world in another context. Often newly promulgated game-protection areas which benefit by a sudden cessation of hunting undergo a rapid increase in game stocks, both apparent and actual. The distinction must be made since animals soon become accustomed to their new security, and so become quite tame and are therefore more visible. Another factor in this increase is often immigration into 'safe' areas from neighbouring zones where they are still hunted. Furthermore, it can also happen – when for instance natural predators are eliminated by the various human irruptions – that the ecosystem's checks and balances are disturbed or destroyed, so that some surviving species increase in number to the point of 'population explosions', with catastrophic results for their habitat, and ultimately for themselves. But we will look at this and other problems involved in protective conservation more closely in a later chapter. The point worth making here is that such a degree of ecological destruction invariably requires far greater forces and impacts than are ever applied by traditional subsistence hunting alone, when not motivated by commercial intent.

This 'rotation' of hunting grounds can be regarded, in some measure at least, as a parallel to the rotational agriculture of the forest-clearing subsistence farmer. He too can have the effect of destroying nature's acquired equilibrium of species in a natural stand of forest. What grows up again, or fastest, once his axe has passed on to clear fresh fields, may well be species which were less dominant in the original mature tree association. But here again, over time an 'equilibrium of successions' might also establish itself.

The farmer's activities can also sometimes be beneficial to forest wildlife. Like humans, many animals live on the fringes and in clearings, rather than in the depths of the forest. The regrowth of disturbed, secondary forest offers such animals more, and more accessible, sources of nourishment and shelter than virgin high forest. Tony de Vos, a Canadian professor of ecology who recently worked in Africa and South East Asia, reported from Gabon (where practically all the lowland forest is regrowth of exploited, thrice-worked-over humid evergreen forest) that leopards were 'pullulating' in some areas, and that buffalo, elephant, chimpanzees and many antelope were still plentiful.

Other experts report that there are still large areas where gorilla populations exceed those of humans. But these last, the greatest of the apes, prefer untouched, undisturbed jungle, unlike chimpanzees, leopards and the rest, which thrive in secondary regrowth.

Indeed all accessible forested areas of Gabon are now covered in secondary regrowth. Even when Albert Schweitzer wrote at the beginning of this century that he was living 'on the edge of the primaeval forest' at Lambaréné on the River Ogoové, he was already indulging in poetic licence. Even in his time the forests around Lambaréné had nothing 'primaeval' about them – they had already been fully worked over, and all that remained in this early French colonial administrative and trading centre was purely secondary or tertiary regrowth.

Forest functions

In the highlands, however, many kilometres from Schweitzer's land, Gabon enjoys even today an important share of the earth's remaining undisturbed tropical forest. It will be a tragic loss for all mankind, and not just the poets and sentimentalists among us, if it should disappear. For, oddly perhaps, it gives irrational hope and pleasure to many men and women imprisoned in the concrete bounds of cities to know that forests still exist on our planet, though they may see and experience them only rarely in person. This is reason enough to preserve them – ignoring other 'practical' reasons or material values – wherever we can and by whatever means. And reason, too, to look to city dwellers for help in finding the means required to do so. Only by preserving their habitat – by ensuring a world fit for apes to live in – can we hope to ensure free-living primates' continued existence, along with that of a wealth of other creatures great and small, which share with us a common global environment.

The forest, everywhere, performs many useful functions. Holding together – indeed even creating – the fertile layer of topsoil on which we depend for our sustenance has already been mentioned; as also the functions of absorbing and retaining rainfall, and distributing seasonal rainfall over a larger part of the year. Equally important are the emission of oxygen, the absorption of carbon dioxide and the fixation of nitrogen.

Filtering dust from the air and the retention of moisture vapour below the forest canopy also play a role in cleaning the air and controlling local climatic conditions. And the most important function – in fact most obvious, although usually forgotten – that of providing shade, a chance to escape the overpowering tropical sun's rays, is one which makes life tolerable for human and beast in what would otherwise be unbearable exposure.

Scientific research has lately revealed more complex functions and relationships. Scientists believe that the evapo-transpiration of woodlands – the 'breathing' of the trees as they take up water from their roots in the ground and then release it as vapour through their leaves – generates rainfall by re-introducing ground-water to the atmosphere.

The continuing rampant deforestation of the tropics should frighten all of us, and not only those whose good fortune it is to live in the tropics. People everywhere will be and are being affected – perhaps directly affected by similar exploitive processes in their own immediate environments, but more certainly indirectly by the effects which devastation and impoverishment of the unique ecosystems of this critical region, central to the globe's interrelated environments, will have on our own different parts of the inescapable whole.

'Spy-in-the-sky' satellite measurements have recently revealed correlations between the degree of reflection of solar radiation impinging on the earth's surface, at any given point, and the amount of rainfall that area receives. In brief, the higher the reflectivity, the lower the rainfall. The reason probably has to do with absorption of energy into the ecosystem and its conversion into vapour and wind currents, in complex relationships not yet fully understood. Scientists call this the 'albedo effect'.

Stripping forest canopy, a low reflector (or high absorber) of solar energy, to replace it with open monocultures, grassland or very often simply bare ground – in rising order better and better reflectors of solar energy back into space (without its serving much useful purpose here) – brings about a progressive decrease in the amount of precipitation the farmer, hopefully settling on newly cleared land, can expect to grow his crops. The stable cycle of meteorological and ecological conditions breaks down, and an irreversible downward trend commences. One FAO expert defined this as 'farming downhill with a vengeance'. Not only this, however; in West Africa the rainforest belt along the coast has an influential – if not, as some think, a controlling – function with respect to monsoon rainfall reaching areas far to the north, in the marginal Sahel and beyond. Already hard hit by regular droughts, this zone is becoming uninhabitable at a rate which correlates more or less directly with the rate of disappearance of the forest. Similar processes are under way – or in some cases, already completed – throughout the 'Third World' tropical countries (the two adjectives are almost but not quite synonymous).

Of dozens of examples which might be cited, let us limit ourselves here to one of the more tragic from Latin America. At risk here are not merely the apes and other wild creatures which have always lived in the tropical forest, but the men, women and children of tribes like the Kayapos group of 'stone-age' Indians of the Amazon jungle in today's Brazil – another colonial creation. The fate confronting these people, at the mercy of the developers, is genocide – the same met with by Hottentots in South Africa, Aborigines in Australia or the vast majority of North American tribes, when the Christian explorers arrived to gaze upon the wealth of their 'unused' lands. Quoting a heart-breaking report of the resistance of the Megkronotis tribesmen of the Kayapos group by Jean-Pierre Dutilleux, Norman Lewis wrote in 1981:

> For tribes such as the Kayapos group this has been the century of genocide. They have been massacred in their thousands by the mercenaries of illegal settlers, by hired gunmen [he does not explain the distinction] and aerial attack, by such devices as supplying them with food laced with arsenic and clothing infected with the viruses of deadly diseases, and by forcible transfer from their homelands to barren territory incapable of supporting human life. This rancher-settler attack has reduced an original population estimated at four million to 120,000 at the most.

Such figures are comparable with the German mass-murder of Jews up to 1945, when they managed to destroy some six million of the 11 million Jews at their mercy. They managed this in less than a decade; the ongoing Brazilian effort at genocide has already lasted three quarters of a century.

Dutilleux describes the courageous, futile last stand of the survivors. At last, sickened to desperation by a lifetime's history of broken promises and land-grabbing by government and white settlers alike – a history forming a neat, shameful parallel to the trickery, deceit and robbery with which white men grabbed and destroyed the lands of North American Indians and Eskimos during the nineteenth century – they began to fight back, killing 11 woodcutters sent illegally to clear forest from land forming part of the Indians' promised reserves. He quotes their leader, Raoni, chief of the Megkronotis tribe:

> If we lose our land, then the whites will destroy the whole forest. Where will we go to hunt the tapir, the ant-bear, the panther? What will we eat? There will be no game left.

Raoni and his people would rather be killed than lose their land. That is the heart of the problem. As Dutilleux points out, 'the survival of the Indians is entirely bound up with the problem of the land'.

He says further:

> Four years ago, anyone who visited Raoni's tribe . . . who live by the Xingu river in the Mato Grosso, would have flown over virgin forest for three hours. Today the same visitor looks down on a desert of ashes and calcinated tree trunks for two hours and forty minutes: nothing moves except an occasional herd of cattle in search of scattered tufts of grass. Then suddenly the forest appears, a majestic sight, bathed in the morning sunlight, with sheets of mist still clinging to the treetops. You have to fly low and follow first one river course and then another.

Norman Lewis describes the seizure and despoliation of such land by burning down the forest, a major ecological tragedy which benefits no one. The thin Amazonian layer of topsoil, like that under African tropical forests, is only inches deep and will only grow tropical trees, with the loss of which the soil fertility is lost. The average Brazilian ranch in such country is designed for quick profits; after three or four years it is abandoned, leaving behind desolation and impoverishment – of both land and people. The Brazilian forest, containing one third of the world's trees by some estimates, and producing a quarter of the oxygen we breathe, is an international resource which we should all do our utmost to defend, if only from the narrowest self interest. It is unworthy to leave the struggle for our future survival to the desperate bravery of a handful of naked Indians armed with little more than wooden clubs and bows and arrows.

Less is more

Can we really do anything about all this? Forest exploitation and the extension of farming are going to continue; we will go on demanding timber, meat, agricultural produce from these lands, and people there will be forced to continue producing them. Can we really expect our fellows, as we know them in the rich countries, to accept voluntarily paying higher prices, or consuming less? To accept, in effect, a cut in our standard of living?

These are large and important questions – perhaps the most important posed by this book – and an attempt will be made to answer them in the last section of it. Here let me merely say, as a 'statement of faith' perhaps, that more and more people are coming to believe that many, sick of our mindless 'throw-away' society with its built-in obsolescence, in which, as Tim Robinson has pointed out, (*New Scientist*, 30 November 1978), consumption has become the most important activity an individual can take part in, would accept just a little less of everything, once they came to understand that our wealth and well being are founded on – indeed extracted from – the misery of others.

Awareness of the problem of how the selfish system works is already a vast stride forward. Equally important is awareness of the need, if we wish to avoid worldwide ecological disaster, to allow the inhabitants of poorer lands to retain – against our aggressive commercialism and the urgings of our 'productivity-fixation' – fairer, much larger proportions of the wealth they and their resources produce. Give Kofi a better price for his cocoa, more truly related to the price of the tractor he thinks he needs and the labour and care he expends; or leave Raoni and his people to live their peaceful lives in the forests that are their home, and which protect the environment of us all.

Have a gorilla

In this search for a 'world fit for wild apes', it might be worth returning to these creatures for a final example of how the 'Third World' is robbed even of such an exotic resource as its gorillas. In 1976 Dr Arnd Wünschmann, at that time one of the directors of Munich's publicly owned Hellabrunn Zoo (now Chairman of the German Chapter of World Wildlife Fund), made a trip to Cameroon, and returned home with a pair of baby gorillas. It must have been pure coincidence that just then, a German financed development aid team was assisting a group of Cameroonian wildlife experts from the Wildlife Management School at Garoua to carry out a feasibility study requested by another German zoo director, Bernard Grzimek. The last-named had proposed a project involving capturing six gorillas which he wanted, for reasons of his own, to transfer to Tanzania. These Garoua experts described in their report the methods used by native hunters – working on commission mainly for expatriate animal exporters who usually supply on loan the arms needed for the operation.

The method employed to capture a young gorilla is essentially the same as that described earlier with chimpanzees – by killing its mother. There is one very important difference, however. A group of chimps, if attacked, will scatter in disorder; gorillas, on the other hand, tend to move and stay in defensive family groups, sometimes of several nursing mothers together, with their 'adolescent' young, accompanied by a dominant male. When attacked, members of the group will try to defend the shot mother ape, and even to recuperate the young orphan when she is mortally wounded. So that this method necessitates, in most cases, killing the whole group of adults and intractable juveniles, in the hope of capturing an ape young enough to be defenceless. As with chimpanzees, many of the baby apes die of wounds or capture trauma in the process, and many more die from mishandling or ignorance during the long journey back to the dealer.

One of the Garoua experts estimates that, while the average size of groups killed amounts to five animals, for each young animal surviving long enough actually to reach the hands of the dealer, an average of 29 others have been killed. This includes the 'abortive' killing of groups which failed to yield a sole survivor; also young apes orphaned in the hunt but which escape capture, only to die alone (for the higher primates need years of 'schooling' to learn jungle survival techniques); and the captured animals which die on the journey back to base. And again, these figures take no account of the fact that as with chimps, the great majority of adult animals so killed are female, in the middle of their breeding life on average; their latent breeding potential, as also that of female sub-adults killed or captured, is also totally eliminated.

The cost to wild gorilla stocks in Cameroon of Wünschmann's efforts to attract and entertain visitors to his Munich zoo can be estimated: apart from the immediate casualty toll of 60 animals – for the two exported are effectively dead as far as Cameroon's wild stocks are concerned – the breeding potential of the females can be reasonably assessed. Incidentally elimination of the males has no direct effect on the species which does not form lifetime 'pair-bonds'; a 'widowed' female gorilla or chimp will carry on breeding.

A gorilla's life expectancy in the wild is around 25–30 years, and females start breeding between six and nine years old; thereafter they will produce offspring every three and a half to four and a half years (thus at rather longer intervals than chimpanzees' average of every three). The female gorilla can be expected to produce no more than six offspring in her lifetime. If half of the casualty toll is assumed to be female, at midpoint in their breeding lives, the loss of unborn apes to future stocks can be roughly assessed at a further 45 unborn animals; in 'next-generation' terms (supposing the creatures had been left undisturbed by commercial attack) wild stocks will therefore have lost a total of around 75 gorillas for each one surviving as far as our zoo. In Munich's case, the pair cost the actual and future elimination of up to 135 wild gorillas, projected over the next 25–30 years.

While these figures and likely future impacts may, again, be questioned as being 'theoretical', or dealing in hypothetical 'potential' – and they are not put forward here as firm estimates of course – they do serve some purpose. They indicate at least the scale of financial losses to the Cameroon's treasury and local economy which results from such decimation. (The word, much favoured and abused among conservationists and animal lovers, is used here throughout in its original meaning of killing about one in ten.) At the time of the Garoua team's report, licences for officially-approved gorilla exports (such as Wünschmann's) were being issued at the rate of 30 per year, this figure covering all animals passing through customs, and upon which a small export duty was paid. No attempt was made to estimate the number of animals smuggled over the country's extensive and largely uncontrollable land borders and sea coast without permits, nor of those smuggled through the port or airport of Douala with falsified documents, though one member of the team was convinced that at least as many went out illegally.

Customs dues and a proportionate share of hunting or capture licences brought the Cameroon authorities the equivalent of about DM100 for each exported gorilla. Wünschmann, back in Munich, showed me from his records that he paid DM18,500 for each of his 'babies' – DM37,000 for the pair – to a German dealer, a former taxi-driver who settled in Kribi, a derelict port on the Cameroon coast.

In a more recent example of this furtive international 'monkey business' a Dutch journalist and his wife, Jan and Ineke Bonjer, bought a seven-month-old female mountain gorilla in Belgium, with the connivance of the Dutch World Wildlife Fund. They obtained the animal, by masquerading as wealthy Germans, from a Belgian wild animal dealer named Corten, of Westerloo. It had been illegally captured and smuggled out of Ruanda – one of the last 200 survivors of this sub-species in the mountainous region between that country, Zaire and Uganda. Bonjer reports the dealer's shedding 'crocodile tears' on parting with the creature. More cynical observers might have seen them as tears of pure joy, as he counted the wad of Deutschmarks handed over – amounting to the agreed sum of DM37,900. This figure in itself is a graphic illustration of the point made earlier by my anonymous Ghanaian informant on the inflatory effect of the WWF-IUCN 'ban' on such trading. Wünschmann's Cameroon ape purchases were perfectly legal – he obtained the necessary permits to carry his pathetic booty home. Only subsequently, in 1978, did the Cameroon's government stop all export permits for this species. The price paid by Bonjer's WWF sponsors – more than twice Wünschmann's 1976 prices – indicates the redoubled incentive given to the shady trade by such unenforceable decrees. Many eyebrows will doubtless be raised at WWF's trading in the market they are so loud to condemn. At the time of writing the ape is still being nursed by Bonjer's family, at a hiding place kept secret from competing journalists; while most of Europe's zoo directors – WWF collecting boxes to the fore – intrigue fervidly to offer a 'temporary' foster home for the animal, until someone suitable can be found to take it back to Africa.

No one pretends to know how many lowland gorillas still survive in Cameroon. The Garoua experts and their German colleagues did not even attempt to hazard a guess. And IUCN's 'Red Data Book' of endangered species (once stigmatized by Alistair Graham in *The Gardeners of Eden* as the 'Death Row Calender of the Church of the Pleistocene Overkill') classifies the species in the more reassuring category of 'vulnerable', as against the mountain gorilla's classification as 'endangered'. However, IUCN produces no statistical evidence for either classification.

One thing is certain. Unlike chimps, gorillas breed in captivity only with difficulty; they are expensive to house and feed, and are susceptible to a wide range of human diseases which can prove fatal to them, and against which they must be protected. So that the future survival of this species, in contrast to that of their lesser cousins, depends almost entirely on their survival in the wild. They are also, as has been mentioned earlier, more susceptible to habitat change or disturbance than chimpanzees, which will thrive and multiply on disturbed forest or secondary regrowth. Gorillas tend rather to migrate, as long as there is somewhere undisturbed to migrate to. The limited areas known to contain gorillas in Cameroon, and their need for space (each troop, depending on the nature of the country and the size of the troop, needs 10–40 square kilometres of territory, with a population density ratio as low as one ape per square kilometre), imply that the most favourable estimate cannot exceed a few thousand. It is probably very much less.

On this basis, 'decimation' expresses the massacre mildly. Remaining wild stocks cannot sustain such rates of wasteful culling for more than a few years, however many the 'few thousand' may turn out to have comprised. Yet many people, not only in the western world, are weary of the jargon-ridden 'oversell' of extinction-fixated animal protectionists, and wonder if it really matters – since the only gorilla they are ever likely to see is safely behind bars in their local zoo.

Leaving ethical and ecological considerations aside, such

people will be startled into awareness of how much it does matter, when they begin adding up prices and numbers involved, and realize the scandalous scale of loss involved to a poor, developing country in cash terms alone. At current prices, and in the absence of a rational marketing policy, the loss of this potential natural resource to Cameroon can be spelt out in millions of dollars, over the few short years that remaining stocks are likely to last. The actual wanton exploitation by foreign commercial interests, of what could in other circumstances be a renewable, sustainable national source of income – as well, under proper management, as a permanent source of limited supply of gorillas for those legitimately requiring them – can only be qualified as neocolonialist looting of the most piratical brand.

And yet rational alternatives exist, offering ways of frugal utilization of these natural riches, as well as a rational, incontrovertible case for their preservation for their own sakes. Tony de Vos, reporting on neighbouring Gabon's wealth of wild animal resources, also drew up a simple and inexpensive plan for creating plantations of maize, bananas and other fruit trees especially for gorillas. He proposed siting these in suitable clearings in totally protected forest reserves, sufficiently extensive to support permanent gorilla populations. Suppression of hunting and other disturbance would ensure that the animals rapidly lost their well-founded fear of humans, and thus became more visible than they are in natural conditions in deep jungle.

Such reserves could make an unique tourist attraction (although it might be that the people would have to be sheltered in some sort of cage to protect them from any vengeful apes with particularly long memories of human antagonism) and could make an important contribution towards development of a currency-earning tourist industry. They could also eventually lead to controlled cropping, using improved, humane live-capture methods, of the surplus reproduction of wild stocks. For on such limited areas, when fully occupied by permanent populations of apes, any increase in overall numbers (with the elimination of many natural hazards) can be considered as 'surplus'.

On the other hand, many people doubt that turning wild animals into a free-living zoo attraction is the complete answer. Tourism development is also a contentious issue, and brings its own cultural and social pollution and economic strains, all problems to be examined in later chapters. As will the moral question implicit in our utilizing and manipulating the biosphere and its other living creatures purely for our own selfish purposes. At this point, let us only be certain that, however crowded our world becomes and however few seem to be the alternatives, woodlands and forests are a vital, indispensible part of our 'life-support system' on earth.

We may be able to survive the take-over of modern technology, on a denuded, degraded planet. The prospect lacks appeal, however, to most of us, and there is no certainty that we would even want to try. Our choice is either to preserve wild things in their forest habitat, which serves us too in so many ways – and control the reasonable utilization of both, if use them we must – or to relegate our natural history to past history, and join the poet Tennyson in his lament:

The sedge is withered on the lake, and no birds sing.

8. Wildlife alternatives

Le léopard est un méchant animal: quand on l'attaque, il se
défend.

du Chaillu

If I were a cassowary
On the plains of Timbuctoo,
I would eat a missionary,
Cassock, bands and hymn-book too.

Bishop Samuel Wilberforce

The famous white hunters of the nineteenth and early twentieth
centuries were hailed by their contemporaries, and still are by
some nostalgics today, as great sportsmen. In reality they were
avaricious necrophiles, motivated to a man by greed, carnivory
and a lust for killing. Following up the discoveries of empire-
building explorers (George Schaller has written that 'a country is
said to have been "discovered" the first time a white man –
preferably an Englishman – sets foot in it') who were themselves,
with few honorable exceptions, dedicated slaughterers of both
black men and wild beasts, hunters opened up the 'virgin'
hinterlands of colonial Africa, in the hope of finding an easy
fortune 'on-the-hoof'. Their main target was the elephant, large
numbers of which roamed vast spaces of savannah and woodland,
and whose teeth – more valuable then as trade commodities than
now – provided the profits which fuelled their bloodlust. Profits so
great, and at the outset so certain, they made gold and diamond
prospecting (the other main lures of avaricious trail blazers) pale
in contrast as riskier and more onerous ventures.

Men like Frederick Courtenay Selous and 'Karamoja' Bell
penetrated intrepidly into areas as yet untrampled by the white
man's boot; indeed, even after Major Bell's passage among the
Karamojong in today's Uganda, some areas remained free of
bootprints at least. For he was wont to remove both his boots and

his trousers when on the hunt, often then rubbing himself from head to foot in the freshest elephant dung he could find. This enabled him to approach the unsuspecting herd without his giving off the prior warning of man-smell before his assault; and subsequently facilitated the chase of survivors or wounded animals through dense bush, often liberally sprayed with liquid excrement discharged by the panic-stricken fugitives.

Most eminent hunters of this period kept records on their individual contribution to the massacre. Some even recorded profit-and-loss accounts, measuring rewards from ivory sales in tens of thousands of pounds (when pounds were gold sovereigns) after their months-long 'safaris', against investments in equipment, servants' wages and supplies usually amounting to a thousand or two pounds. Many published their reminiscences in their latter days – memoirs of braggarts, redolent with bloodshed and profitable slaughter.

The devastation caused by this kind of commercial hunting, which began with the first main wave of invasion of southern Africa in the sixteenth century, slowed down appreciably over most of the continent with the establishment and extension of colonial regimes and European or Asian settlers and traders after the 1914–18 War. From then on, the hunters' destructive activity was increasingly regulated and restricted wherever any wild animals were left, the authorities having recognized that considerable profits could accrue from the slaughter of the rarest, most desirable species as a rich man's luxury. Before this occurred, however, in vast regions particularly of the densely colonized areas of southern and northern Africa, where the Portuguese, Dutch, British, French and Germans held sway, the more accessible herds had already been eradicated. They were saved from total extinction in a few fringe areas – known to ecologists as the *Grenzwildnis* – by dawning awareness among Boer leaders like President Krüger, that an important part of the country's natural heritage was being savaged and destroyed. His promulgation of game laws setting up game reserves – originally conceived to preserve the king's game, and later to become the basis of national parks on the US model – inspired similar moves among the rulers of other African colonies. The creation of parks and preserves became a status symbol, and through game-protection and licencing laws which accompanied or preceded them, turned indigenous traditional hunters into law-breaking poachers over-night by decree.

The natives were still allowed to hunt more or less freely any animals not desired by their white rulers. The settlers were allowed to hunt practically anything on their own land. But the latter considered as desirable 'game' species only those which had become rare enough – or were naturally large, fierce or elusive enough – to present considerable difficulty (and a modicum of carefully regulated danger) in their killing.

Game in fact fell into two categories in such safari hunters' eyes. Big game, especially the white hunters' renowned 'big five', variously defined as elephant, rhinoceros, lion, leopard and buffalo (with some substituting giraffe or the larger, more spectacular antelope – eland or the greater kudu – or even in areas where they exist, gorilla, cheetah or okapi for one or other of the above), were sacrificially slaughtered under a laid down ritual for the tusks, horns, hides and other trophies they yielded, and were considered in the main to be inedible. Even the 'trophy' buffalo and antelope were hardly luxury food for such spoilt tourists, being selected for slaying because of their spread of horns, an indicator of age, and consequent toughness and rankness of the meat.

Small game, on the other hand, is distinguished more by the animal's similarity to species considered edible by European taste. Smaller antelope qualified, as did various species of wild pig, hares and various birds. Zebra, on the other hand, were generally considered inedible – by the British, at least, probably because of their equine appearance – but were shot for their skins. Crocodiles were too, while ostriches were shot for their feathers; hippopotamuses, baboons and other monkeys, hyenas, jackals and a host of other smaller creatures were 'permitted' small game, but were mainly shot for target practice – or the pure pleasure of bloodletting. (The past tense is used here since we are dealing with the safari hunting situation between the wars, and during the postwar colonial period. Most countries still permitting sport hunting today impose wider restrictions on species which may be shot, some being theoretically totally prohibited. Despite this, white hunters in the field operate far from the superficial and over-stretched supervisory services these poor lands can afford, and a steady traffic in forbidden trophies still continues.)

In addition, such hunters generally justified the practice of shooting at least up to the limits of their licenced quotas with the excuse of 'shooting for the pot'. They not only expected to feed themselves with the booty of their weapons during weeks of camping in the bush, but they were also invariably accompanied, apart from the white-hunter guide who managed the catering and led them within range of the creatures they had paid so dearly to kill, by a small army of servants, drivers, cooks, trackers, skinners and general dogsbodies. All these expected a large daily meat ration, the joviality of their services depending in large measure upon the copiousness of bounty supplied by the master's gun. More blasé tourists, satiated with killing, would sometimes even order their white hunter to undertake this chore.

Wastage of wildlife was not only a result of such 'consumerist' safari hunting. Karamoja Bell, in his time, wrought devastating havoc among elephant stocks, but in doing so he also fed his multitude of 'boys' on a pure meat diet whenever he could, game meat being among the cheapest provisions available. Apart from this he also required thousands of fresh hides, from anything on four legs – from giraffe to antelope – to wrap the tusks his porters head-loaded for weeks on the long trek back to 'civilization'. The green skin, sewn around the tusk – which weighed anything up to 150lbs – shrank as it dried and made a tight, protective covering for the ivory against the hazards of the long journey to market.

South Africa's 'trekboers' were even more wasteful of that region's indigenous fauna. They massacred hundreds of thousands merely for their hides or feathers, to finance their cancerous spread northward, into lands beyond the hated colonial reach of the British.

During the years of the Great Depression between the wars, the rate of individual slaughter slowed down remarkably, but to counterbalance this there was a manifold increase in the number of freelance commercial hunters. Game preservation and hunting laws reduced the damage to more accessible and easily supervised herds; and the more conspicuous products of the business – ivory, trophies and skins – were to some extent controlled at the marketing or exporting end. But there were many ways a white man with a gun could live by preying on Africa's wild animals – and with any luck, live well.

Hunters of this generation – men like 'Iodine' Ionides, 'Rufiji' de la Bere Barker (the self-styled 'Jungle Hermit', whose progeny are dispersed throughout East Africa), George Tasker or 'Uncle' – were able, through discreet abuse of a colonial system fairly liberal for whites at least, to lead a life which seemed affluent to the natives whose resources and labour they exploited – and like romantic adventure to those at home brought up in the traditions of heroic Empire. There were several ways of doing this. Simplest was to obtain a licence allowing the shooting of one (or sometimes two) elephants, among much other game. Costing less than £100, it was a lucrative investment with the price of ivory constant at around £1 per pound weight, and elephants carrying tusks weighing 60 lb each still being common – and teeth of up to 160 lb or more were not yet uncommon. The chances of showing a fair profit were assured, while 'making a killing' was always a reasonable hope. Few professional adventurers were satisfied with such legitimate returns, however.

All those I met boasted proudly (some even recounting in their published memoirs) of their stratagems in bending the law. Usually they shot as many elephants as possible, selling the ivory surreptitiously on the black market run by Asian traders, and omitting to enter the kills in their licence forms, as the regulations stipulated. This slaughter continued until they were obliged by an official's awareness of their latest kill (or by fears of denunciation by unfriendly natives in the neighbourhood) to enter their latest success on the form. Most reckoned to 'stretch' each elephant hunting permit to cover the slaughter of nine or ten animals. Ionides, while serving as a colonial army officer and later as a Game Department official, regularly spent his leaves from service in Tanganyika, poaching elephant in this way over the border in the neighbouring Belgian Congo – sometimes hunting without any licence at all. His other passion, until he took up catching and exporting snakes, was to seek out and slaughter the rarest and most beautiful creatures in today's 'Red Data Book of Endangered Species' – helping them to qualify for this title and in the process filling Nairobi's Coryndon Museum and many others with the mummified bodies of gorillas, okapis and various rare gazelles.

Crocodiles were classified as dangerous vermin throughout most of this period. A licence to shoot gave the right to kill unlimited numbers of these now rare creatures, the belly skin of which sold at the time for up to 25 shillings an inch. The most valuable skins come from immature animals around five or six feet long, and a good night's hunting could produce as many as 40–50 skins. Hunting was usually carried out at night, by the light of an acetylene or battery-powered lamp strapped to a headband – a prohibited but widespread practice, the headlamps being on open sale in every general store. Usually the hunter would drift by canoe, in darkness, close to a river bank or lake shore. When the lamp is switched on, the eyes of any crocodiles lying on the bank reflect a luminous red target down the beam of light illuminating the sights of the hunter's rifle. Shooting indiscriminately at these reflections he would be sure to hit some, and hope that many of these would die on the spot. After 'doing his rounds' in the dark, the hunter would then return at daybreak to collect the corpses of any that had failed in their instinctive struggle to reach the water. These were skinned, and the flesh was left for the carrion eaters.

Night shooting is generally illegal, being too easy, non-selective and deadly for many other creatures as well as crocodiles. Offenders were rarely caught, however, and any neighbouring fishermen who might have denounced the law-breaker were likely to maintain silence in return for the supply of free meat – to them most acceptably edible. Moreover, when the densest crocodile populations were shot out, as they rapidly were all over the continent, many hunters turned their hand to skin trading to supplement their income. They left the more onerous killing of dispersed survivors to the local inhabitants, who used nets, lines, traps, poison, spears or the antique muzzle-loading muskets which most such villages possess. Such trading aided a mutual interest in avoiding the authorities' notice.

At different times and places the authorities declared many other species to be vermin – placed beyond the pale of limited protection and exposed to the full fury of the passionate hunter. Zebras and buffaloes suffered this fate in Kenya, Rhodesia and elsewhere before the last war, as did also lions in many places and, on some occasions leopards, for competing with, infecting with disease or preying upon the white man's cattle. (Black cattle herders have never paid much heed to laws enjoining them to protect predators – and still don't today.)

Wild pigs, warthogs, wild dogs, hyenas, jackals and snakes have all been awarded the brand of outcast from the living world, from Sudan to South Africa, from Senegal to Somalia – as were also many species of birds, practically all rodents, and most other reptiles apart from the snakes and crocodiles already mentioned. As for the wonderful world of insects and lesser life forms, anyone even suggesting a measure of protection here was considered slightly insane. This latter view is still prevalent.

Lions were considered as vermin in cattle-raising areas of Southern Rhodesia (today's Zimbabwe) when I first went there in 1957; the appearance of a pair on a friend's farm there even occasioned an invitation by radio to a 'flying doctor' in Lusaka in Northern Rhodesia (today's Zambia), to fly down and join in the grand sport of shooting them. The following year, in Tanganyika, I found that baboons and various semi-terrestrial monkeys, which can do considerable damage to a field of ripening corn, were not only 'free' game, but a reward was paid for killing them. This 'bounty' was paid for each severed monkey hand delivered to the local Game Department office, while the farm workers were delighted to dispose of the rest of the cadaver.

Slaughterhouse shock

Having dealt at some length with the gorier realities of big-game hunting, in the hope of countering some of the romantic mythology with which its practitioners and advocates surround and ennoble it, it may be worth introducing a personal note here. For the development of my own ideas regarding our relationships with the living world which sustains us, and in particular with the other animals in it, was largely governed by experience in the field. It was deeply influenced by listening to, and later reading, the reminiscences of great hunters like those quoted above, and even more so by the writings and conversation of men like Ian Parker, Brian Nicholson and several others who knew most of them better than I. This led me to reflect in general on the exploitation of our natural world's resources for our survival and profit, and on the limits and restraints we should accept in this.

Growing up, as I have said, between the wars when the imperial tradition held sway, and when hunting was a socially acceptable – even snobbishly desirable – pastime, one dreamed frustratedly in a middle class urban environment of owning a gun and the right to shoot over someone's land. Occasionally during my boyhood, friendly farmers would allow me to clear their fields and woods of 'vermin' (which in England in those days included wood pigeons, rooks, crows and birds of prey, rabbits and any small predators except the fox) and lend me the weapon to do so.

I first went to Africa under the conviction (which I still hold today) that to kill for the purpose of eating deserves no moral censure or opprobrium. Killing merely for pleasure or profit, on the other hand (even as a vocation, as with slaughtermen), is always heinous. Being of this mind, I occasionally hunted over the years in Africa, usually alone or with a like-minded friend, and make it an inflexible rule never to kill any animal not intended for my own or others' consumption. The only exception to this rule was the shooting of vermin, where official approval made a socially acceptable pleasure out of their killing, especially when I was cattle farming.

In the Southern Highlands Province of Tanganyika in the late 1950s, wild animals on the farm were viewed as competitors with or for our cattle, carrying various infectious diseases – foot-and-mouth, rinderpest (both introduced to Africa with the introduction of cattle) and rabies, or a range of enzootic tick and fly-borne diseases like East Coast fever or trypanosomiasis. Pastures could be cleared of these costly plagues in time, by regularly dipping the cattle with insecticides, and rotating their use of pastures on a regular schedule. The cattle pick up a large proportion of the insect vectors each time, and these are killed in the dip. As long as no new infestations are brought in by wildlife using the same range, ticks can be wiped out in a year or two, and the pastures effectively 'cleaned'.

With veterinary services generally inadequate, and expensive when they were available, the marginal economies of beef farming in Tanganyika at that time demanded that all such precautions against infection should be strictly enforced. Building up a breeding herd, and consequently loath to sacrifice our own beasts, we were naturally glad of the supplement which any such unfortunate wild creatures contributed to our own and our cattlemen's diet. Predators, on the other hand, represented a costly menace, especially when building up a breeding herd, when calves tend to comprise a higher than average proportion of the livestock.

Our cattle farming venture failed after three years of struggle, during which the seasonal rains failed entirely in the region. The expense of trying to keep the cattle alive by trucking drums of water from a permanent river over 40 miles away, mounted to the point of exceeding any residual value of the sickly, staggering hide-covered skeletons which thus far survived on the impoverished, eroded land. Final dissolution of our hopes came when the lease on the land was revoked, under newly independent Tanzania's policy of expropriation of expatriate-held land and collectivization of agricultural production – a policy which seemed a reasonable option at the time, but which has contributed importantly to the country's present penury. Tanganyika and Zanzibar were on the whole relatively well off in terms of the people's diet, choice and earning opportunities at the end of the British mandate there. (Until 1919 Tanganyika was a German colony.)

Mulling over the reasons for our defeat, we recalled that even during the worst of the drought, the buffalo and antelope we hunted appeared to be thriving, as fat as butter and as plentiful as in lusher rainy years. We concluded that we had been farming the wrong animals in that environment. There followed a period of intense, though intermittent study – at first directed towards the concept of domestication of indigenous species, and breeding them in the classical farming context, as substitutes for cattle, sheep, pigs and poultry. Jean Dorst in Paris first guided my quest through the published literature then available. There was little enough at that time, though as I was to discover, the idea had already been explored in practice many times during the preceding half century or more, usually on a small scale, except in South Africa where thousands of farmers were (and still are) making a good living out of game and ostrich farming.

Following this, after an interlude back in Africa, some years spent in Rome occasioned further guidance from Thane Riney, then running the Wildlife Section of FAO's Forestry Division and, more importantly, from several of his expert colleagues. Most diligent, patient and generous among these helpful people was Tony de Vos, a Dutch-Canadian Professor of Ecology and Forestry, who was arguably the most knowledgeable wildlife utilization expert then active in the field. Research revealed many past and current initiatives based on the idea of farming or 'cropping' indigenous animals, and not only in Africa. From New

Zealand and Australia, through North and South America, China and the Ukraine, to Scandinavia or Scotland, the practice appeared to have been working for decades at least (in Askania Nova, for instance, for three quarters of a century), on a very wide scale.

Our use of such animals for human purposes has acquired its own trade jargon. It has become a specialized sector of the new discipline of nature conservation, and given the title of 'wildlife utilization'. The techniques and practices involved are usually summed up under the heading 'wildlife management'; the aim is invariably stated in the professional pidgin as being production of meat and other products, or of hunting and game-viewing facilities 'on a sustained yield basis'. As in all such hybrid language, these terms are misnomers, leading to confusion and obscurity of purpose, and frustration of results. 'Wildlife' has become restricted to meaning all the higher animals, mammalian and avian – but excluding aquatic (whales, manatees and crocodiles excepted), smaller life forms from insects to bacteria, and the whole world of plant life – which do not fall under the heading of 'domesticants', i.e. the usual 'farm' animals such as cattle, horses, donkeys, pigs, sheep and goats, poultry, rabbits, and in some regions such creatures as camels, elephants, buffaloes, yaks, llamas, alpacas and reindeer – as well as the more common household pets.

The margins between these latter classifications are frequently vague, and distinction is often made between the 'wild' and 'domesticated' versions of some species, 'wildness' being dependent on the user's definition of 'domestication', or the form or method of 'utilization'. A full list of creatures falling into these marginal categories would be practically endless. We have employed an astonishing variety of animals over the centuries for an equally surprising number of tasks or purposes. Elephants have not only been in use – probably for thousands of years – for transport and heavy lifting; in Hannibal's time and probably long before, they were used as war machines as well. The ancient Egyptians harnessed and tethered (i.e. presumably raised in domesticant conditions) a great variety of bovids, antelopes, felines, canines and birds; while the modern fur industry, which raises a number of predatory northern mammals and rodents for their pelts, including mink, ermine, martens, foxes, beavers, rabbits and chinchillas, may well be following in the footsteps of much earlier trappers and fur traders, who sometimes bred from live-caught animals to add to their supply of pelts. Ostriches have been bred and intensively farmed for more than a century at least (it is uncertain whether the ancient Egyptians or other Middle Eastern civilizations actually farmed these birds although they certainly kept them, and the possibility is not to be excluded), first in Algeria and later spreading across the world, to Australia, California, Texas, and even to Hamburg, as well as to South Africa, which continues today to raise around 100,000 of these great birds annually for their feathers, skins and meat.

Fish have also been intensively farmed for thousands of years, principally in the Far East but, throughout our current millennium at least, in Northern Europe too, and more lately in America. The practice of pisiculture today is a world-wide industry, profitable enough even to attract the attention of such giant petrochemical concerns as Shell and others. Fishing itself has involved another form of domestication – that of cormorants in the Orient, where the bird is made to dive after individual fish, a ring placed round its neck preventing swallowing. Oysters, mussels and several crustaceans have long been farmed artificially, and goldfish and many other decorative fish bred and kept in the closest 'domestic' captivity. Dolphins and killer whales, though not yet bred in captivity for the purpose (although this is inevitably being attempted at the time of writing), can surely be considered 'domesticated' as they carry their keeper for a ride around the 'dolphinarium' – or in the even more gruesome and furtive activities of the US Navy, which has taught them to fetch and carry in pursuit of submarine warfare.

The avian world has contributed far more fully to human service than its mere exploitation as poultry for meat, eggs, and sometimes feather production. Here again, the number of species used makes a surprising tally. Apart from the universal chickens, ducks, geese, turkeys and pigeons, more specialized bird farmers breed quails, pheasants, partridges, wild ducks such as teal and widgeon, Guinea-fowl, ptarmigan and and other grouse, emus and, as already mentioned, ostriches. Experiments are currently being carried out in Argentina to breed penguins for their flesh and fats, protests about this development being drowned earlier at the time by the general hullabaloo about the Falklands War.

Not only have birds been domesticated for their flesh, eggs or feathers, but many decorative species are widely bred in captivity for trade, and must be considered effectively domesticated. These range from the common cage-birds – budgerigars, canaries and other finches – to parrots, cockatoos and the flamboyant peacock. We might also note that at least one of each of these 'productive' or 'ornamental' categories served supplementary functions in other days. The pigeon, endowed with a homing instinct, has been used for carrying messages, especially in wartime, and still serves today as the object of the international sport of pigeon racing. The canary served as a warning system of accumulations of poisonous gas, both in the early days of coal mining before the invention of the 'Davy lamp', and again in war.

The last major use humans have made of the avian world relates to hunting, and concerns the raptors. Most birds of prey – from eagles to barn owls, though more generally the hawks and falcons – have been tamed and trained to hunt and retrieve small terrestrial and avian prey, though I have been unable to find any record of their being regularly bred for this purpose.

Hunting is also a major motive for the domestication of some other mammalian species, one of which is today principally a household pet, and basis of a lucrative world-wide trade and breeding industry. (The whole subject of the modern 'pet syndrome' and the trade which battens on it will be reviewed at length in a further book, at present in preparation.) Quite who domesticated whom, however, is not altogether clear. Historians often suggest that dogs were the first animals to be domesticated. But Ian Parker, a Kenyan wildlife specialist, has postulated that their domestication may have occurred 'in reverse' – that in a sense, dogs may have 'domesticated' us.

The middens and offal of primitive early settlements must have provided rich scavenging for the wild dogs of the time (not to be confused with the African wild or hunting dog, which hunts in packs well away from human habitation, and is only distantly related), as they do today for jackals, coyotes and the half-wild, ownerless pye-dogs of most Asian and Middle Eastern countries. These skulk around the littered fringes of villages and towns, living off whatever edible rubbish, sewage (or occasional stolen foodstuffs) they can find – usually rewarded for this useful carrion clearing function with a blow or a thrown stone whenever they come into range, and making moonlit nights hideous with their howling.

Parker suggests that rather than people having tamed and purposely domesticated such dogs, the boot may well have been on the other foot. The dog's opportunism, and its instinctive submissive behaviour if confronted by a more powerful opponent, may have driven it closer and closer into contact with human habitations, until the people realized that the creature's presence offered useful advantages, and stopped throwing sticks and stones. Once having achieved tolerance, the dog would instinctively 'adopt' the human group and its habitation as part of its own pack and den – and defend them ferociously against intruders, as is its nature. People would be quick to appreciate and exploit this. Furthermore, dogs soon proved invaluable aids in hunting, vastly extending the hunter's range, improving the sensitivity of his tracking, and adding force to his attack. They almost certainly facilitated the capture of the first herbivores to be domesticated, and were rapidly enrolled in the task of herding and protecting them, extending their instinctive protectiveness of human habitation to include their cattle as well.

A factor in such (still hypothetical, but reasonably probable) development which Parker fails to mention, is that since early times dogs also provided us with part of our meat diet directly – apart from their help with hunting and herding. Many early remains of human settlement contain bones of dogs, showing signs of their consumption by the inhabitants. To this day, dogs are eaten in many parts of the world – and some of the rich world's most popular pet breeds first evolved as 'eating' dogs – King Charles spaniels in Europe, and the chow-chow and pekingese in the Orient, to name but three. Their meat value alone may have been sufficient incentive to allow the pye-dogs of the time to ingratiate themselves into human communities.

Indeed, the same early remains also show unexpectedly large numbers of hyena bones. It is even conceivable that early humans may have developed a similar tolerant cohabitation with this much more powerful species. (White farmers and hunters have frequently tamed and raised hyena puppies as house-pets.) But the dangers inherent in close contact with such a powerful creature may, as life became easier with the development of human survival techniques like agriculture and animal husbandry, have outweighed any advantages.

Perhaps, to continue the hypothesis, it proved impossible, given its lower level of intellectual development than the dog's, to induce the hyena to inhibit the instinctive urge to chase and attack fleeing livestock. This would render it useless as a herder's aid, and probably also as a hunter's. It should also be remembered that modern domestic dogs are often guilty of harassing sheep and cattle, while each year brings its reports of children – and adults too – being savaged, sometimes killed and, more rarely, even eaten by dogs.

Domesticating wheat

We have seen then what 'domestication' is *not*. It is not merely 'taming', and does not invariably entail control of breeding of the animals concerned. Nor is it merely manipulation of creatures' lives, habitual behaviour or natural functions. What the word does imply, on the other hand, is a much more fundamental change – more subtle and far less reversible, influencing the animals' gene inheritance. This genetic manipulation occurs in several ways. Initially, in the first domestications, it was purely by human selection, probably largely unwitting or even unintended. Indeed, if Parker's theory of dogs' 'domestication' of humans has any truth, it may even have occurred involuntarily, against humans' will – a 'pest' transforming its own image in human eyes.

Similar processes are involved in domestication of other natural life-forms – of 'wildlife' in the broader sense, which also includes the world of plants. It might be useful to illustrate this here by a parallel process in a common plant. Many have suggested that our progress toward an agricultural society first involved the shift from a 'hunter-gatherer's' economy to that of arable farming, through the domestication in particular of cereals, which provide us with nutritious food reserves easy to store over long periods of time. This marked, in their view, the first step towards modern civilization.

Domestication of animals was, in this view, a secondary phase (some even claim a degenerative phase), primarily motivated by the need of animal traction power for arable farming – for ploughing, harrowing and as pack animals, or to draw sleds and carts to transport the harvest, as well as to tread it in primitive threshing. It is unlikely, however, that progress in such complex issues was ever so causally clear-cut; more probably, the two processes – plant and animal domestications – took place in differing order, or even simultaneously, and at different rates (with possibly at times some exchange of ideas or 'inter-group feedback') in the very diverse habitats occupied by our earliest ancestors.

The example of wheat – the most important grain crop today on the international commodity markets – has been studied thoroughly by archaeologists and plant breeders. The earliest natural wheat, which evolved around the Eastern Mediterranean Basin, bears little resemblance to today's commodity crop. Its seedhead is a loose assembly of hairy, barbed grains, unlike the hard, densely packed hairless wheat familiar to most of us – more like today's barley in its whiskery appearance.

In nature, wheat's barbs and whiskers made each individual seed into an aerodynamically perfect 'dart', an image perfected by a sharp, horny tip to the seed. These ensure that, on being dislodged from the seedhead at ripening, the seed will plummet down to penetrate some way into the soil surface. The tip itself is furnished with angled hairlike barbs, which on penetration catch between the grains of soil. They not only ensure the seed's fixation there, but under action of the wind shaking the 'dart's' protruding whiskery 'tail-feather', cause it to burrow deeper into loose soil until it buries itself completely. Such evolutionary adaptations favour wild wheat's natural survival, procreation and dissemination. They are often disadvantageous for the farmer, however.

It happens that one wild plant in a million or more is a genetically stable mutation of the wild variety. In the case of wheat, this 'mutant' carried seeds packed more tightly in the seedhead, and more firmly fixed to it. As a result, they withstood better the harvesting of sickle-wielding early farmers (who used elegant dressed stone blades set with natural glue into a wooden shaft), during whose reaping, bundling into sheaves, and carrying home, many of the 'normal' wild grains would spring loose of the ripe heads and be lost to the harvester, before he could get them home. This factor alone produced a selective tendency, in that proportionately more of the mutants survived the harvesting process, resulting in more of them ending in the corn-bin or granary – and becoming next year's seed corn when agriculture developed beyond mere gathering of wild crops, to become the purposeful planting of chosen seed. Over the 10 to 12 millennia that this practice continued, the mutant variety tended to predominate, and finally ousted normal wild wheat altogether. Later, active selection followed, farmers similarly 'breeding out' by conscious selection the barbs and whiskers – no longer an advantage when the grains are artificially planted, and indeed something of an uncomfortable nuisance, as anyone who has hand-harvested or threshed similarly bearded barley will remember from experience. The end result of the process is the modern wheat grower's familiar crop.

It probably happened in a very similar way to that whereby early domestic animals selected themselves – first through the mechanism of genetically governed instincts and temperament more suitable for human needs or purposes. The example has already been given of the dog's greater suitability than the hyena's for sheep herding or hunting – and one might extend the hypothesis to the case of the wolf in northern areas.

In the case of herbivores, the best instinctually adapted to herding and droving would be the natural choice – that is to say, the more gregarious among them. The phlegmatic temperament of most bovids is an obvious example. This characteristic, which, among other things, has the effect of the herd's 'damping down' individual reactions to any traumatic contacts suffered at human hands (a solitary animal like a kudu would probably disappear over the horizon after branding, while a steer will hide itself back in the herd, its panic and anguish soon dissipated by the latter) would certainly be reinforced in the initial stages of domestication, by a self-selecting process similar to that described in plants.

The capture of more aggressive cattle, or raising calves from aggressive strains, would prove less easy than with beasts of a more placid temperament. Hunters would probably kill them for meat rather than try to capture them; and herdsmen would take a similar view of bullocks or heifers growing more aggressive with age. Later, purposive breeding would enhance the genetically linked behavioural traits desired. Aggressive or other undesired traits would submit to the predominance of more placid 'genotypes' selected for breeding, and become submerged. In an ultimate stage, where husbandry techniques have evolved so far as to diminish the importance of such characteristics in domesticants, and breeders' selectivity seeks to bring out other desirable qualities – such as improved meat or milk production, better hides, resistance to disease, or improved fertility and breeding rates – the traits considered undesirable by earlier breeders may re-emerge. This tendency can be seen most clearly in modern dogs. Some races – the St Bernard or the German shepherd or Alsatian – have in recent years been bred for appearance rather than for their temper; as a result many individuals of these races have become dangerously savage and unpredictable.

A few examples from the phylum (class) of arthropods (insects) will round off this summary review of our more intimate exploitation of the animal world. Although we have used insects or their products for many different purposes – decorative (butterflies and others), religious (scarab bettles, considered divine in ancient Egypt), culinary (cochineal for food colouring), sport (maggots bred for anglers), amatory/medical (cantharides or 'Spanish fly', used as an aphrodisiac, sometimes with dire effects), comestible (honey from bees), illumination (bee's wax – though again, this often also had religious connections through the burning of church candles) or even entertainment (as in the oriental use of crickets for their 'music') – none of these can be considered as truly domesticated except the bees, and also silk worms (this being in fact the caterpillar of the Chinese moth *Brombyx mori*), the breeding and life cycles of both being largely controlled or influenced by humans, as well as their productive activity.

Taming the wild

Proper scientific study of the practical use of African animals, which had been attempted innumerable times during the colonial period in a desultory way and on a small scale, began in Southern Rhodesia – today's Zimbabwe – in the early 1950s. The Henderson brothers there owned a ranch of some 120,000 acres, half of which was already developed as a cattle ranch. The other half still carried large numbers of game animals. They first planned to shoot these out. But two American scholars,

Raymond Dassman and Archie Mossmann, persuaded the Hendersons to study 'cropping' these animals, with a view to turning the area over to permanent commercial production of game meat, instead of beef. Wild animal cropping, another term which has entered the jargon, is often used interchangeably with culling, and implies shooting (or otherwise slaughtering) an annual crop or harvest of animals at or under the rate of annual increase in herd numbers. Cropping, however, should be understood to imply purely quantitative selection of animals to be eliminated; culling, in contrast, includes the application of qualitative parameters – selecting the victims on the basis of set criteria such as age, sex, state of health or value, although not necessarily implying elimination of the weakest, least desirable specimens for the improvement of the remainder, as culling does in normal usage of classic animal breeding.

Results over the first two years were marginally convincing, and could have been improved by higher stocking rates, for which the land had potential. But the venture failed as a result of marketing problems. The meat was mainly sold as 'boys' meat' – work-contract rations forming part of the emoluments of native employees prescribed by the colonial labour administration (the 'boys' were not considered capable of spending their own money on food if paid a full wage).

Initially the Rhodesian meat-marketing authority handled consignments of field-shot antelope carcasses without difficulty. Eventually however, cattle farmers viewed the venture as unfair competition for their more expensive beef (with some justice in purely commercial terms), and demanded the imposition of equal hygienic standards for all meat using their marketing channels. These were impossible to attain in field conditions, and alternative marketing systems proved inadequate to cope with the problem economically.

Dassman and Mossmann left (the former to end up as IUCN's Chief Ecologist), and the Hendersons turned the game ranch (which was never more than a trial cropping operation, making no attempt at either domestication or at stock and range improvements through selective culling and management) into an exclusive commercial 'safari hunting' park, offering a guaranteed weekend's shoot to Salisbury's business visitors. These were helicoptered in for a quick blood-letting, with a hearty meal around the campfire to follow. So successful was this scheme that the brothers had to restock regularly, even buying in and introducing new species such as the greater kudu to make the hunters' choice of targets more attractive. They replaced their depleted game stocks from as far afield as the Transvaal where thousands of large farms are ranching game animals (over 3,000 then, by some estimates), often jointly with cattle or sheep, but many raising one or two species of indigenous antelope alone. The most common game animals there are springbok, blesbok and bontebok, the last saved from extinction by commercial ranching, after being hunted almost out of existence before its potential for making money had been realized.

In many parts of Central and East Africa, farmers have attempted to raise a number of native species, from buffaloes, eland and kudu to a wide range of lesser antelopes – with varying degrees of success and various intensities of domestication. It may be worth defining this term for readers not familiar with the trade jargon. Domestication means more than taming. An animal is tamed, especially an aggressive or fugitive species, when it has learnt to accept human proximity and contact without attacking or fleeing. Domestication does not necessarily imply that the domesticant breeds under human subjection. The female Asian elephant is turned loose for mating with wild relatives and often to give birth, and returns or is recaptured. (Few uncastrated males are used – and indeed, gelding a bull elephant is in every sense a major operation.) Working elephants can nevertheless be considered as domesticated. The hunting cheetah is another borderline case for similar reasons.

Many wild lions have been tamed in Africa, but cannot be called domesticated. On the other hand, Jimmy Chipperfield's lions, of which he once claimed to own over 3,000 in 'safari park' zoos and circuses around the world – more than are under the control of any single national park or game and wildlife authority in Africa – may well qualify for the title. Breeding in captivity with awesome fecundity, they created a glut on the world market until an enterprising game meat wholesaler in Bavaria spotted an up-market opportunity, and came to the rescue. He discovered in the sated German luxury food market an eager opening for lion flesh, and today sells deep-frozen, plastic-wrapped lion quarters – from around 140–150 beasts per year – to the gourmet restaurant trade.

He told me he also delivers complete 'oven-ready' carcasses by special order, 'in the skin' – if so required. His source of supply is the numerous zoos and 'safari parks' throughout Europe. Indeed, Chipperfield recounted that a new park in Holland produced over 600 surplus lions in the first four years of its foundation.

Such manipulations are characteristic of an intensive degree of domestication – usually associated with the practice of 'zero grazing', with keeping animals permanently in close confinement and bringing their fodder to them. At the lowest degree of domestication, captive herds under the charge of a herdsman graze more or less at will over pastures selected by him or by his overseers responsible for their management, and are culled or cropped at regular seasons. The range progresses through management involving increasing measures of manipulation and restraint, where the animals are available for such operations as dipping and other veterinary handling, supplementary feeding, dehorning, castration and selective breeding, branding or marking, milking, shearing, plucking or (in the case of feather cropping) clipping, and eventual sale or slaughter. Finally in the most intensive sphere animals are handled like stud bulls in cattle farming, which allows full control of choice and timing in breeding. This last example illustrates the point that domesticants need not *per se* be 'tame'; many other stud males, apart from bulls, are dangerously aggressive unless kept under rigid safeguards. Similarly controlled are elands, favoured for experiments in domestication, partly perhaps because of their cow-like size and general aspect, and the relative tractability of most females. Their popularity has certainly been prompted by the success of Russian breeding of an eland herd at Askania Nova in the Ukraine, where they have been raised for milk (whose properties hold many advantages for humans, including medical) and meat since 1892. The Russians were not even the first in modern times to do so. Lord Derby – remembered more often for his devotion to horse racing and his taste in hats – bred them in England in the 1830s.

Since these early beginnings, but still before the First World War, a Rhodesian farmer had domesticated eland and several other antelope. He also caught and tamed zebras, to the point of using them as draught animals for ploughing. Many others experimented with this species around this time, but most concluded that zebras were not constitutionally robust enough to sustain the heavy working regime of more familiar draught animals. Where methods are recorded, however, it is clear that they expected the zebra to subsist while working on its normal wild forage diet, failing to take account of the interruption of normal grazing routine and the animal's consequent need of supplementary feed, as would have been provided for horses or mules.

Belgians undertook a similar experiment in their immense Congo colony, which failed for similar reasons – but is mainly interesting for its success with other creatures. During the precolonial Belgian occupation of Zaire, when the huge territory was formally part of the private estates of King Leopold (having been annexed for him by the Welsh-American explorer Stanley), attempts were started to exploit local animals more intensively than merely by gunning them down. Leopold set up a research station in the Ituri Forest to test domestication of elephants and buffaloes (as well as zebras), at first gaining few results before finally succeeding.

Several failures by imported Indian mahouts to adapt classical Asian techniques to the very different temperament of the African elephant, led at one point to a desperate attempt to import four Indian elephants as a possible solution. These were to be marched overland after landing at Dar-es-Salaam. Three died on the journey, and the fourth shortly after arrival at the station, their deaths probably due to lack of immunity to enzootic African diseases which local elephants tolerate. Another eventual Ituri station success was domestication of African buffalo – again after early setbacks and a similar unsuccessful attempt to substitute the Asian species for them. The elephant training station has survived the vicissitudes of Zaire's recent turbulent history, relocated near the country's northern border. Much run down during the post-war colonial period of advanced mechanization and cheap petrol, it may still serve as a model for local imitation.

Incidentally, an effectively domesticated herd of about a dozen red forest buffalo – caught wild, and reputedly the more implacably savage of the two African varieties – existed for many years during Belgium's colonial and post-colonial periods in Antwerp Zoo. They calved regularly, and their keepers handled them exactly like a herd of cows, driving them about and moving unconcernedly among them while 'mucking out' their enclosure and stall. The whole herd died in the early 1970s, victims of a Belgian animal disease transmitted, it was thought, via the boots of a visitor from some rural area.

During the same period, Paddy Hopkirk in Southern Rhodesia kept a large herd of eland with cattle, while several smaller scale ventures were tried in East Africa. More recently in Kenya, John King not only proved again the 'domesticability' of buffalo and eland – even dehorning some of the latter to reduce damage to his fences and corrals – but also of the much rarer oryx and addax, two graceful large antelope more at home in the desert than down on the farm. He found that these can be tamed, herded and handled as easily as free-ranging cattle, and that herds of 60–100 antelope can be managed by teams of four herdsmen, allowing three to supervise the herd with one off duty. Labour costs in this are higher than for cattle similarly run, but the economic balance was restored by far lower veterinary costs. This factor could be an asset to the many African countries labouring under a dearth of veterinarians, but with a surplus of potential herdsmen.

King demonstrated that in the dry country of Galana where he worked, oryx so herded are far more productive, in economic terms, than Boran cattle, sheep and goats. H.P. Ledger, however, advises caution before accepting comparisons of productive efficiency. 'Efficiency indices' – as overworked in conservationists' utilization advocacy as that other old favourite, 'biomass carrying capacities' – are suspect without precise definition of their parameters and methods of measurement. Most comparisons are made, he says, between exotic domesticants on marginal land and game 'not messed about by management practices originating in better areas'; or between entire (i.e. non-castrated) game and castrated domesticants, which affects carcass composition. For example, the meat-to-fat ratio of a steer's carcass, and also the weight ratio of its fore and hind quarters, are lower than those of a non-castrated bull.

Protective opposition

Conservationists are by no means all advocates of this use of wild animals, although most of them today pay lip service to the idea of 'wildlife utilization'. The examples to be cited below show clearly that the bitterest enemies of this method of conserving otherwise endangered species are not among the beef-men and developers, but entrenched in the ruling establishment of the conservation movement itself.

Serengeti, a vast strip of upland savannah plain near Tanzania's northern border with Kenya, halfway between Mount Kilimanjaro and the great Lake Victoria, has long been recognized as a hunters' paradise. Its pullulating herds of game and their attendant predators are one of nature's most exuberant gifts. A paradise too for film makers and affluent animal lovers, the former often share with us their wonder at the spectacular seasonal migration of hundreds of thousands of free creatures, to and from the neighbouring rich grasslands of the Ngorongoro Crater.

It was first put on the television in all its colourful glory – and thus 'put on the map' for most of us – by a former official of Nazi Germany's Ministry of Food and Agriculture, turned zoo keeper, whose zoo-catching expeditions and imperial nostalgia occasioned his trying his hand at film-making in Africa's ex-German colonies. Bernard Grzimek's name became a household word among animal loving TV viewers and early conservationists (and also crossword puzzle fans), and his remarkable early films had a huge success. Profits from the first paid for a small aeroplane. With his son Michael at the controls and the help of Alan Root, a gifted Kenyan photographer, he made some of the first aerial films of wild African herds, showing their milling panic as he swooped low among gnus, gazelles and zebras peacefully grazing, or busy dropping their calves and foals. This made sensational footage – apart from giving awaiting packs of predators splendid opportunity to come amongst the disorganized herds. In the process he invented the modern biologists' sport of aerial game counting.

Grzimek's most successful film, *Serengeti darf nicht sterben*, was an important element in raising general consciousness of the endangered status of remaining stocks of wild animals in Africa, and indeed elsewhere. On the other hand, the reasons he propounded for this threatened status were far wide of the mark. Wholeheartedly propagating the classic views of his white hunter friends and their game-protecting successors (many switched roles easily) that the threat stems from native hunting, which he and they invariably vilify as 'poaching', he doggedly ignores the disastrous effects of western-style development on wild areas, except warmly to endorse the trend when occasionally touching on the topic.

His first major film success, however, had the immediate effect of countermanding the Tanganyikan colonial administration's proposed alteration of the Serengeti Reserve's boundaries to allow Masai cattle herders access to their former pastures, a move which would have cut across migratory routes of wild herds between Serengeti and the Ngorongoro Crater. Thenceforth, Grzimek looked upon Serengeti as something of his own creation.

In the early 1960s, two German developers, Sachs and Glees, aware of Tanzania's crying need for cheap meat supplies (where average total animal protein consumption is still estimated at less than two kilograms per head *per year*), set up a scheme to 'crop' surplus antelope (mainly Thompson's gazelles and gnus) and zebra spilling out of Serengeti's protection zone, to feed the country's undernourished people. It frequently happens, when human predation of wild herds is totally suppressed in restricted areas, that animals undergo a rapid 'population explosion', increasing in numbers until they destroy their own pastures before dying of starvation or associated diseases. In unrestricted natural conditions, emigration of surplus animals and the cyclical rise and fall of predation first described by the English amateur biologist David Lack, resolve the problem. But where 'protection' and the wider habitat where animals are tolerated are geographically limited, the sensible course seems (to advocates of utilization, at least) to crop or cull the 'overspill', with quotas of the off-take carefully measured to maintain optimum viable stocking of the protected area. This also prevents wild animals from spreading to become a competitive pest in lands used for other human purposes.

Sachs and Glees, sharing this opinion, started cropping meat in areas each side of the long, corridor-shaped park. Thinking further, they perceived possibilities of turning the meat into an export commodity (the German army, for instance, imported large consignments of canned game meat from Rhodesia at this time), and set up a small-scale field cannery to solve problems of transport and import controls. (Canned meat, sterilized during the canning process, is not subject to restrictions limiting fresh or deep-frozen meat imports in the rich countries.)

They had the canned products tested for taste and quality in Hamburg with impressive results. 'Blind' olfactory tests using a panel of ordinary consumers clearly showed a marked preference for gnu goulash or jellied zebra over a range of conventional canned meats bought in Hamburg's supermarkets.

Grzimek saw in this development a threat to his beloved Serengeti. Instead of interpreting it, as its supporters did, as an encouragement and motivation for Tanzanians to maintain and protect the fountain-head of this natural resource against the cattlemen's continuing pressure to take over the land, he had it stopped. The administrative 'mechanism' for doing so was simple enough. Serengeti had at this stage been given national park status. Sachs and Glees found, after some years of research, that the best area for cropping, permitting a constant off-take of carcasses as needed for continuous production of the cannery, lay on one side of the park. But the cannery, built in the early stages, lay on the other. Under national park regulations, possession of wild animals or anything deriving from them is absolutely prohibited within its confines. Although a special transit dispensation was sought – the only communication between cropping area and the plant being the national trunk road which crosses the park – and could have been made for such an officially approved, priority food-production project, none was forthcoming.

Similar scandalous neocolonialistic interference with Zambia's chosen use of its own resources, by another highly placed conservation-establishment figure, caused the far more expensive disruption and eventual abandonment of another major 'wildlife utilization' initiative a few years later. The Luangwa River drains the whole length of Zambia's eastern border, which runs along the watershed of a mountainous strip of country forming Malawi – the former Nyasaland – bounded in turn to the east by the 350-mile-long Lake Nyasa. The river then runs parallel to Zambia's south-eastern border with Maputo (formerly Mozambique). Rising near the triangular northern junction of Zambia's and Malawi's boundaries with that of Tanzania, it flows over 700 miles to join the waters of the mighty Zambesi at another triangular junction of boundaries in the south – this one those of the ancient Tete Province of Maputo with Zimbabwe.

Hardly a great stream as Africa measures her rivers, its catchment area was left untouched by colonial development. The Great North Road, fulfilling Cecil Rhodes's imperial dream of a route from Cape to Cairo, runs parallel to the river some 70 miles to the west, above the Muchinga Escarpment which forms the western boundary of the basin, carrying traffic from Lusaka to the Tanzanian border town of Mbeya, and on to Dar-es-Salaam or Nairobi. Criss-crossed by a network of smaller tributaries, and with most of its basin infested with tsetse flies, the Luangwa's well-watered alluvial plains were largely uninhabited, and game herds thrived when Livingstone passed through the neighbourhood about 1855. They continued to do so for the next century.

Since early colonial times, and particularly after the Second World War, the Luangwa Valley provided the Copperbelt, the rich mining complex in Zambia's north-eastern corner, plus Lusaka and other major population centres, with large supplies of game meat. Great herds of buffalo and elephant were common in the valley, and the river and its manifold tributaries echoed with the noise of a multitude of hippopotamuses. One of the first initiatives of the new Zambian post-Independence government was to try to rationalize their exploitation as a food source. This implied improving their butchering and transport to market to meet more acceptable standards. They therefore built a slaughterhouse in the valley to this end. Once it was set up, the project attracted support from FAO, mainly channelled through the Wildlife Section of its Forestry Division. Foreign loan capital was obtained to extend and equip the plant, and later, deep-freezing equipment was installed, and a 'cold chain' of stores and refrigerated trucks ensured that the produce was carried to its distant markets in desirable condition.

The main game areas of Luangwa Valley had by then been taken over as a national park. Within this tourists were conducted on 'walking safaris', an idea conceived by Norman Carr – a white hunter whose concession comprized all of the eastern half of Zambia. No hunting was allowed within the park of course, but Carr found ready demand for his tours from visitors prepared to walk all day and simply wonder at the animals around them. They were protected by an armed game-scout, and their baggage was transported from camp to camp by a team of 'boys' who took care of their needs and nourishment each evening.

The cropping scheme ran simultaneously, without much friction with game-viewing tourists. A separate road network was set up for the transport of carcasses, which were discreetly covered by tarpaulins. Care was taken to keep visitors away from the active cropping areas – not a difficult undertaking given the enormous area of the reserve. Animals were killed by various methods according to species being cropped, and were chosen purely for their efficiency as productive slaughter methods, no consideration being given to the sport hunter's sacred rules. Needless to add, all the shooters were professionals employed by the project. Thorough surveys were first made of existing animal stocks and their 'population dynamics', as the jargon has it. This latter is assessed usually by killing a sufficiently large cross-section of the animals present, establishing their age (through a study of tooth-wear, horn or tusk development and a number of other indicators) and dissecting their genitalia. Old scar tissue visible in the womb or ovaries of an adult female will show how many young she has borne; the presence or absence of motile sperm in the testicles will establish fertilizing capacity and age extremes of males. The experts thus established an accurate idea of breeding and survival rates, and drew up cautiously conservative shooting programmes, with large safety margins to allow for eventual miscalculations.

Hippopotamuses were shot in the water in daytime, when the huge submerged beasts surfaced briefly for air, by marksmen using telescopic sights. Showing a minute target for such a massive animal – a snorted plume of water vapour signalling the brief appearance of the black nose tip and the protruberant eyes, ears and vulnerable cranium – the telescope was necessary for accurate snap-shooting from a swivelling tripod rifle-rest. A disadvantage of the method is its lack of selectivity. The shooter, swinging towards the snort of exhalation, has little possibility of judging anything but the size of the quarry before firing, and no means of telling male from female from this target alone. A lactating female with a nursling submerged beneath her is indistinguishable from any other animal on this brief appearance, unless her offspring surfaces simultaneously, which fortunately, it usually does. Only long and careful study of positioning and drift of individuals in the herd before making attack can increase the shooter's chances of selecting a suitable adult. In practice, however, problems rarely arose from this cause.

On impact, the animal submerges instantaneously, and dies underwater. Cessation of eructation – a constant accompaniment of herbivores' digestive processes – causes rapid buildup of gas in the bowels, and after an interval of some 20–30 minutes, the inflated carcass floats to the surface. An awaiting dinghy or canoe, equipped with an outboard motor, would then tow it as rapidly as possible to the nearest low bank, for a tractor or truck to winch it aboard a flatbed trailer for the journey to the processing plant.

Buffalo, on the other hand, were shot at night from hides near their waterholes, with the aid of headlights. Disturbance caused by daytime shooting of buffaloes rendered survivors too wary to approach. Night shooting, on the other hand, troubles them much less, as long as they do not learn to associate the sight of men with gunfire and death. Indeed hunters have found that shooting from a hide or at night leaves survivors or succeeding herds of many species practically undisturbed, to the point that they will sometimes pass cadavers of their fellow creatures shot earlier – near a waterhole, for example – without trace of alarm.

Elephants present a very different problem. In the early stages of the scheme they were 'darted' with an immobilizing poison which left their flesh edible. Succinyl choline was used to incapacitate the great beasts, which were then winched aboard a flatbed truck, brought to the abattoir and dispatched by opening the jugular artery. The method was chosen as being more 'humane', and for causing less disturbance to remaining elephants than the sound of heavy gunfire would. The dart was a flighted hypodermic syringe activated by a heavy plunger, injecting its contents on impact. It was propelled by a very much smaller explosive charge than required by the large-calibre bullet, and consequently made much less noise. However, major disadvantages soon appeared with this method. It is difficult to approach a wary herd near enough to shoot the dart accurately, the range being limited to under 100 yards by the tiny charge employed. (A larger charge would smash the syringe, or cause it to discharge prematurely.) Furthermore, a successfully darted elephant will often travel for many miles, the drug taking 10 or 20 minutes to take effect. It will mix unidentifiably with the scattering herd in the process, so that the hunters may be confused as to which animal to follow. Worse still, unlike other gregarious species, elephants do not usually abandon a fallen member of the herd but, like the gorillas discussed in an earlier chapter, often gather to defend it, sometimes for hours, and attempting the while to raise it to its feet. To prepare an animal for butchering in such circumstances proved equally trying for the cropping team.

The worst disadvantage, however, lay in a sadly mistaken understanding of humaneness in slaughtering. For it was eventually pointed out to the experts that their chosen drug effectively immobilized or paralyzed the elephant, but left it fully conscious. It was quite evident to all participants in the operation that the helpless creatures were fully aware of what was happening to them from the moment of painful impact right through to being hoisted by heavy-duty crane and cables onto the abattoir's concrete floor.

Another avoidable error – committed despite the available experience of Ian Parker and others in Kenya – was to attempt culling individual animals from standing herds. Ten years earlier, Parker had contracted with the Kenya government to reduce the heavy over-stocking of Tsavo National Park, where 30,000 elephants confined to an area capable of safely carrying half that number were rapidly destroying their whole habitat. With human settlements on all sides, there was no possibility of expanding the park. The only alternatives were to let the herds continue their devastation until the number dropped dramatically in a massive mortality, as most of them starved to death, or to shoot the surplus. Parker soon discovered that shooting one or two selected elephants from each herd didn't achieve the massive reduction needed. Apart from upsetting the age and sex ratios of the herds, he found that even a single surviving elephant would, as he put it, 'spread the bad news to neighbouring herds, and spook out the whole country'. The solution was to choose separate family groups of up to eight or ten beasts, usually from the air. Using his black-painted Cessna, he tracked and drove them into the firing range of his waiting shooters, who then killed the lot. Immature animals died alongside their progenitors, there being no kindness in allowing defenceless creatures to starve or to die more savagely at the fangs of some other predator.

The economics of Parker's early operations, being organized under Game Department supervision on a commercial basis, were also extremely interesting. We will look at this aspect further – here, suffice it to say that they were anathema to the 'animal protectionist lobby'. Despite this, the Luangwa team were forced to adopt similar methods, and eventually achieved a satisfactory cropping level. Carcasses were delivered at the planned rate to the abattoir, and a fleet of trucks distributed frozen meat which was well received by consumers in urban and mining centres.

Initial problems having been largely eliminated, an eminent British visitor participated with his daughter in a Norman Carr 'walking safari'. Peter Scott is an ornithologist more widely reputed among the British public for his wildfowl sanctuaries than his knowledge of African elephant ecology or 'population dynamics'. He learnt of the cropping programme, and instantly decided the experts were all wrong. Son of a British national hero and personal friend of the royal hunting princes who founded and run WWF, Scott is himself an influential office holder in many bird and animal protection societies. He found ready access to the ears of Zambia's President Kenneth Kaunda and his ministers. A member of the British High Commission staff then in Lusaka told me of a meeting between Scott and Kaunda reported to him by a participant. Scott assured the President that unless elephant cropping was halted, he would personally make every effort – using his considerable influence with the media – to tell the world that 'when African countries achieve Independence, they first turn to wiping out the wild animals we have protected for so long'.

The project was immediately scaled down to a field-trial basis, despite the many years of experience already acquired and the millions of dollars invested. A sequence of FAO team managers fell foul of local authorities by defending the project too vigorously, were declared *persona non grata* and promptly deported. FAO soon realized the futility of struggling against such establishment machinations and withdrew. Within two years the costly installations, which Zambia is still paying for, had fallen into irretrievable ruin. Zambia turned to importing beef from secessionist Rhodesia for those of her countrymen who could afford to buy it, while elephant poaching boomed.

Zambia, like so many other impoverished former colonies, was left with trade patterns revolving around a single commodity – in this case copper. Richly endowed by nature with large, though finite, deposits of the metal, so essential to industrialized nations, the country's economy is dominated by their exploitation, and consequently by the international 'mafia' of brokers and bankers who deal in such commodities. During the wars of liberation on three sides – in Mozambique, Rhodesia and Angola – Zambia's copper exports were blocked by the interruption of her links with sea ports, a situation only slightly relieved by China's building the Tanzam Railroad to Dar-es-Salaam. The world price of copper climbed to a dizzy £1,500–1,600 per ton, while land-locked Zambia struggled against bankruptcy, with ever-mounting debts and accumulating interest to the international aid industry.

With the ending of these wars (at least on Zambia's southern borders) the copper flowed once more, and its price slumped. Worldwide depression shrank demand and, together with increased supply, this chased prices down to half what they had been. Zambia's economy approached collapse. The near-collapse of local food production followed, as currency was lacking to pay for the imported chemical fertilizers, pesticides and machinery to which this once-prosperous sector has become hopelessly addicted. The illegal ivory and game-meat trade flourished openly – becoming the country's most thriving and profitable activity as control services lapsed into despair and apathy, their salaries and supplies unpaid, and their vehicles and equipment falling into disrepair for lack of spare parts.

Ian Parker recently made a thorough study of the ivory trade, and points out quite reasonably:

> Today the . . . poacher can obtain 25–30 per cent of current market value for ivory ($74 per kilogram). A pair of 10 kilogram tusks will raise $370–$444. The minimum urban wage . . . is $45 a month, and rural wages are $26 a month. Thus in a week's work to get (kill or find) a pair of 10 kilogram elephant tusks a man stands to make the equivalent of 8–17 months wages.

He further suggests that contrary to the general impression, poachers receive far greater relative benefits from the trade than anyone else in the train of raw ivory traders. Thus laws depriving them of such a source of income inevitably cause general resentment. He continues:

> The leniency of sentences for poaching in Africa is a frequent source of conservationist complaint. In 1978 a Zambian poacher killed five elephants which produced ivory worth several thousand dollars, and was fined $154 . . . what is not taken into account in the complaints is that the fines are low through a general sympathy with the poacher.

In a despairing proposal to combat the Zambian poaching problem, one German veterinary development assistant working there at the time of the Luangwa scheme's final collapse, concluded that the only way to halt the massacre was to saw off their tusks. He had large supplies of surplus 'M99' – the morphine-based drug most generally used in the live capture of large animals not intended for slaughter – and proposed darting elephants as they approached maturity, and releasing the mutilated amputees to live out their lives without fear of ivory poachers. His argument quickly revealed its fallacy as he went on to calculate the value of the 'crop' of ivory and the 'residual' value of the stump which would continue to grow during the maimed creature's lifetime. This proposition – put forward in all seriousness – not only ignored elephants' normal use of their tusks and trunk for feeding, digging and various delicate manipulations, not to mention their use in defence or wrestling whereby they establish their place in the elephant 'hierarchy'; it demonstrated a lamentable ignorance (in someone officially engaged in the matter) of poachers' mentality and motives. For the latter, a tusk stump is, weight for weight, as attractive a proposition as a whole tooth – or even more so, the stump being the heavier part, and easier to secrete and smuggle than the whole – while the carcass and hide of the defenceless animal, perhaps easier to approach in safety, is still no mean attraction. The proposal, as idiotic as it was obscene, received short shrift from the Zambian authorities – although the veterinarian's masters in Bonn long toyed with the idea with interest, circulating it to interested enquirers as a potential solution to the poaching problem.

The latest news from Zambia is that in a desperate search for new food-producing lands in that hard-pressed country – once a prosperous exporter of agricultural produce – the Luangwa Valley is currently being sprayed with chemical insecticides in an attempt to wipe out the tsetse flies which have kept it green thus far. It is zoned by the development planners for settlement by mealie farmers (who produce the country's staple, maize). Other parts are planned as cattle production areas. Unfortunately for them, wild elephants, hippos and buffaloes mix comfortably with neither of these activities, and the demise of the survivors is assured. Scott's 'protection' of these once-mighty herds can truly be said to be taking effect.

Simultaneously with Parker's study of the ivory trade, another Kenyan elephant expert undertook a continental survey of Africa's remaining elephant stocks. Iain Douglas-Hamilton found that Zambia has in all some 150,000 elephants left (where by most informed estimates, they were numbered in millions in Livingstone's day). A count in the Luangwa Valley in October 1979 showed a 40 per cent reduction on the last count undertaken for the cropping scheme in 1972. He deems poaching the main cause of the decrease.

Factors of failure – signs of success

What then is the answer? The manifest bankruptcy of classic 'protectionist' conservation in a world where free animals and their lands are disappearing ever faster, and the history of failure haunting development aid's rare sponsorship of initiatives in what the jargon calls 'rational utilization', both raise the question of what (if anything) can be done in practice to stop the rot? Most aid fund controllers and other investors, even with the best will in the world, can be forgiven for viewing this history of expensive waste, ineptitude and emotional contention with sinking dismay, and for passing over proposals for more of the same in favour of less schismatic projects.

In regions enjoying less sophisticated food supply systems, meat indeed represents an effective extension of human resources. Its growth is an efficient way of converting the elements and life-force of the sun into human food. Grasslands unsuited to agrarian crops – or desirably left untrammelled by direct human intervention for any of several other excellent reasons – produce great quantities of vegetable food not directly conducive to human consumption. This resource is freely turned into human food by way of animals as 'primary converters'. As 'secondary converters', we and other predators obtain access in concentrated form to vast stores of natural nourishment.

We can profitably examine the deeper motivations of opponents of the concept of so using free creatures for our purposes, before looking at some internal causes for past failures, and finally, looking to a more hopeful future. Direct opposition stems most obviously from proponents of classical animal husbandry, as it has evolved today. Classic here includes the latest 'high technology' breeding methods, highly productive (at the cost of widespread animal suffering) in the expensive cash economies of the 'advanced' world, and currently being inflicted on poorer countries by the development aid lobby. 'Intermediate' or 'appropriate technology' groups also specifically advocate the introduction or extension of classic domesticants in their activities.

The reasons for this open opposition are clear cut. Wild animals represent competition with cattle and other livestock in several ways. They often reduce available forage, include or attract predators which can also threaten cattle, and carry a number of diseases to which they are immune or resistant themselves, but which can infect livestock, often fatally. More fundamentally and subtly, cattle development is based on the concept of property. The word 'cattle' can be traced back to mediaeval Latin's 'Capitale' and denotes property ownership. Nomadic pastoralists' livestock were correctly referred to in an earlier chapter as their 'capital-on-the-hoof'.

Wild animals on the other hand, are by definition no one's property – they are ownerless. Historically they have often been declared the exclusive property of the monarch and his nobility – the 'King's Game' – but in practice they have generally been treated as a common resource, belonging to none. The idea of investing in or developing a resource which is 'free for all' therefore runs counter to the aims of societies dedicated to property ownership and personal enrichment. This factor is equally apparent, incidentally, in the socialist or 'centrally-planned-economy' countries, the state taking on the status of monarch in this respect.

Another major factor in open opposition to development of wildlife utilization is to be found at official or administrative levels. Inheriting the whole panoply of monarchical prohibitions and restrictions, and indeed expanding these on previously laid down constitutional bases – including those deriving from the 'King's Game' concept – modern administrations (particularly post-colonial ones continuing their previous masters' legal systems) suffer from an ingrained conservatism and resistance to change. This produces administrative inertia (sometimes defined as 'masterly inactivity') when confronted with the need to review and modify the status of 'non-proprietary' animals. In contrast, cattle development can be quantified, forecast, and its short-term profitability estimated with reasonable assurance. Administrators invariably prefer a predictable, and hopefully favourable, 'bottom line'.

Internal causes contributing to past failures in wildlife utilization can often be found in the confusion of motives and aims. Utilization advocates and practitioners are most commonly ecologists, biologists, foresters, veterinarians, wildlife technicians, nature conservationists and the more engaged and ecologically aware administrators and functionaries – all imbued with a certain streak of romanticism. The majority see in 'utilization' primarily a method of *conserving* wild animals.

We have touched several times above on the trade jargon which has grown up around the field. The point of greatest importance here is that it embodies distortion or confusion of purpose, and can mislead fatally and expensively. Key words here are 'wild', 'nature' and 'ecology'. More confusion and contention has arisen through lack of perception of the true implications of these comprehensive concepts than any others in the field. 'Wild', in relation to animals, is used as synonymous, variously, with free, savage, indigenous or native, feral or endemic; and as antonym for tame, domestic, domesticated (the last two having different meanings), exotic, and farm animals. One even comes across such semantic make-shifts in the literature as 'domesticated wildlife' or 'wild domesticants', which reduce language to a state which only compounds confusion.

Having examined in detail several past failures, and mentioned in passing some successes, we should look at the reasons for the latter, as far as they are identifiable. The largest number and greatest scale of positive results have been achieved in South Africa, where several thousand farmers are breeding game animals commercially – mainly in the Transvaal but also several hundred in Natal, Cape Province and elsewhere. In all of these, success seems to have arisen out of a fortuitous combination of favourable circumstances, all serving self-interest. Conservation considerations were an incidental afterthought, despite the saving, through its commercial breeding, of one species – the ungainly bontebok, a pied sub-species of the dorcas gazelle *Damaliscus pygargus*.

Even the utilization success embodied in South Africa's national parks, regularly cropped for meat as well as live animals for relocation in more depleted reserves, cannot be considered devoid of an element of self-interest. Created as pure conservation zones, they (and all such designated areas) serve a practical purpose in terms of their 'alibi function'. This in effect enables developers and limitless-growth advocates to point to them as areas in which wild nature's interests are expensively catered for – and thereby deflect protest over their further depletion in the rest of the country. People are even encouraged to go and visit these areas in droves, to see for themselves small corners of this vast country (less than 1 per cent of its area is under such 'protection') still untouched, bringing devastation with them. A parallel sequence has occurred in North America, and is under way wherever natural areas of any economic potential remain to be consumed.

Australia offers further examples of commercially motivated 'utilization' success, although most of these hardly relate to *indigenous* wildlife. One third of the 'beef' exported by Northern Australia is in fact buffalo meat. This derives from feral or 'redomesticated' Asian buffaloes imported in the late nineteenth century as work animals, and later turned loose to run wild on the collapse of early development attempts in the region. They thrived and multiplied in the swampy tropical regions of northern Queensland and the Northern Territory, and after the Second World War a small local industry grew up around hunting for their meat and hides. More recently, their capture (by lasso-wielding cowboys riding cross-country motorcycles), redomestication and breeding for the same purposes have become more profitable than merely shooting them. Two government licenced slaughterhouses were set up for processing the meat for export, mainly to Japan.

Exotic ostriches were also profitably bred in Australia, until the First World War wiped out the greater part of this worldwide breeding industry with the collapse of the feather market. Indigenous emus are still farmed there on a small scale, for meat and eggs. Feral camels too are an exotic introduction – again first as a domestic work animal but later abandoned. Today they form the basis of a local industry, as they are hunted for the production of petfood.

Not only has the confusion of aims worked against the success of utilization initiatives, but an injudicious mixture of methods has reinforced the effect. Game viewing by animal-loving tourists obviously mixes poorly with efficient cropping – usually a bloody, noisy business at best. And the cost of a separate infrastructure of roads to transport carcasses, for example, adds a heavy burden to the finances of an experimental scheme sufficient to nullify any economic benefits such tourism may bring. A related problem in mixed schemes – and even in 'centrally planned' pure ones – lies in the question of who benefits from the proceeds? If mounted (usually as a *conservation* measure) to provide local people with motivation for maintaining wildlife in their lands, they serve little purpose if the profits – instead of benefitting the locals – end up contributing towards the costs of centralized administrations, or worse, in the pockets of the powerful in distant cities or abroad.

One pragmatic wildlife expert, reviewing an apparently promising utilization proposal, commented: 'It will only work if someone like a "hard-nosed" Texas cattleman could be brought in to run it.' Such a 'hard-nosed' approach involves systematically defining aims and priorities, and sticking to them. Main objectives can be: meat production (with other by-products); making a profit; earning 'hard' currency in countries with balance-of-payments problems; conservation or environmental protection; development of a tourist industry. Experience has shown that no scheme can satisfactorily achieve more than one of these aims – generally to the exclusion of the others except as incidental minor activities. Meat production requires narrower definition. Is it to be primarily for the hungry poor, the dispersed rural or concentrated urban slum populations, for the 'cash economy' markets or again, as an export commodity? Is the aim to use local meat supplies as substitute for imported meat in the richer markets, or is it to supplement this and increase meat consumption by broadening the choice available to those able to afford it? The answers to each set different conditions of financing, and differing parameters and standards for operations, processing and distribution, all of which can influence success or failure fundamentally.

Even the question of profitability, which may at first glance appear a clear-cut aim, requires examination in terms of objectives. The Henderson brothers in Rhodesia, for example, were primarily interested in economic returns from their land. In the event they found that while meat production, from both beef and wild animals, was profitable, bigger profits could be made by turning it over to 'safari' hunting – any meat produced then being purely incidental. Furthermore, combining tourism development and 'conservation' produces grave conflicts, often mutually destructive although in practice tourism usually wins the contest, largely destroying the environments it touches.

Some of these examples – the ostrich in particular – clearly demonstrate the danger of regarding utilization of wild animals as a conservation method without taking into account its underlying commercial background. However exotic the ostrich may have been as an introduced species in Australia, it is now extinct there. South African farmers in the Little Karoo district of the southern Cape Province now own what is probably the largest single assembly of these great birds on earth – around 100,000 of them. All of them are of exotic strain, incidentally. Having wiped out most indigenous ostriches by shooting them for their plumes, farmers stocked up with Syrian and North African birds when the feather market was booming at the turn of the century, these having commercially far more valuable feathers than the local strain. With the collapse of the market in 1914 the remnants of the latter were culled out, and their genotype has to all intents and purposes disappeared.

An example from another continent of the felicitous combination of circumstances and interests is the domestication of the capybara. Largest of the rodent family, this pig-sized amphibious hystricomorph is native to Central and South America, where it has been successfully farmed or ranched for decades, especially in Venezuela and neighbouring countries. Tony de Vos has reported that this 'elephantine guinea-pig' is four times better at converting grass into meat than cattle, and would be a better choice for exotic introductions for meat production (assuming that local species are not available) than the developer's usual preferences. The exploitation of such species, however, faces similar problems to those of any classic livestock species under similar conditions. Dangers inherent in injudicious insertion of any exotic species – 'wild' or domesticant – are always to be feared, and avoided wherever a locally indigenous alternative offers itself. Wild animals, even native species, often lose their natural tolerance of local diseases, particularly when shielded by husbandry from disease vectors. Introduced species can be hardy within their home range, but vulnerable to enzootics in new habitats – as King Leopold possibly discovered with his Asian elephants in the Congo.

A European example of exotic introduction for wildlife utilization, the Soviet Union's eland herd, has become inbred. The original small breeding stock not having been supplemented from external sources, the animals show signs of genetic deterioration, particularly in hereditary birth defects such as crippled hooves and twisted horns. Injection of a new 'bloodline' by importing a stud-bull eland from elsewhere would rapidly correct this however.

The illustration underlines the interest breeders ought to take in the preservation of genetic diversity of all species. The Russians might be encouraged to subsidize African countries preserving such species in the wild. One site for mutually profitable collaboration in initiatives of this kind could be Cameroon, where elands are still not uncommon in some limited areas, but are inadequately protected at present. Issues of such universal importance to human and beast alike should override political considerations, where these play a role.

A considerable advantage to be derived from using animals coming from wild stocks is the possible 'conservation effect', where preservation of the wild 'gene pool' becomes motivated by users' need to assure future sources of renewal and improvement. But as has been emphasized above, this neither makes an effective basis for success in utilization, nor does (or should) it constitute sufficient grounds for conservation of wildlife for its own sake. Gene pools or banks are well enough in their way – and the desirability of establishing and guarding them is in no way contested here – but they invariably fall into the hands of powerful agribusiness interests which control and manipulate our global food supplies (as has already happened in the plant world).

To sum up, practical utilization, where so intended, should be a commercial end in itself, with well defined, selected aims. It should be not encumbered with extraneous configurations, inappropriate restraints and justifications such as 'conservation of genetic stocks' or 'preservation of diversity' – or even conservation of land and landscape. It may achieve any or all of these, if this is at all possible, but only as incidental to its primary purpose.

Comparative limits

Before abandoning the difficulties which lie in the way of intensive use of wild creatures, another suggestion of Ian Parker's is worth mentioning. He advances the possibility that we may have long since domesticated all those creatures fitted for this process and for our purposes. Any animals not so used, however suitable they may appear superficially, may contain some 'hidden flaws' – some traits of character or biology inherent in the species – which render them unsuitable in practice. This interesting proposition – impossible to establish or disprove without undertaking test programmes of scope and duration beyond the capacity of any existing body in our present world – has nevertheless to be seen in the perspective of *purposes*. It is patently true, at least, that until very recent times – until the industrialized world's 'population explosion' and subsequent intolerable demands on global resources – our domestic animals fulfilled adequately all demands we placed upon them. But the world has shrunk. Now it is no longer possible for people in lands still disposing of vast spaces little touched by human demands, to partake so liberally of the food these produce. Wildlife hitherto enabling them to do so has come under attack from all sides, as have the lands themselves – from developers, consumers and, ironically, conservationists. The perceived need to domesticate new species should be seen in the light of altered circumstances in the global community. With changed parameters the suitability of species for such use also changes.

Parker himself warns – as does H.P. Ledger quoted earlier – of the trap of not comparing 'like with like'. In experimental stages of his first elephant cropping programmes, he once shipped ten tons of deep-frozen elephant meat to London's Smithfield meat-market – merely to show it could be done. Despite this, his early operations ran into considerable marketing difficulties, the Asian Nairobi butchers frequently failing to turn up with their trucks at agreed cropping sites, or arriving with too few or too small trucks to transport the agreed quantities. This led to a certain degree of waste and financial loss, since Parker's company had paid large advance royalties to the Kenyan government – £17,000 for the Tsavo scheme, in which the ivory was also handed over to the government – and planned to recoup this and other outlays from the sale of meat. In the event he was able to recoup these losses by selling the elephants' hides to the 'speciality' market. But as he points out, such 'speciality' sales offer no basis of comparison for assessing relative economics of elephant 'farming' and beef production, the products and their outlets being dissimilar.

Domestication for other than classic farming, transport or industrial purposes is commonplace in history. Some such uses can in fact be called classic within this context. Zoos and circuses have bred tamed animals and trained them practically at least since Roman times, their use for human purposes (however abhorrent to most modern taste) being clearly a 'domestic' one of economic motivation. Modern zoos' claims to the 'preservation of endangered species' are entirely specious, as John Perry, director of Washington's Smithsonian Zoo has pointed out lucidly and often. As stated earlier, they breed large quantities of more common, hardier species which will reproduce anywhere, but as far as rare wild creatures are concerned they have until today been the greatest single influence in their extermination – far greater in fact than any subsistence hunting, which attacks far easier targets.

Apart from the widespread 'classical' breeding of European game animals for restocking the squire's hunting preserves various countries have used their indigenous wild animals in ancient traditional ways, as well as in modern developments. In the central Asian plains the saiga deer (*Saiga tartarica* and *S. mongolica*) have been cropped for meat for centuries, their horns nowadays being ground for feeding to battery-farmed chickens. The horn is composed largely of chitin, necessary for the production of a good yellow egg yolk; free-ranging chickens obtain most of their requirements of this for themselves, from beetles and other creatures they find. And further east, China and Tibet have many intensive deer-breeding operations based on long tradition, main interest lying in the deers' antlers, which are sawn off when newly grown and still covered with 'velvet', for use in traditional human medicine.

In most 'Third World' countries, however, game meat production and distribution is generally ignored by development planners. They usually claim it is unimportant as a food source; and simultaneously, that there are no firm data to allow quantification and realistic costing of proposals, in order to forecast likely returns on investments. Eduard Neumaier of West Germany's GTZ (Agency for Technical Co-operation), a leading advocate of 'hard' chemical pesticide use to clear large areas of cattle diseases, recently wrote: 'The numbers of wild game in West Africa are so small that their usage for the local population is inconceivable.'

Hungry Africans' views of what constitutes edible or huntable 'game' are widely at variance with those of western hunting tradition. Rats, bats, reptiles and monkeys, birds of all kinds and even insects and their larvae, together provide West Africans with far more protein (and other nutrients) than more impressive big-game hunters' targets, although the latter are also eaten wherever they still exist. According to various estimates, from 20 per cent of total protein intake (including plant protein) in some cases, up to 60 per cent of animal protein consumed in others, comes from 'bushmeat' and fish (and most fishermen will consider themselves lucky if they chance to catch a manatee or a crocodile). In hunter-gatherer people such as the bushmen or pygmies, this figure can reach 100 per cent.

Traditionally, before slave traders and other colonialists forced Africa's entry into the 'market economy', hunting was effectively controlled by customary restrictions – closed seasons and reservation of hunting rights in particular areas, with a share of the 'bag' for the rights-holders – and by the 'cost benefit' dynamics of hunting effort in relation to hunting success discussed in an earlier chapter. When all easily huntable species have become rare the hunter will turn to fresh areas. Surviving members of reduced species will rapidly repopulate their former habitat, either by breeding up from survivors' stocks or by immigration. In this way, an ecological equilibrium was maintained by wildlife stocks in relation to human populations using them for food.

Planned attempts at wildlife cropping usually aim for a more constant yield, around the optimum production rate of the ecosystem. But modern hunting of 'bushmeat' is rarely based on rational planning – mainly because of the colonial inheritance of laws prohibiting most native hunting to preserve game stocks for the colonial ruling class. These laws were taken over uncritically by newly independent Africa, and most countries apply them as before, under the pressure and encouragement of western animal-loving and nature-conservation groups. Indeed, many of the latter appear to find virtue in the preservation of wilderness for its own sake, at whatever cost to the local inhabitants.

In planned developments the bottleneck, as we have seen, is often marketing. In the earliest attempts before the First World War, meat marketing standards of hygiene were not particularly stringent, where they existed at all in the colonial countries. Marketing of game meat was no more 'bedevilled' with sanitary regulations than was marketing the butcher's more conventional products. But increasingly since the Second World War, public health authorities have raised standards of slaughter-house practice and marketing to the point where field-shot game would constitute a risk of contamination if marketed together with butchery produce.

Advanced countries have developed separate game marketing systems (often combining game and poultry marketing), while in most of Africa game meat marketing has grown up entirely in the informal sector. Furthermore this informality, coupled with the fact that much of the produce starts through the system in contravention of wildlife protection and hunting control laws, means that authorities and developers usually prefer to turn a blind eye to this sector. The inevitable result is the present dearth of official statistics about game meat production and consumption, and about the market value of what meat is commercially traded. Several African institutes are currently planning to fill this gap. UNCTAD-GATT's International Trade Centre is surveying the advanced countries' game-meat trade, and potential export markets for 'Third World' game-meat products. This led to the planning of an inter-university study aimed at surveying regional West African markets and an inventory and assessment of actual and potential production.

This initiative is a more constructive response to West African meat supply problems than that of many conservationists, who also express widespread public concern about side-effects (in terms of human health and environmental dangers) of most disease eradication being undertaken today. Using hazardous chemical weapons these massive operations cost West African taxpayers enormous sums, with little guarantee of success as experience has shown. They also create an inevitable obligation – should these campaigns meet with any success – to export the produce in order to earn currency to pay for it all. Critics of such developments generally tend to be negative or restrictive in their approach. Most often they wish to stop harmful actions.

The inter-university group's viewpoint takes a more constructive line: it aims to provide a factual basis for the development of viable and ecologically desirable alternative meat sources. Not intended as substitutes for existing traditional animal husbandry, nor for its improvement within present geographical limits (potential for improvement is certainly still far from exhausted), it is aimed at supplementary meat sources and methods of using areas not traditionally consecrated to commercial meat production for various reasons.

The institutes taking part cover three aspects which rational control of game-meat production and marketing demands. The Inter-State School of Veterinary Medicine and Science of Dakar is examining hygienic and animal health aspects of the trade. The Garoua Wildlife School in Cameroons trains game and wildlife department officials. Its director, Andrew Allo, has a long-standing interest in domestication of various indigenous species for the purpose of commercial meat production. Garoua's special interest is in the administrative side of regulation of the game-meat production and marketing sector. The Wildlife Management Department of Ibadan University's Forest Resources Faculty has previously carried out several local studies in this area, and is West Africa's leading centre of expertise in practical utilization, headed as it is by Sunday Ajayi whose large-scale experimental domestication of edible giant rats – a much appreciated delicacy sometimes available even in Ibadan's Senior Staff Club restaurant – aimed at providing Nigerian villagers with a method of breeding these cat-sized creatures for home consumption.

Despite critics' claims, much data already exists on the trade and consumption of meat from wild animals in East, Central and

Southern Africa. In West Africa such studies as have been made only examine local markets, and are unco-ordinated and diffuse. The regional survey will assemble and amplify these on a standard base, and provide an effective first step towards countering utilization opponents' more materialistic arguments. As Professor Ahmed Lamine Ndiaye has said:

> This inventory will make it possible to draw conclusions capable of correcting numerous errors which have been made. Apart from this, it will permit the definition of the potential of production of meat which the wildlife of Africa represents, and so constitute a sound basis for the elaboration of viable projects in this domain.

Conceptual confusion

The true root of confusion lies in our attitudes towards an important spectrum of essential components of our living world. We define them as 'pests'. The concept pest – and its plant-world counterpart 'weed' – is one of civilized human creation. Essentially, pests are non-human members of the natural order in places where people do not want them to be, in quantities we find intolerable, and which conflict with our material interests or comfort. Pests can be anything – from the familiar range of insects (mosquitoes and midges, tsetse and house-flies, wasps and hornets, ants and termites, moths and the larvae of butterflies when they are eating our cabbages) through a range of small mammals and birds to such larger animals as lions, leopards, zebras, buffaloes or indeed, most game animals.

Pests have existed only for as long as human societies have concentrated on specialization. For people unaccustomed to 'civilized' comfort and protection, such irritants are part of the natural order of things, not recognized as vectors of disease or avoidable nuisances. When early farming began to cause the first stages of desertification (human activity having influenced or extended most desert areas), creatures previously living off the vanishing 'bush' turned to people's crops, and thrived on the rich pastures they found there; the first locust swarms and other 'biblical' pests began to plague us.

The process of civilization's creation of pests can still be observed today. The quelea, a sparrow-sized weaver bird nesting in vast colonies throughout the Sahel, normally forages for its preferred food in the semi-desert scrub. As this is destroyed by overgrazing (fostered by 'development') the quelea's natural food goes too, and flocks numbering tens of thousands descend, *faut-de-mieux*, upon neighbouring crops, driven there by our destruction of their natural food resources. FAO and the petrochemical industry have recently 'declared war' (the military terminology is of their own choosing) on the quelea. They deploy the whole horrifying range of military technology against them and their nesting colonies, including aerial bombing with high explosives, napalm and chemical poisons, and biological weapons, in a futile attempt to reduce their number.

The same alliance declared war too on a whole range of other wild species which disturbance of the natural 'ecosystem' has turned into dangerous or expensive hindrances to people's civilized purposes. We have already discussed the tsetse fly and the production of resistant strains of mosquitoes and consequent spread of malaria epidemics through misapplication of pesticides. But locusts, termites, rats, mice, voles, moles, badgers, coyotes, jackals, dingoes, kangaroos, rabbits, foxes, stoats and weasels – and any carriers of rabies, which can range from bats to hedgehogs, or even cows – have all come under concerted attack at some time, and survived. It would almost seem, on attempting to compile even the most summary list, that anything and everything has once qualified for our condemnation, and attempted extermination.

Chaffinches in Europe are currently undergoing a transformation similar to that of the quelea – from tolerated or even welcome birds to pests – though in this case through greater availability of preferred food supplies rather than their destruction. Bird protection laws and the poisoning of their predators (especially sparrow-hawks and other raptors) have caused their numbers to increase remarkably. But their pest status among fruit growers has developed as a result of monoculture of certain varieties of apples. In old-fashioned mixed orchards chaffinch damage to fruit was limited to certain trees, and the farmer harvested most of his crop. In modern orchards a single hybrid variety is usually grown, and the birds find a feast. Starlings are another European bird passing through a similar transition. Much vitriolic ink has been spilled on the subject of Italian bird hunters whose activities add many small birds to their autumnal menus. Such attacks – often perverse and erroneous – fall wide of the mark, and indeed are aimed at the wrong targets.

Dr E. Gwinner of the Max Planck Institute's ornithological research station at Radolfzell near Lake Constance, demonstrated with maps of established migratory routes and patterns that the network these form, when various species' routes are plotted, largely avoids Italy in any case. Far more of our northern visitors pass over southern France and Spain, or else over Greece and the Aegean Islands to Turkey, Asia Minor and East Africa. In all these areas, birds are seasonally shot, trapped or netted in far greater numbers than in Italy – yet the Italian hunter has to bear the main brunt of North Europe's bird-loving reproaches. In reality the Italians' attack on migratory species has a limited impact, the season of autumnal overflight being brief. Today's two million or more Italian hunters certainly make no more impact on migratory flock numbers than did their forefathers – practically all of whom enjoyed the sport in ruder days. The birds have continued to return, year after year over the millennia, indeed in increasing numbers of late. Gwinner says for instance that nightingales are noticeably on the increase. Cuckoos are certainly much more common in recent years.

The last two are both solitary birds, however, while the bird hunter's 'bag' is filled with gregarious species migrating in flocks. Estimates have been made that in many species of these, only ten per cent of individuals leaving their summer breeding grounds survive the round trip to breed again the following year. They fall victims to a wide range of natural perils, from storms and unfavourable winds (leading to exhaustion and starvation) to the natural enemies lying in wait to pick off weaker stragglers. The whole 'winnowing' process demonstrates the natural law of 'survival of the fittest', and the hail of hunter's shot (or even his fine strung nets) is more likely on average to take its greatest toll on failing, exhausted creatures unlikely to survive the long, hazardous journey rather than the fittest and fullest of strength.

Far more deadly is the assault – unintended but not unremarked upon – of development aid's pesticide spraying exterminators on the birds' wintering quarters. For here the few survivors of the outward journey die in their thousands from eating poisoned plants and insects. Those which do not succumb to these hazards, return the following spring with an accumulated load of deadly chemicals stored in their body-fat which reduce their breeding ability, and even kill them outright as they burn up their own poisoned energy reserves under the stress of long-distance flight or brooding.

Having emphasized sufficiently my own opposition to killing for pleasure, be it song birds or elephant – or even intensively raised pigs and poultry – it seems to me more probable that two million Italian hunters (and a similar proportion of all western populations along the migration routes) will more easily be brought to share my present view by reasoned persuasion, rather than by shrill and bitter polemic. Concerned people everywhere would do better to turn their efforts towards forcing through legislation (and assuring its enforcement) to prohibit our industrial and commercial interests from destroying animals and habitats for their own short-term private profit, and from producing and dumping in more defenceless lands the evil products we are wise enough to prevent them using at home. As for the pests these agencies claim to combat – and in reality, create or aggravate – they are usually better regarded as a resource within a system. At the simplest level, creatures like locusts and termites can be (and often are) consumed in many places. In Uganda, each termitarium has its designated 'owner', who takes a crop twice a year, the land on which it stands producing twice as much edible protein in this way than it would through cattle. The quelea could be netted in flocks, as are European migratory birds. And even 'pests' like the tsetse fly serve to protect certain habitats from inappropriate human encroachment, and thus protect another food resource, and ultimately our whole environment.

Mankind's oldest relationship with animals was symbiotic, and basically it has not changed today. To the extent that other living forms, of any sort, impinged on our interests, they could be considered as competition; symbiosis on the other hand occurred when our fellow creatures and plants offered some advantage to our survival and development purposes. In a more generalized sense, symbiosis occurred where the rest of the natural world – neither of direct use nor offering any discernable threat – merely shared and formed part of the range of ecosystems which constitute our global environment.

The highest degree of direct use, as also the most manifest degree of direct menace, was offered in the main by the most highly evolved members of the natural order. Mankind's domination of the latter, and the development of our influence in creating or modifying environments, commenced with our acquiring mastery over the most practically useful life forms sharing them, while at the same time acquiring effective defences against those offering visible menace. Modern science or technology has little of value to add to this developmental process, and when profit alone rules their end effects are inevitably negative.

I am reminded of a slogan proposed by Lee Talbot, recently sacked as head of the IUCN as a result of the intrigues of the animal-lovers' lobby which controls the World Wildlife Fund, paymaster of IUCN. Defining the shift of policy he tried to introduce into that august, arch-conservative body of nature protectionists under his short-lived leadership, he accepted as inevitable the continuation of 'development' as such; the main thrust of his reasoning – which is that of many other enlightened conservationists – was that such development should be redirected to take into account its impact upon our environment, and where this was seen to be unacceptably negative, to modify it through the efforts of the development planners themselves. As he put it: 'If we can't beat them, we must get them to join us.' A variation on this suggests itself in relation to pest control: 'If you can't beat them – eat them.'

9. Beating the system

It is the whiteman's burden,
As everybody knows,
To teach the black to feel ashamed
And then to sell him clothes.

Graham Laidler ('Pont') in *Punch*, 1939

It is the whiteman's burden,
It cannot be gainsaid,
To steal the Black's materials
And then to give him aid.

Geoffrey Rowell in the 'Bull's Head', 1981

This book has looked in some depth at a few of the negative aspects of development aid, which is its central theme. There are a multitude of others – both of negative aspects hardly touched on here, and of examples from every part of the 'Third World' – but a compendium of them all would not only require a work of unmanageable size, but would also make an unbearably depressing reading. (As mentioned previously, Curry-Lindahl's 1979 report to the Swedish government on the ecological damage produced by its development aid runs to 500 pages.) The examples given here are reasonably typical of what is happening throughout the world-wide development aid industry; the flaws that lie at the basis of operations like those described here are general, and at the root of much of the damage being done. Must it always go wrong? Is there really nothing that we can do – for each other?

Before even suggesting an answer, I must first repeat once more the caveat which was interposed at several earlier points in these pages. While remaining extremely critical and dubious about the intentions as well as the effects of the vast majority of projects and programmes which our masters label as aid, nothing I have written anywhere in this book should be taken to imply anything other than the greatest respect, and admiration, for the commitment, generosity and goodwill of people advocating – and actively extending – the offer of a helping hand to those in need. The fact that such genuine goodwill has become institutionalized, and misappropriated for sinister purposes, does not detract in the least from the generosity of their intentions; it merely magnifies the guilt of those with the power to effect the malversation of such benevolence.

Perhaps, by the nature of the system and of institutions modelled on a hierarchy of power, it cannot be otherwise. But even this does not mean that it is impossible to help. In the meanwhile, let me give a concrete example – again the story of an individual, given here as an indicator of direction rather than the 'model' for which most linear-thinking aiders search so desperately. It points to one of the most promising ways I have yet seen of overcoming the 'North-South' *impasse*. For all its faults (mighty as these may be), the 'North' (or 'West') has something of value to offer to the 'South' – as a small measure of compensation for the immense wealth it drains from the defenceless 'Third World' lands. Having so frequently turned to Africa in quoting the negative sides of the aid effort, let us stay in that continent for this final example. We turn again to Ghana.

Fraud of freedom

It is necessary still to depict more of the depressing historical background of recent developments there, in order to give a truer perspective of the inestimable value of this small initiative. We touched in earlier chapters on the problems of Ghana's cocoa farmers, lake fishermen and meat producers. But for all those who knew Ghana, in its heyday of freedom from colonial rule in 1957, the country today presents a sorry spectacle. For gone is the music and the laughter, gone the carefree confidence that a new and better world was about to open a cornucopia of riches to accompany the long-sought Independence. The exaggerated and often naive expectations and hopes which were awaited by those who chanted 'Free-dom! Free-dom!' to greet 'Verandah-Boy' Kwame Nkrumah wherever he appeared in the Gold Coast that turbulent year, were inevitably doomed to disappointment. Some of the more ambitious or innocent hopes of immediate results, held by many unsophisticated Gold Coasters, were documented at the time by Henry Thompson, a former editor of *Drum* magazine and one of the most brilliant and objective journalists of Nkrumah's Ghana.

These pre-independence dreams ranged from the notion that the police force and the army – both institutions of the colonial power – would be disbanded forthwith; through such glowing expectations (and the rumour was widely believed) that fares on railway and bus services (run by colonial administrators) would be abolished; down to the nice calculation that, with so many thousands of white civil servants and expatriate traders to be thrown precipitately out on the country's attaining freedom, their inflated emoluments would be collected into a national 'kitty' and divvied up annually as a stipend for all free Ghanaians. Good (if wishful) thinking, perhaps, but unavoidably due for disillusionment in the harsh reality of the post-independence world.

Thompson's survey never saw print, being considered too tendentious for publication in his South African-owned paper. Moreover, his outspoken dedication to truth, coupled with his remorseless public exposure of what he saw as the dangers of Nkrumah's incipient megalomania, eventually led to a clash with 'Osagyefo' (The Redeemer) and his disciples in the political arena, as Thompson helped to found a united opposition party to oppose Nkrumah's plans. This ended dangerously, with a murderous attempt to silence him permanently (to which I was a witness), and finally, eight years of imprisonment in Nkrumah's infamous political jails. He was released when the military first took over power – wiping out 'Osagyefo's' Russian bodyguards in the process, as they attempted to hold the fort for their master, who was away on a state visit to Hanoi at the time (1966).

At this stage the army had no intention of ruling permanently. A junta of military and police, headed first by General E.K. Kotoka (his name is commemorated in that of Accra's international airport) and later, after his death in 1967, by Generals Afrifa and Ankrah, merely sought to end Nkrumah's excesses – both economic and political. They had inherited a situation of near bankruptcy, mainly the result of Nkrumah's grandiose plans to turn Ghana overnight into a westernized industrial power. Abandoning his leftward-leaning central planning policies, the junta opened the country's doors to all comers, unleashing a free-for-all surge of highly speculative short-term investment which effectively mortgaged any uncommitted resources remaining in the land. The ensuing goldrush – almost of Klondike proportions – included Lonrho's successful takeover of the Ashanti Goldfields' Obuasi goldmine, said to be the richest in the world, and a long-standing bone of contention between Nkrumah and its former imperialist owners. This shady, shabby deal was shepherded through the official controlling services and ministerial approvals by R.S. Amegashi, a West Coast dealer and 'fixer' of uncertain nationality who was nevertheless Commissioner for Ghana's Lands and Mineral Resources. Having pulled off this profitable deal, he left the ministry to become Lonrho's right-hand man and chief representative in Ghana – an appointment which was certainly as rewarding as the chain of luxury restaurants he runs all along the West Coast.

The Lonrho takeover did not go through without some popular resistance, despite the good offices of Mr Amegashi. It was opposed by miners' strikes – which were broken by police bullets leaving at least three dead and 28 wounded – and by a series of legal actions, which were eventually settled fairly inexpensively out-of-court with the aid of Lonrho's 'fixer'.

In 1969 the military handed power back to a civilian government, headed by a former sociology professor at London University, Kofi Busia, following an election during which the left wing was excluded from campaigning or voting. Busia was even more friendly towards foreign investors than his military predecessors, and leaned heavily on British aid in trying to cope with the massive debt he inherited. Despite this, the debts grew by leaps and bounds during his tenure of office.

Then, as now, cocoa exports represented over 60 per cent of Ghana's foreign currency earnings. In 1971 the cocoa price offered by the western agribusiness commodity markets plummeted. With this, the widespread corruption and open nepotism of the Busia regime became an intolerable burden on the ordinary Ghanaian, whose standard of living had suffered a continuous, vertiginous plunge since the boom year of Independence. With general popular support – and following a wave of nostalgia for the 'good old days' of Nkrumah – the military intervened once more, this time as a junta of 'young Turk' officers of middle rank, headed by the Ashanti Ignatius Kutu Acheampong, then a colonel. They inherited an economy staggering under a burden of long-term external debt amounting to almost $700 million, and immediately due short-term debts of around $300 million – this figure including interest payments alone of some $60 million a year. And this, as it happened, was one of the few good years the country has had in the past three decades, which was even able to show a small balance-of-payments surplus – largely a result of the US monetary authorities' decision to 'free' the previously fixed gold price, which then rocketed around the world with some small benefit to producers like Ghana. These were, however, the last surpluses that the country was to see.

One of Acheampong's first moves, after condemning eight leading opponents to death and jailing most of Busia's ministers pending investigation of their speculations, included an initial attempt to disclaim the previous regime's more fraudulently incurred debts (an attempt which was briskly slapped down by Ghana's 'aid-dispensing' creditors in the West). His early initiatives were very well received by the population, even when they involved a programme of austerity – belt-tightening as regards imports, diligence in exporting whatever the country could sell abroad, and above all striving for self-sufficiency in food production, in pursuit of national autonomy.

In exemplary mood, Acheampong and his ruling colleagues took to travelling in a fleet of Peugeot 504s, instead of the more customary luxury of ministerial Mercedes Benzes. A trivial gesture, perhaps, but taken all in all, the country and its friends began to hope that a way out of the vicious circle of indebtedness and poverty might at last be distantly in sight. Then came the 'oil crisis'.

Starch and sedition

Contrary to the popular mythology among most development economists, outside Ghana as much as within, this did not have very much *direct* effect on the country's balance of payments. Compared to its neighbouring countries which do not benefit from such 'grandiose follies' as Nkrumah's Akosombo hydro-electric dam, Ghana imports a relatively limited proportion of its energy requirements. Furthermore, the impact of corresponding price-hikes for petrochemical-based fertilizers was to a very large extent offset by the phenomenon of an 'overproportional' increase in agricultural productivity by any application of 'artificials' in fertilizer-starved Ghanaian peasant farming (as compared to the marginal effect of such increased inputs in 'high-tech' farming areas). Thus any increase in domestic food production resulting from the more expensive chemical imports would have more than substituted for the food imports (running at $25 million a year then) whose price was far more severely affected by the petroleum price – as indeed was the clandestine intention of the petroleum company cartel which organized the whole 'oil crisis' charade. (There was in reality no oil shortage in 1973, nor any other year; the mighty oil company cabal merely needed, and so created, an excuse for quadrupling the prices of its products. Indeed, when it is borne in mind that the cost of crude oil accounts for only ten per cent of the cost of petrol in your tank, the rest being absorbed by transport, refining, marketing and delivery costs, not to mention taxes, then it becomes abundantly clear to what extent this is true.)

Indirectly, however, Ghana's economy was hard hit by the inflation of manufactured import prices, which the industrialized world not only passed on to their captive 'Third World' markets, but even tried doubly to inflate, in order to minimize increases on their shrinking domestic markets. The ruling military junta could offer nothing against this worldwide movement other than clamping down even harder on imported manufactures and consumer goods, cutting down food imports (mostly meat and animal products), and exhorting even harder the raising of domestic food production. For a time, such campaigns as 'Operation Feed Yourself' were remarkably successful, at one point eliminating the need to import starchy staple foods such as maize and rice. But the regime also adopted the all too common and usually mistaken expedient of trying to hold down food prices artificially, by imposing official controls. As so often happens, this merely created a disincentive for food production – particularly among smaller farmers around the subsistence level – while encouraging larger-scale farmers to sell their produce abroad, usually illegally, as it was smuggled over frontiers with the connivance of border officials and suitably 'dashed' customs services.

Such policies are designed to appease the clamorous and powerful pressure groups constituted by the concentrated urban masses – the poor slum-dwellers and unemployed among them – at the expense of the even more destitute but spatially dispersed (and therefore voiceless and politically impotent) rural population, who are the prime producers of the country's wealth. The result was to create major food shortages throughout the land. A rudimentary, inefficient and inequitable rationing system of essential foodstuffs failed to make any impact on the problem, except to ensure the diversion of what food was available to a thriving black market open to those who could pay – and also to open further wide avenues of profitable corruption to the functionaries charged with its administration.

After six years or more of such austerity, grinding poverty, mismanagement and open corruption, the inevitable result was the final evaporation of any remaining good will Acheampong's regime may have enjoyed. Having promoted himself in the meantime to the rank of general, the Chairman's personal popularity had by then plunged to the point where he found it advisable to abandon his '504' for a bullet-proof Mercedes Benz.

His zeal for rooting out corruption had diminished equally. By 1977 the whole of the military junta had succumbed to the temptation to ensure a comfortable retirement through a little private enterprise – perhaps understandable in view of the likely cancellation of their military pensions in the event of an overthrow. In that year an American financial adviser in Accra claimed that at least one third of Ghana's total foreign currency earnings never reached the country, but was being creamed off into bank accounts in London and Zurich held by these officers and gentlemen, or else by their ladies. (As a result of indiscreetly mentioning his discovery, the US official was promptly declared *persona non grata* and shipped off home.)

To add to this financial drain – estimated by the Americans at over $300 million a year – which was bleeding the country white, the final nail in Acheampong's coffin was provided by the weather. For to top off the misery, the monsoon rains of 1977 failed completely in the northern provinces, where famine and starvation replaced the general food shortages. And this in one of the potentially richest and agriculturally most productive lands of the tropical world. The despairing populace was by this time being held down by military force. Widespread strikes and agitation, and the approaching collapse of public order, led to arbitrary dismissals of prominent dissenting civil servants, mass arrests and treason trials of the most outspoken opposition leaders. The universities were closed, after a students' strike at the instigation of Ghana's Professional Bodies Association.

Responding to the government's closure of the universities, these middle class professionals then joined the students' strike in a display of elitist agitation which they hoped would awaken mass support from the trade unions and the country at large. The dismal lack of response from the people, and virtual absence of any trace of solidarity on the part of the trade unions, were not so much their expression of any divergent view of the regime; it was rather an indication of the yawning gap between rich and privileged professionals (among whom Ghanaian students already count themselves) and the working (or would-be working) classes and small traders. The latter generally regard such 'upper-crust' cavorting as a private pantomime, played out among the powerful to decide who will rule over and exploit them next.

With such a disparity of opposing interests and forces, it became clear to both the regime and most of its opponents that a parliamentary system of government based on anything resembling the Westminster model – such as the British had imposed on newborn Ghana – could not have the slightest relevance in confronting the country's problems.

No way to win

In an effort to keep the economy from total collapse, by attempting hopefully to repair the country's disunity, alienation and total disillusionment, the Supreme Military Council (as the junta called itself) offered a plebiscite on a form of Union Government, with power to be shared by the army, the police, and elected representatives of the people – in that order. Only some two million of the twelve million inhabitants bothered to turn out, slightly more than half of whom voted in favour of the governing SMC's proposal – corresponding roughly to the number in government employment in the country and their families.

By this time the junta was living in increasing isolation in the army headquarters at Burma Camp or the ancient colonial Christiansburg, the former residence of British and Danish governors. Their contacts with the outside world were practically limited to senior functionaries and visiting diplomats, and infighting among them inevitably grew with their growing insecurity. For they were well aware that their figurehead leader Acheampong was becoming an increasing liability. Insiders with access to the Burma Camp were at this stage convinced that he would willingly have relinquished power, if he could safely have done so. He even attempted to leave for a holiday in London with his family, to tend his bank accounts. His colleagues on the SMC refused to let him leave the country, suspecting him of hoping to achieve a 'Gowon' solution to his problems. (His former counterpart from Nigeria succeeded in escaping from his eminent office by a similar flight, and settled in England with the connivance of the British government to live and study in comfort, while several subsequent rulers were duly overthrown or assassinated, until one more favourable to his return to his homeland came to power.)

Throughout this period the International Monetary Fund, worried about the prospects of Ghana ever being able to pay its astronomical debts, repeatedly pressed for a loosening of restrictions on foreign investment and a drastic devaluation of the local currency – IMF's standard formula for dealing with the problems of poverty. In 1978 the SMC yielded, and sacked Acheampong to replace him by another of their number, General Fred Akuffo. This was, however, too little and too late in the way of a change. By June of the following year, a new and vital revolutionary force appeared on the scene, in the person of Ghana's present leader. Then a 32-year-old Flight Lieutenant in Ghana's airforce, Jerry Rawlings headed a new group of the military which, utterly sick of the spectacle of depravity of their national pride engendered by their seniors, carried out a further brisk putsch and bundled the whole boiling into jail. Within two months, Rawlings had caused eight of the most heinous to pay for their crimes before a firing squad (although lacking the courage to mete out the same fate to any of the Levantine and European businessmen of Accra who inspired and largely financed their corruption), carried through a general election, and handed over power once more to an elected civilian government.

Inexperienced in the ways of power and its effects upon people, he was bitterly disappointed by the results of his idealistic attempts to reform the democratic process by draconian example. The new head of state, Hilla Limann, backed by another university professor as vice-president, the eponymously named de Graft Johnson, engaged in a spree of graft and spending to make that of the Busia regime pale in comparison. One of their first acts was to rusticate Rawlings, sacking him from the airforce – a step which he accepted as unavoidable if the new rulers were to be given a chance to show their paces. After less than two years, the disastrous speed with which they set about Ghana's final ruin was more than he could stomach, and on New Year's Eve of 1981 he was obliged to repeat the process, and take over once more.

Since then the change in Ghana has been deeply refreshing for all those of good will who care in the least for the future of this great-hearted land. Space here, and the time Rawlings has yet had to effect change, precludes me from saying more at this point than that he has, undoubtedly, restored hope to the country, and its faith in an indomitable ability to climb out of the morass by the people's own efforts. To this end he has renounced 'aid', as it is offered by the 'North', and has inspired his admiring people to seek their own autonomy through self-sufficiency. Only time will tell if he – and they – will be allowed to complete this forbidding task.

In Nkrumah's laughing, balmy days, the red dust roads of Ghana were boisterously navigated by a colourful fleet of 'mammy lorries' or 'trotros' – Bedford J1-type truck chassis with locally built wooden bodywork, which formed the principal public transport system of West Africa at the time. Each of these was decorated with a personal slogan, a beautifully lettered statement of the 'trotro' owner's or driver's view of life or in commemoration of some happy event – and often containing a cryptic *double-entendre*. Most of these excellent and highly adapted vehicles have disappeared today, victims of the kind of 'development' which replaced an important indigenous coach-building industry with ready-made 'minibuses' imported with all their built-in obsolescence from the rich industrial world. But some of the more famous slogans (*Still Christians Leading; One Man No Chop; No Time To Die*) still survive – if only in the memory of an aging generation.

Little is possible

This then was the scene, at the height of Acheampong's power and in the middle of one of the worst droughts in living memory in the Sahel, just over Ghana's northern border, into which appeared a remarkable couple and their children. Johan Spee is a Dutch peasant, coming from generations of peasant forefathers. He left school at 13, to work first on his father's farm and then on his own. His wife Ada, also of rural stock and a woman of equal resource, is a trained sociologist; Johan's own further education and considerable culture were acquired by self-teaching. They have a daughter, Tineke, still studying, and an older son, Maarten, who is handicapped and works with his father. In 1974 Johan Spee was practically self-sufficient as farmer of two and a half hectares of rich Dutch land, which supported his family and a small herd of white goats, the milk of which also provided them with cheese in sufficient abundance for him to be able to sell the surplus, in order to pay for the clothing, tools and other articles they could not make themselves. Having heard so much in the Dutch media about the hardships being suffered by the Sahelian drought victims, they decided to go and see what they could do about it.

After a first look around Ghana, during which the Spees found a promising site in the northern village of Dibuyiri, not far from the border with Upper Volta, they returned to Holland to collect their goats. With 20 pregnant white nanny-goats packed in specially made crates, and a little financial support from a small private group of friends and acquaintances, they all set off again the following year.

The village chief at Dibuyiri was delighted to accede to Spee's request for a couple of acres of land to start farming. He had recent memories of a now-defunct German agricultural project in his neighbourhood, where the rich, free-spending German development aiders had brought into his realm a lifestyle and a gleaming array of all the good things of western life, such as rarely find their way into the remoter bush areas. He was soon to be disconcerted, however, by the very different reality of these particular visitors.

Having chosen his piece of land, Spee then squatted down in the dust with the village elders and asked them what to do next. At this they were flabbergasted. They had previously only known white men as distant, lofty beings who had always arrived, accompanied by rich accoutrements, to tell them what to do; to find one apparently as poor as themselves, and asking them what he should do, was an unfamiliar and initially perplexing experience. Spee explained that while he knew all about growing things at home, here everything was different – the crops they grew, the weather, the soil, the methods. He spent hours in such long and patient discussions, sketching explanations and ideas in the dirt with a twig or straw, as peasants do all over the world whenever the language barrier intervenes. At the outset his command of English was rudimentary, as was too that of the villagers. But as he explains, peasants everywhere recognize each other instantaneously, and can overcome any barrier of language, race, culture or climate to arrive at rapid understanding of common problems and interests.

In this way he acquired the knowledge he needed, learning all he could of local crops and seasons before buying the seeds he needed to start planting. Then he asked: 'What do I do next?' His African hosts had expected him to bring in a tractor to start his ploughing, and were duly consternated to find that he did not have the means to do so. They showed him rather sceptically how they dug their own fields with a heavy hand-hoe; the scepticism changed to astonishment when Spee and his family took up their hoes, and prepared their patch of ground for its first crop with the same back-breaking labour that they invested themselves, year after year.

In the beginning, Spee kept his farming strictly to the local methods, all the while asking endless questions and learning from the Africans. Only very cautiously and discreetly did he start, after a time, to introduce minor variations or improvements which he knew from home, and which he felt might work beneficially. His principal modification was mulching. The productivity of dryland farming is entirely dependent on the water regime. And the natural water regime of such hot-country soils depends – after the amount of rain that falls – on the humus content of the soils. Soil humus can absorb ten times its own dry weight of water, and retains this for long periods during later sunny periods, especially if the ground is shaded. Moreover a surface mulch, while absorbing and retaining water itself, lowers the soil surface temperature appreciably, thus reducing evaporation (and also the rate of bacterial action, which is often too rapid in hot tropical soils). The mulch also hinders weed growth, reducing competition for the crop's nutrients; and it provides worms with material to draw below ground to feed on, thereby augmenting further the soil's humus content and fertility. The practice was unknown in Dibuyiri until Spee arrived. But the beneficial effects were rapidly apparent in his crop – and the villagers began to take notice.

The second way of retaining as much precious ground-water as possible, especially valuable in the early stages of growth when the young plant's roots are shallow, is to obtain as rapidly as possible a complete coverage or canopy over the soil surface by the plants themselves. Spee achieved this by two methods. One was by sowing weeds. A local plant, the Crotelaria, sinks its roots deep into the subsoil, so reaching and feeding upon (and bringing up to its surface parts in the process) the invaluable phosphates which are leached out of the topsoil by permeating water. Its roots serve to penetrate, condition and bind the soil, and it also has the virtue of fixing nitrogen from the air. It grows very rapidly to cover and shade the soil – more rapidly indeed than most crop plants, which earns it the label of 'weed'. Spee found that by sowing seeds of Crotelaria (called in the local language Winne Lebbego, which means 'God which returns') shortly before the onset of the dry season, his land retained a plant cover and the soil its condition until the next planting season, to the benefit of both. The Crotelaria was then chopped off at ground level, to make an excellent green mulch, and the roots left in the soil to help create a good structure.

A variation of this which he later applied involved some more marked deviation from customary local farming practice, and did at first arouse some derisive opposition. Maize and millet both grow two to three metres tall, and are usually spaced in rows one metre apart to give them sufficient space to mature. It is a long time, however, before the plants' lateral leaves have grown out wide enough to meet across the rows, and so close the shady canopy; during this time a lot of bare soil is exposed between the rows, and a great deal of soil moisture thereby lost. Spee's answer was to plant at half a metre between rows, the crowns of the young plants then joining far earlier. His African neighbours were quick to point out his error in scorn. But when asked why they always planted at one metre intervals, they said that this was what their forefathers had always done, and had told them to do in their turn. This is a powerful argument in such traditional societies, where the wisdom of the ancient lore, entrusted to the elders, is held in unquestioning respect. Spee's answer was typical – and indeed the only effective one open to him. He replied that his own grandfather back home in Holland had told him to do it this way, at half-metre spacing. This was of course unanswerable, without showing a discourteous lack of respect for their visitor's unknown ancestor, and the villagers held their peace, and waited to see the outcome at harvest time.

They did not have so long to wait, however. With the conservation of extra moisture which the method permitted, Spee's crop grew faster and thicker than usual – and as soon as the plants began crowding each other, he commenced cutting out one row in two, leaving the roots in the ground as soil conditioners, and fed the cut maize plants to his goats. As these waxed fat and produced a plentiful milk supply for the village children, he was able to show an all round profit in every respect for a little extra work – and his corn crop yield was better than those of his neighbours into the bargain. The goats, in contrast, did not in the long run bring him any such resounding success. The region had always suffered an annual epizootic disease which regularly decimated the local flocks of sheep and goats. His exotic Dutch breed had no immunity at all to this, and eventually all succumbed. Undaunted, and adaptable in all such things, Spee decided to abandon goat raising and turn his land into a model horticultural and agricultural plot, to show the people how his bio-ecological adaptations of their traditional practices could improve both their yields and their lands.

He developed simple methods of composting in heaps, and silage making to store the surplus 'intercropped' forage maize, which is of course cut over a short period at the right point of growth, to give a seasonal abundance; but the goats need it all the year round. He also introduced the villagers to some basic but highly refined European farm implements – particularly the scythe. Having learnt to use the traditional cutlass-like chopping knife (called a 'panga' in East Africa) as effectively as any African, he showed how a Dutch scythe could cut the same area five times as fast. He found, too, that the long-handled Dutch hoe was more efficient – and easier to work with than the heavy short-handled local tool – for certain jobs like weeding and cultivation.

By this stage he had been 'adopted' by a faithful young assistant named William, who drank up the knowledge he had to impart as if it were nectar. William quickly learnt to use the European implements, and when Spee's friends sent some spares for lending out, he proudly undertook the task of showing his fellows how to use them properly.

Apart from his penchant for weeds, Spee is also passionately fond of worms. A further fundamental initiative he took on was to develop a simple technique for counting them. These most visible and familiar of the myriads of creatures inhabiting any healthy ground are a key indicator of the state of the soil. By simply counting the number of worms picked or sieved out of some small measured patches typical of the area under study, and calculating from this the average number per square metre, he taught the Africans to assess the current state of their land by a simple and comprehensible test available to any who wanted to try. He says, in fact, that good ground should show a minimum of at least 500 kilograms of worms per hectare. And it hardly needs pointing out here that worms are one of the first victims of agrichemicals.

The death of his goats was not the last trouble Spee was to meet from these capricious experiments. The village's surviving native goats were mainly in the hands of the village chief, who kept a large herd of them – as an important personage should in Africa. He kept them closely corralled alongside his house at night, but allowed them to roam and forage freely during the daytime. Consequently they regularly ravaged the garden which Spee was trying to establish. With the aim in view of producing the greatest possible impact, he had chosen his land as near as possible to the centre of the dispersed village. To make casual visiting easier, he had not fenced it either. Thus when the goats invaded it, he could only counterattack, repulsing them with sticks and stones, to the unbounded merriment of his neighbours.

For several weeks they found it a great joke to watch this wiry, white-bearded white man dancing around, chasing and throwing stones at the chief's goats. Despite their hilarity, Spee persisted chasing off the intruding flock. Gradually, as time went by, a subtle shift occurred, and a gradual alteration in the direction of the joke became apparent as the villagers switched their humour towards the owner of the goats – the village chief.

This development displeased that dignitary, who felt a discomfitting loss of prestige at becoming the butt of village derision. It left him also in a dilemma. He could hardly stop Spee from defending his garden; yet to make any change would be to admit fault, and bring a further loss of face. One morning as the Spees awoke, they found on the verandah of their simple house some rolls of chain-link wire fencing – sufficient to enclose the garden – which had appeared there mysteriously during the night. Spee ignored them and continued chasing goats; with the rolls of wire simply left where they lay, the joke became even richer as village hilarity knew no bounds. It finally became too much for the chief, who called his council of elders around him, and dressed in their finest robes they called in state at Spee's house.

Asked to explain why, since he had been given the means to do it, he did not fence in his garden, and save himself so much trouble, Spee responded politely that a garden should be a place for all to see, to visit, to admire the plants in it and the work being done. If he fenced out the goats he would also be excluding the people too. Better, he courteously suggested, that the chief fenced in his goats and had their fodder brought to them, than that he should fence out the people. The chief cut the seance short, and left discountenanced. During the night, however, the wire mesh rolls disappeared as mysteriously as they had arrived, and the next day Spee saw with tightly controlled satisfaction that the goats were securely enclosed in a chain-link fenced paddock.

Unfortunately, some of Johan Spee's adversaries were of heavier calibre and their insidious methods more powerful and ruthless than marauding flocks of goats and recalcitrant village chiefs. For his philosophy and teachings clearly ran counter to the policies promoted by all the official aid agencies and industry, including their local partners or 'counterparts'. Indeed, everything he stood for was diametrically opposed to the thrust of the aid industry. The latter did not, of course, take this lying down. The difficulties deriving from its machinations ultimately caused him to decide to return to Holland.

The various means by which such small-scale private initiatives can be administratively sabotaged – especially in a country in the grip of a military dictatorship (as Ghana then was) working hand-in-glove with the aid 'donors' – need not concern us here. Suffice it to say that they are numerous, effective and extensive. Reticence on this point is by no means motivated by any desire to shield the nefarious agencies and people which undertook such avaricious obstruction and undermining of this unique little demonstration of the possible. It is rather to protect the survivors; for the Spees earned the respect, admiration, and even love of very many people in the area, who still carry on applying their ideas. To point the finger and name the names at this stage would serve no useful purpose in furthering their efforts, but would on the contrary cause useless and destructive recriminations at the very least.

Spee's influence continues to spread around Dibuyiri; some time after his departure, a colleague visiting the area came across a barrow-shaped compost heap beside a field many miles away from his demonstration plot. On questioning the boy who had made it he learnt that the lad had been shown how by his father, who had learnt it 'from the old white man with the long white beard'. Furthermore, the effect on Dibuyiri itself was remarkable. William took over the model garden, and continued to run it successfully and to teach, although not a native of the village, having moved there with his family from some miles away. But as all the villagers took to using the improved methods, their crops and their lands improved so much that even young men who had quit the village and land as hopeless, and gone to seek their fortunes in the cities, began to return to take up farming again. So many, in fact, that the neighbourhood rapidly ran out of unused farmland, and envious eyes were cast upon the piece – now the best in the region – being farmed by the 'foreigner' William. In consequence he decided to strike out anew.

Collecting together 60 like-minded families from his natal village, William and his family have set up a new village on another abandoned piece of their tribe's customary land, to apply the bio-ecological farming system for themselves. He wrote to Spee to tell him: 'We love you as a father, and will always respect your advice. But we don't want you to come and help us this time.

We must stand on our own feet, and do it ourselves.' This was not the only letter Spee received from Ghana, nor by any means the end of his connection with that country. For shortly after his return to his own small farm in Holland he received a petition from Nene Nagai Kassa VII, Chief of the Shai people of Agomeda in the Accra Plains, halfway between Accra and the Akosombo Dam. Word of his work had reached the chief who, after due consultations, decided to request that the Spees come to his southern village to set up another project. Knowing that such official letter writing is a weighty matter among the traditional tribal societies of such lands, accompanied by much deliberation and even ceremony involving the whole village, Spee had no hesitation in taking this seriously. He packed his family up once more – this time without goats – and set off again for Ghana.

The Accra Plains are a narrow coastal strip of low grade man-made grassland stretching from the sea to the scarp which forms the limit of the Central African Plateau, some 50–60 miles inland. Before colonial times it was covered by dense tropical rainforest; the early slavers' and traders stations' demand for logs, building timber and firewood cleared most of it, and the subsequent demands – mainly for firewood and food crops – of the coastal cities which grew out of these early settlements denuded it almost completely of trees. The grassland is maintained free of bush regrowth by wandering Fulani herdsmen droving herds of slaughter cattle from the distant north to the coastal markets, and who regularly burn the grass to promote the tender shoots of regrowth which follow and which their herds prefer. More recently the burning has been taken over to a large extent by the 'Sunday hunters' mentioned in an earlier chapter.

Such excessive burning has degraded the land, by eliminating many desirable highly productive annual plants (such as *Panicum maximum*) while fostering the spread of less valuable fire-resistant species such as *Imperata cylindrica*. The increased albedo and decreased evapo-transpiration resulting from the disappearance of the forest has caused a 70 per cent decrease in rainfall, as well as a decrease in soil humus (or organic matter) from 12 per cent to under 2 per cent – and its annual supply by the remaining vegetation from about nine tons per hectare to around one ton per hectare per year.

Against this background, Spee once again sat down with the

elders of Agomeda and discussed their farming problems at length. They decided to create a demonstration farm or garden of one hectare in area, accepting this time the necessity of surrounding the whole with a cleared fire-break two and a half metres wide, with a dense flame-proof hedge on the inside. He created the latter with a deep-rooting nitrogen-fixing Cassia variety, pollarded Dutch willow-style at four feet high to give a bare stem carrying a dense crown. The crown could then be harvested two or three times a year by pruning, to produce phosphate-rich mulch, compost or firewood. He filled the lower storey at ground level with densely planted sisal, which not only provided a cheap and effective spikey barrier impenetrable to any marauding beasts – wild or domestic – but also produces fibre for a cottage industry rope and cord production. Much of the garden was planted with fruit trees, to tap deep subsoil nutrients, interplanted with maize, beans, groundnuts and sunflowers to provide immediate returns.

In order to achieve a rapid improvement in the soil structure of this demonstration plot, Spee found that apart from returning to the soil all the plant material grown over his one hectare, he also needed to harvest the waste material from a further four hectares – before the arsonists got to it. Once the soil was stabilized, his hectare produced a surplus of vegetable matter which could be used for improving or reclaiming other areas – a system long in use in Holland for newly reclaimed sandy soils.

After much deliberation, the people of Agomeda decided to call the plot the 'Maarten Garden', after Spee's son who worked so well with him in its creation. Again, Spee used no chemicals, but found just as effective several natural, commonly occurring products, such as the leaves and berries of the poisonous Neem tree (*Azadirachta indica*) which, soaked in water overnight, make an excellent insecticide. (So for that matter do cigarette ends – but all the Spees are non-smokers.)

Since then Spee spent several years 'commuting' between the Maarten Garden and his own farm in Holland. With the fortunate 'complementarity' of the agriculturally important half of each year in both places, he was able to spend the different growing seasons where he was most needed, with the aid of a young Dutch assistant to look after his farm in winter, and another young Ghanaian, Joseph, to run the Agomeda garden in his absence. His total commitment to the project is witnessed by the fact that he even abandoned his beloved goats at the Dutch end.

Approaching softly

In degrading lands such as Spee went to work with, the pressure of destruction can only be halted by reversing the process. He showed in fact that this can be done. The land of all tropical countries – even the desert fringes – is capable of producing great wealth, if people care for it and nurture it, using it skilfully in ways respecting the limitations and demands of its ecological nature. Where our approach is that of violence to nature with blunt instruments, as is the case when we deploy the chemical and mechanical weapons of 'high technology', the tendency is always to spread destruction – to level more forest and dissipate ever more topsoil, where the true roots of human culture are to be found.

The ancient cultures of Europe – and even more so, of the Orient – have something of value (though far less than many technologically arrogant westerners imagine) to offer to impoverished lands in Africa and the New World. But it will only meet with acceptance if offered in modesty and friendship – and above all in the spirit of mutual education.

Postscript

A book of this kind can never be a solo effort. Although the writing of it and the necessarily limited selection of events and examples given in it are entirely my own – and may be called idiosyncratic or worse by critics less receptive of such personal interpretations as I have attempted to give (one of the more unsympathetic to these ideas has already called it a 'work of fiction') – it was obviously inspired by many other thinkers and writers who concern themselves with these problems. And although its writing was completed without any form of subsidy or outside support, apart from a small advance from my publishers and an astonishingly complaisant and noble bank manager, it could never have reached this point without the most generous material support and heartening encouragement of many dear friends in many places.

It is customary to list those contributing to such enterprises, usually at the beginning; I have preferred to do so at the end, for the benefit of those who have borne with me thus far. Having already quoted the work of several of the people who inspired this book in the text, I can do no better here than to list most of the generous supporters and influences – adding the equally customary disclaimer that they bear no responsibility for any error in fact or interpretation I may have made (and some indeed are known not to agree entirely with one or other of my views on various aspects). This list could never be complete – and indeed I have purposely made some prominent omissions to avoid the embarrassment of worthy and most generously helpful people still 'in the firing line'. My heartfelt thanks, therefore, to them all including:

Carl Amery and Maryjane; Sunday Ajaji; Zach Akum; Andrew Allo; Anneliese Barry Barclay; Agnes Bertrand; Erna Bennet; Bernard Bull; F. Burger; Alfred van Binsbergen; Dieter Brauer;

David Bull; Goof Bus; John Burton; Egon Christensen; Gil Child; Robin Cook; Justin Cooke; J.W. Copius Peereboom; Kai Curry-Lindahl; Huup Dassen; John Davoll; Michael Dover; Erhard Eppler: André Gunder Frank and Marta; Peter von Fürstenberg; Teddy Goldsmith; Susan George; Yvette van Giap; Philip Hadjor and Bramford; Heinrich; Don Hinrichsen; Gerrit Hekstra; David Helton; Hans Jahnke; G.C. Kellas; Russel Kyle; Bart van Lavieren; Raymond Lloyd; Simon Mapangou and Marie; Arthur Mbanefo; Otto Matzke; Bloke Modisane; Sigi Menzinger; Pat Mooney; Nancy (Moustique); Bon Okanta; Walter Ormerod; Piet van Pelt; Ian Parker; Pietro Rava; Lucas Reynders; John Ringwood; Geoffrey Rowell; Valerie Sackey; Johan Spee and Ada; Uli Spielberger and Ingrid; Roy Smith and Val; Henry Thompson; Martin Urban; Barbara Veit; Tony de Vos; Henrick Waltmans; Chris Wardle; Wolfram Ziegler. And above all others, Angelique van Pelt.

Index

OTHER BOOKS FROM PLUTO

AID
Rhetoric and Reality
TERESA HAYTER with CATHARINE
WATSON

In a powerful follow-up to the long-out-of-print
Aid as Imperialism, Teresa Hayter and Cathy
Watson argue that existing forms of aid from the
West to the Third World are *not* in the interest
of the poor.

The most influential 'aid' institution is the
World Bank; it sets the pattern for almost all aid
given by western countries. Its radical rhetoric
– and reputation – are entirely without
foundation. 'Aid' is channelled to keep right-
wing governments in power, to subsidize
exports and to ensure that Third World
countries stay within the capitalist world
market. Even where 'aid' is specifically
targeted at the poor, most of it is lost along the
way in waste, corruption and elite consumption.

In the face of this reality, alternatives are
evaluated and a strategy of 'Solidarity not Aid' is
sketched out.

320 pages
0 86104 626 9   £4.95 paperback

THE CREATION OF WORLD POVERTY
An Alternative View to the Brandt Report
TERESA HAYTER

This book challenges the assumptions that the west, through its aid agencies, is 'helping' the rest of the world to develop. Far from rescuing the countries of Asia, Africa and Latin America from their supposed backwardness, the rich countries have accumulated vast wealth at their expense.

'It makes a stirring and outraging read.'
Times Educational Supplement

'Crushing analysis of the Brandt proposals. It's shooting from the hip and welcome for it.'
Oxfam News

128 pages
0 86104 339 1   £3.50 paperback

HARD TIMES
The World Economy in Turmoil
BOB SUTCLIFFE

More people are unemployed today than ever before. The miracles of the post-war boom are forgotten and production stagnates. Governments everywhere are cutting already inadequate welfare services.
Hard Times shows how this economic nightmare has resulted from the capitalist system's need for profit.

128 pages
0 86104 505 X   £2.50 paperback

DUE SOUTH
Socialists and World
Development
JEREMY HILL and HILARY SCANNELL

Underdevelopment is the world's most pressing
economic problem – and capitalism's greatest
scandal. *Due South* shows what *we* can do
about it.

It criticizes both existing international
institutions and policies, and alternatives such
as the Brandt Report and the Alternative
Economic Strategy. Its own proposals centre on
a greater integration of domestic, foreign and
development policies, and on popular
mobilization.

At the time of writing the book, both authors
worked for Third World First.

'A refreshing, realistic assessment.' *Third
World Quarterly*

128 pages
0 86104 507 6   £2.50 paperback

Pluto books are available through your local
bookshop. In case of difficulty contact Pluto to
find out local stockists or to obtain catalogues/
leaflets (telephone 01-482 1973).
    If all else fails write to:

Pluto Press Limited
Freepost (no stamp required)
105A Torriano Avenue
London NW5 1YP